Aquinas in Dialogue

Aquinas in Dialogue

Thomas for the Twenty-First Century

Edited by
**Jim Fodor and
Frederick Christian Bauerschmidt**

© 2004 by Blackwell Publishing Ltd

First published as volume 20 issue 1 of *Modern Theology*

BLACKWELL PUBLISHING
350 Main Street, Malden, MA 02148-5020, USA
108 Cowley Road, Oxford OX4 1JF, UK
550 Swanston Street, Carlton, Victoria 3053, Australia

The right of Jim Fodor and Frederick Christian Bauerschmidt to be identified as the Authors of the Editorial material in this Work has been asserted in accordance with the UK Copyright, Designs, and Patents Act 1988.

First published 2004 by Blackwell Publishing Ltd

Library of Congress Cataloging-in-Publication Data has been applied for

ISBN 1-4051-1931-4

A catalogue record for this title is available from the British Library.

Set by SNP Best-set Typesetter Ltd., Hong Kong
Printed and bound in the United Kingdom
by MPG Books Ltd, Bodmin, Cornwall

The publisher's policy is to use permanent paper from mills that operate a sustainable forestry policy, and which has been manufactured from pulp processed using acid-free and elementary chlorine-free practices. Furthermore, the publisher ensures that the text paper and cover board used have met acceptable environmental accreditation standards.

For further information on
Blackwell Publishing, visit our website:
http://www.blackwellpublishing.com

CONTENTS

PREFACE

In our era of dialogue and heightened awareness of the other, theologians seem to be rediscovering a rather odd resource: the thought of the thirteenth-century Dominican friar, Thomas Aquinas. This seems odd because of the picture of Thomas that still prevails in some quarters: the one who reconciled faith and reason so that dialogue becomes unnecessary because there is nothing new to learn, everything being dogmatically determined beforehand. But for those who actually read Aquinas' works, it is clear that he is constantly aware of and engaged with the heterogeneous voices both within and beyond the Christian tradition.

In the various places where Thomas discusses the "argumentative" or "artful" nature of *sacra doctrina*, he suggests certain guidelines for the variety of ways in which dialogue might take place. With those who accept the scriptures, or at least part of them, one may begin from these first principles to rather secure conclusions. But with those who accept only the principles of natural reason, one can only answer their objections to specifically Christian beliefs, though one could presumably argue more securely about those theological matters that fall within the scope of human reason. And with those who do not accept the principles of unaided human reason. . . . well, to Thomas this would be madness, but such people might be subject to some sort of persuasion, if not reasoned argumentation.

We might think of the first three essays, by Root, Marshall, and Valkenberg and Schoot, as falling into the category of speaking to those who accept all or part of the scriptures. Of course the Eastern Church and Judaism were two groups of whom Thomas was well aware, and with whom he engaged in dialogue and disputation. The Reformation, however, was still 250 years in the future. But if one views the Reformation, as Michael Root does, as in continuity with the preceding centuries, then we might well imagine Thomas viewing the Reformers as embodying certain positions within the Western Catholic tradition, and would have engaged them accordingly. In some ways, the dialogue between Thomas and the Reformers is very much a "family dispute" within the Western Catholic tradition, bounded not only by the shared text of scripture, but also by the determinative influence of Augustine. The dialogue is in some ways even a friendly one, in large part due to the interest in Aquinas shown by a number of theologians in the tradition of the Reformers.

Thomas' engagement with the Christian East requires a bit less imagination, since he articulated a number of his positions in direct response to Orthodox positions. Still, it is only in the last 200 years, with Thomas' ascendance to the position of *doctor communis* in Western Catholicism, that his views have become a target of critique from the East. The Eastern response, as Bruce Marshall's essay indicates, has largely been negative, seeing Thomas as the apotheosis of a tradition of error stemming from Augustine. Marshall's essay might be thought of as Thomas' reply in the ongoing debate, a reply that, true to Thomas' principles of dialogue, takes the form of arguments about how to think about God's self-revelation in scripture. And, like Thomas' own arguments, it seeks not so much the defeat of the dialogue partner as the shared arrival at a deeper and clearer understanding of scripture.

In their essay on Aquinas and Judaism, Pim Valkenberg and Henk Schoot point to the tension-fraught nature of the dialogue between Christians and Jews—tensions that arise not simply from the shameful history of the effects of Christian anti-Judaism, but also from the mysterious play of identity and difference between these two claimants to the legacy of Israel. Without denying the "awkwardness" of some of Thomas' views on Judaism, the authors also indicate resources within Thomas' thought that might help Christians recognize the integrity of Judaism as a religion (and not just as a preamble to Christianity), while at the same time acknowledging its unique position as Christianity's inseparable dialogue partner. Their attention to the analogy between the "mystery" of the hypostatic union and the "mystery" of the place of Israel in the Christian economy of salvation points to fruitful new possibilities in the Christian theology of the Jewish people.

Islam presents a different sort of partner for dialogue. Though Muslims might consider Christians to be "people of the book", Thomas thought of Muslims as being the same as pagans in rejecting the authority of scripture (see *Summa Contra Gentiles* bk. 1, ch. 2). Thus one must argue with them on the basis of natural reason. But, as David Burrell points out in his essay, Thomas' engagement with Islamic thinkers was hardly an apologetic monologue. Rather, he found in the questions raised by Islamic thinkers a prompting to ever greater clarity in his own Christian beliefs. In a way that may seem counter-intuitive to some contemporary advocates of dialogue, it was precisely Aquinas' unbending commitment to truth as the object of argumentation that led to his striking openness to alien quests for truth.

As Paul Williams notes in his essay, Thomas almost surely knew nothing of Buddhist quests for truth. Yet Williams demonstrates that a deep engagement with two radically different traditions can still yield fruit. Just as Aquinas refused to ascribe to a "double-truth" solution to the confrontation between Augustinian Christianity and Aristotelian philosophy, so too Williams refuses to accept the radical pluralist presumption that Thomist theology and Buddhist philosophy are discrete language games, between which contradiction is impossible. His essay argues that there is in fact sufficient common ground between Thomas and Buddhism to make genuine disagreement, and therefore dialogue, possible.

In the minds of some Thomists, the gulf between Thomas and analytic or "Anglo-American" philosophy is as wide as—or wider than—that between Thomas and Buddhism. In his essay, Fergus Kerr notes some of the reasons for this Thomist suspicion of analytic philosophy and then goes on to demonstrate what one might call the "subterranean" dialogue between Thomas and analytic philosophy. This hidden dialogue reaches back to the origins of analytical philosophy in the work of Brentano, and continues into the modern period in the work of Elizabeth Anscombe and Philippa Foot. One might read Kerr's essay as a plea that this dialogue be brought above ground, for the mutual benefit of Thomists and analytic philosophers.

Denys Turner's essay begins with a dialogue between Aquinas and atheism, but then the dialogue partner shifts from the atheist to the idolater—who today is perhaps the more compelling conversation partner. Turner shows that speaking with atheists is a rather straightforward matter, whereas the issues involved in speaking with the idolater (whether the good old-fashioned statue worshiper or the new-fashioned angel enthusiasts) are considerably more complex. But the very complexity of the issues involved is proportional to the conceptual rewards of sorting them out.

The final essay, by Frederick Bauerschmidt, extends the dialogue beyond those who accept scripture and those who accept reason, to look at how a Thomist might speak with and to a "culture of nihilism" in which the reigning assumption is not the positivist claim that there is no God, but the Nietzschean claim that "God is dead". Enlisting the aid of the "hillbilly Thomist" Flannery O'Connor, the essay argues that in a context in which reasoned argument is impossible, one ought not simply abandon dialogue, but rather adopt a stance of rhetorical persuasion that seeks to apply a "shock therapy" in hopes of overcoming the postmodern blindness to truth, beauty and goodness.

For many modern people, Thomas would get low marks for tolerance of difference. When confronted with a position that contradicts his own, Thomas seeks to defeat it. But he seeks to defeat it by first understanding it, and in coming to understand it he opens himself to the possibility that he must understand his own position in a new way. Thomas challenges our modern valorization of dialogue by asking what the goal of dialogue is. If it is dialogue simply for the sake of dialogue—no more than a way to pass the time while avoiding conflict—then there is no impetus to listen to and learn from our partners in dialogue. But if the goal, however distant, is the arrival at truth, then we have a genuine stake in listening and learning.

Jim Fodor
Frederick C. Bauerschmidt

1

AQUINAS, MERIT, AND REFORMATION THEOLOGY AFTER THE *JOINT DECLARATION ON THE DOCTRINE OF JUSTIFICATION*[1]

MICHAEL ROOT

I. Aquinas and the Reformation Divide

Thomas Aquinas was "the fountain and foundation of all heresy, error, and the obliteration of the gospel (as his books prove)".[2] So said Martin Luther in 1524. The modern observer is not surprised by such a comment. That Luther, the archetypal Reformer, would utterly reject the theologian Pope Leo XIII would later call "the special bulwark and glory of the Catholic faith"[3] is what one might expect. On closer examination and with greater historical knowledge, matters become more complicated. At the beginning of the Reformation, Thomas did not hold the place he later came to hold in Catholic theology. As Bernhard Lohse notes: "On the whole, in the period around 1500, Thomism was represented at only a few universities, and only a minority of theologians followed Thomas."[4] A disproportionate number of Luther's early critics, however, were Dominicans and Thomists of various stripes and some of these critics held up Thomas as uniquely authoritative.[5] In response, some of Luther's harshest comments on Thomas are directed less at particular assertions of Thomas and more at the authority ascribed to him by his adherents.[6] On Thomas himself, Luther's attitude was, at least on occasion, more nuanced. Luther could, in some contexts, speak of Thomas as a "great" or "holy" man,[7] although it now appears that the anecdote about Aquinas which Luther cited as exemplary of Thomas' own humility is apocryphal.[8] On Thomas' theology, Luther could also make differentiations. In

Michael Root
Lutheran Theological Southern Seminary, 4201 N. Main Street, Columbia, SC 29203, USA and
Institute for Ecumenical Research, 8 Rue Klotz, 67000 Strasbourg, France

relation to the doctrine of justification, on which Luther said "stands all that we teach and practice against the pope, the devil, and the world,"[9] his critique of Thomas was "astonishingly limited in its range and intensity".[10] Denis Janz concludes his comprehensive survey of Luther's comments on Aquinas with the statement that Luther showed a "grudging respect" for Thomas as a theologian.[11]

Lutherans have shared Luther's ambivalent attitude toward the Angelic Doctor. When Johann Agricola was gathering books in early 1521 for Luther and others to burn, along with the papal bull excommunicating Luther, he found that the Wittenberg theologians were not willing to give up their copies of Thomas' *Summa theologiae* (or their copies of Scotus' *Sentences* commentary).[12] Oddly enough, as the Reformation controversies hardened into long-term church division, Thomas' standing actually improved. As Robert Preus notes in his study of Lutheran Orthodoxy, a turning point came in the early seventeenth century with John Gerhard, the greatest of the Lutheran scholastics. Thomas ceased to be the source of all heresy; Gerhard "often quotes Thomas to clarify or illustrate a point".[13] Various factors stand behind this change, among them the adoption of a more scholastic method in Lutheran theology and the reception in Lutheran universities of the renewed Aristotle study of the later sixteenth century.[14]

A high point in the re-evaluation of Thomas was the 1656 publication of Johann Georg Dorsch's *Thomas Aquinas, dictus Doctor Angelicus, exhibitur Confessor Veritatis Evanglicae Augustana Confessione repititae*. Dorsch, who taught for most of his life at Strasbourg, argued that Thomas advocated views that agree in some cases better with Lutheran than with Tridentine Catholic positions and that Thomas viewed certain assertions to be non-heretical for which Lutherans were later condemned.[15] Dorsch's large volume, made up mostly of direct citations of Thomas, shows the limits of the discussion. While affirming Aquinas, its structure is patterned on that of Bellarmine's *De Controversiis*. Dorsch's text remains an exercise in post-Reformation polemic. The confessional disputes shape the evaluation of Thomas, even if he is now recruited for the Reformation side rather than attacked as the theologian of Roman falsehoods.

More recent discussion of Aquinas by Lutherans are still usually shaped by the confessional divide. Otto Hermann Pesch refers to "the tenacious desire [*hartnäckige Lust*], indeed the compulsion of Lutheran theologians and Luther scholars to contrast Luther against Thomas".[16] The reasons for this desire or compulsion are not hard to imagine. Lutheranism, far more than any other Protestant tradition, continues to be defined theologically by the sixteenth century debates with the medieval and Catholic tradition. The confessional texts that were produced in those debates remain the criterion of Lutheran identity. (Membership in the Lutheran World Federation, for example, is limited to churches which affirm the Augsburg Confession and Luther's Small Catechism.[17]) If Lutheranism remains defined by those debates with Catholicism and Thomas is held to be the Catholic theologian par excellence, then a Lutheran engagement with Thomas seems both unavoidable and problematic. The problem lies in the difficulty of a Reformation approach to Thomas that is not colored by the dynamic of church division, by the need either to affirm the necessity of the Reformation by placing Thomas and Luther in utterly opposed camps or the need to downplay their differences in the name of the pursuit of unity. Both tendencies are the children of division.

The most recent example of a reading that places the Reformation and Thomas in utterly opposed camps comes from an unexpected source, the post-Christian feminist theologian Daphne Hampson in her book *Christian Contradictions: The Structures of Lutheran and Catholic Thought*. While the form of Christianity to which Hampson is "post" is not Lutheran, her analysis is dependent on a particular tradition of Lutheran theology and, more narrowly, a particular tradition of interpretation of Lutheran-Catholic differences. At least since the early nineteenth century, some theologians have sought to move beyond a piecemeal analysis of the various theological points of dispute between the Reformation and Catholicism by uncovering the single *Grunddifferenz* which will explain and account for the individual disputes.[18] Various *Grunddifferenzen* have been proposed. Some are doctrinal, often related to the doctrine of justification. A Reformation understanding of justification is proclamatory and verbal, while Catholicism is transformatory and causal.[19] Some proposals center on philosophical differences: Aquinas typifies the commitment to a substance ontology, while Luther is at least on the way to a relational ontology. Whatever the particular *Grunddifferenz* proposed, the result is the same: discussion of individual points of dispute is pointless, unless the underlying *Grunddifferenz* is addressed and overcome (or discussion is simply pointless, because the *Grunddifferenz* is so basic that a meeting of the minds is simply impossible). The division of the Western church that resulted from the Reformation (and a distinct Lutheran church and identity) is thus theologically underwritten. The church did not divide over a dispute on some particular theological issue; it divided because the two sides occupied utterly different worlds of thought and belief.

Hampson fits well into this tradition. Her *Grunddifferenz* is anthropological. The Reformation and Catholicism understood the self in decisively different ways. Other differences flow from this source. These differences are so deep that "the two systems are strictly non-comparable".[20] Aquinas and the Reformation represent "two faiths."[21]

Hampson's work is a striking example of the dangers of this sort of analysis. To move Lutheranism and Catholicism into non-communicating worlds, she must deeply distort both.[22] For example, she states that "Catholicism is able to be what it is through making revelation inessential".[23] More specifically, "Thomas can essentially say all that he wishes about the relationship with God within the compass of the doctrine of creation."[24] Thus, the incarnation and the specification of the supernatural destiny to participation in God dependent upon it are rendered merely accidental to our relation to God. The schema of contrast turns into a Procrustean bed of a particularly egregious sort.

The *Grunddifferenz* tradition is not simply wrong, however. Any reader of Luther and Aquinas senses quickly that the two men are quite different kinds of theologians. Individual differences do fall together into comprehensive patterns that are deeply rooted in the way they address the theological task. A more fruitful (and eirenic) understanding of this difference has seen it as one of contrasting perspectives on the same fundamental faith or truth. Perhaps the best known version of this approach is Otto Hermann Pesch's contrast between Aquinas as a sapiential theologian and Luther as an existential theologian.[25] Pesch summarizes this distinction:

> *Existential theology* is the way of doing theology from within the self-actuation of our existence in faith, as we submit to God in the obedience of faith. Its affirmations are so formulated that the actual faith and confession of the speaker are not merely necessary presuppositions but are reflexly thematized. *Sapiential theology* is the way of doing theology from outside one's self-actuation in the existence in faith, in the sense that in its doctrinal statements the faith and confession of the speaker is the enduring presupposition, but is not thematic within this theology. This theology strives to mirror and recapitulate God's own thoughts about the world, men, and history, insofar as God has disclosed them.[26]

Both Luther and Aquinas seek to speak from faith, but they speak out of different moments of that faith. Luther speaks out of the situation of the justified sinner, standing before the judgment and mercy of God. The first person perspective is never lost but, as Pesch puts it, "reflexly thematized". Even when Luther speaks in the third person, the first person perspective persists.[27] As Robert Scharlemann shows in his study of John Gerhard, even in Lutheran scholasticism, or at least in Lutheran scholasticism at its best, these traces of the first person perspective are never lost.[28] For Aquinas, on the other hand, theology expresses the divine wisdom, as human knowledge has been allowed to participate in that wisdom. The faithful self is still speaking; it has not been repressed. The self which speaks in theology, however, is the self which is caught up beyond itself into the wisdom of God and so is able to speak of the divine order, the causes, by which all things are.

> He who considers absolutely [*simpliciter*] the highest cause of the whole universe, namely God, is most of all called wise. . . . Sacred doctrine essentially [*propiissime*] treats of God viewed as the highest cause—not only so far as He can be known through creatures just as philosophers know Him—*That which is known of God is manifest in them* (Rom. 1:19)— but also so far as He is known to Himself alone and revealed to others. Hence sacred doctrine is especially [*maxime*] called wisdom [*ST* I, i, 6].[29]

Thomas is not a "theologian of glory" in the sense that Luther defines in his *Heidelberg Disputation*. In thesis 19 of the *Disputation*, Luther insists that "one is not worthily called a theologian who perceives the invisible things of God understood through that which has been made", i.e., through creation.[30] Both Aquinas in *ST* I, 6 and Luther in *Heidelberg* thesis 19 contrast true theology with an understanding of God on the basis of creation, as described by Paul in Romans 1:19–20. But Thomas is a theologian of glory in the sense that his theology seeks to mirror the glorious wisdom of God by which all things are ordered, a wisdom that has been revealed to humanity. As Pesch puts it: "In accordance with his understanding of the nature of faith and of theology, he [Thomas] intends—so far as this is possible for the man of faith—to look with God's eyes and from God's heights at God himself, and then at man and history."[31]

The fruitfulness of Pesch's eirenic approach was already demonstrated in the detailed analyses of his massive study of Luther and Thomas on justification.[32] It does bring, however, its own dangers.[33] Does an ecumenical desire for unity tend to reduce substantive differences to mere differences of perspective? A false harmonization, according to which Thomas and Luther are always interpreted as somehow "saying the same thing" with different words, distorts in its own way. The Lutheran-Roman Catholic *Joint Declaration on the Doctrine of Justification* (JDDJ), in which the Roman Catholic Church and the Lutheran World Federation affirmed a consensus on basic truths of the doctrine of justification and stated that the condemnations relating to justification from the Council of Trent and the Lutheran Confessions do not apply to the contemporary teaching of the churches as stated in this declaration, comes close at crucial points to falling prey to this temptation. After affirming the consensus in basic truths, the JDDJ states that the "remaining differences" are matters of "language, theological elaboration, and emphasis".[34] This affirmation was taken by many, not least by some of the JDDJ's critics, as asserting that all remaining differences were matters of "saying the same things with different words", although the term "theological elaboration" [*theologische Ausgestaltung*, in the original German] might include genuine differences, even if differences that do not contradict the agreement in basic truths.

Can we move beyond either false contrast or false harmonization? The JDDJ, in both its content and its result, points to a different approach. In terms of its content, the JDDJ spells out in relation to specific controverted points both a consensus that permits one to see Lutheran and Catholic affirmations as capable of being held by persons within a single communion and a series of remaining differences which, if not church-dividing, are nevertheless matters for serious theological discussion and debate. For example, to say that Lutheran-Catholic differences over the sense in which the justified person can rightly be called a sinner need not be church-dividing is not to say that the matter is trivial and not worthy of serious argument. The JDDJ here seeks precisely to affirm both commonality and difference.

Also in its result, the JDDJ points to the possibility of a more balanced assessment. As long as theology operates against the background of a divided church, the assessment by Reformation theologians of Aquinas, the "common doctor" of the Catholic tradition, will inevitably be shaped by the dynamics of division. A pressure exists either toward the defense of one's own confessional identity or toward a perhaps inaccurate downplaying of difference in the name of unity. In a situation in which the differences over justification have been confessionally defused, it should be more possible to deal with this theme and related issues both unpolemically and unapologetically. The continuing discussion should neither be confessional nor ecumenical; it would simply be theological.

The JDDJ and its official ratification do not themselves, however, immediately change the theological situation. They need to be received into the theological discussion. I have suggested elsewhere[35] that a test of the reception of the JDDJ will be whether Catholic and Lutheran theologians can follow the JDDJ in hearing in the condemnations of the Reformation era "'salutary warnings' to which we must attend in our teaching and practice".[36] For Lutherans, this hearing is perhaps most difficult in relation to canon 32 of the Council of Trent's Decree on Justification, which condemns anyone who says that "the justified person, by the good deeds done by him through the grace of God and the merits of Jesus Christ (of whom he is a living member), does not truly merit an increase in grace, eternal life, and (so long as he dies in grace) the obtaining of his own eternal life and even an increase in glory".[37] Here, Catholic theology seems to be speaking a language Lutherans simply cannot understand or, if they can understand, must reject.

Can Thomas help here? Can Thomas' discussion of merit both illumine the meaning of the Catholic affirmation of merit and clarify the challenge that affirmation might present to Lutheran (and, more broadly, Protestant) theology? The rest of this essay will take up that question, if only in a necessarily preliminary way.

II. Aquinas and Merit

One might suspect that merit would have been discussed in great detail in ecumenical dialogues. After all, the Reformation accusation is often that Catholic theology teaches some form of salvation by one's own works, and the teaching that our works can be meritorious would seem central to that suspicion. In fact, the topic of merit has received very little explicit ecumenical attention. The US Lutheran-Catholic dialogue statement on justification dedicated only five of 165 paragraphs to the topic of merit. While the two sides were able to recognize legitimate concerns behind the other's acceptance or rejection of the concept of merit, they could not find a common language to speak of promise and reward. "Both concerns reflect aspects of the gospel, but the tension nevertheless remains."[38] The Anglican-Roman Catholic International Commission statement on *Salvation and the Church* devoted only two paragraphs explicitly to merit and reached agreement on the question.[39] The German study of the condemnations of the Reformation era was able to dispose of the controversy over merit in less than two pages: "Strange though it may seem, the dispute about merit also rests largely on a misunderstanding."[40] The JDDJ treats merit in the context of the place of good works and, while noting the linguistic difference that Catholics refer to good works as meritorious while Lutherans do not (as will be seen, a not totally accurate statement), sees little problem in relation to the concept.[41]

The concept of merit thus does not appear to be a contemporary ecumenical problem (although the conclusions of the various dialogues on this point have not convinced all).[42] The question still remains: What might non-Catholics learn from the Catholic discussion of merit and in what way can Trent's condemnations related to merit be heard by heirs of the Reformation as "salutary warnings"? Here I turn to the aid of Aquinas and ask two questions: What is it to merit? What can be merited?

I will limit myself here to looking at Aquinas' explicit discussion of merit in the *Summa Theologiae*.[43] The question on merit (I–II, q. 114) comes last in the *Prima Secundae*, at the end of the series of questions on grace. The question of merit is clearly a part of that series. The last two questions, 113 and 114, are introduced: "We must now consider the effects of grace: firstly, the justification of the unrighteous [*impii*], which is the effect of operative grace, secondly, merit, which is the effect of cooperative grace (I–II, q. 113, Intro).

Aquinas begins with the obvious question: can humans merit anything from God? Yes, for the Bible speaks of God rewarding persons, and reward and merit refer to the same thing (a. 1c, *ad idem referuntur*). Aquinas thus judges himself compelled to speak of merit because he is bound by the Bible, which uses equivalent concepts. He immediately recognizes, however, the problems he faces. Since merit implies justice, justice in the strict sense [*simpliciter*] depends on equality between agents, and the "greatest inequality" exists between God and humanity, "merit" in the strict sense cannot apply to the divine-human relation. 'Merit" can be used only in a relative sense, i.e., relative to the "proportion of what is wrought by each". But since "the mode and manner of man's virtue are due to God", any human merit must rest on "a previous divine ordination". This divine ordination is

of such a kind that by his work and action man is to obtain from God as a sort of reward [*quasi mercedem*] that for which God has allotted him a power of action. So too creatures in the physical world obtain by their movements and actions that for which they have been ordained by God. There is a difference, however; for rational creatures move themselves into action by free choice, and so their actions have a meritorious character; this is not the case with other creatures[44] (q. 114, a. 1c).

These sentences are decisive. As Joseph Wawrykow argues, the divine *ordinatio* is rooted in God's wisdom, which rightly orders all things.[45] Crucial to this ordering is the relation of each thing to its end. God will bring things to their ends in a way appropriate to their natures. But humans are actors, agents; they move themselves. God will bring them to their end in a way that maintains their nature as agents. And the relation of free and responsible agents to their ends must, in some sense, be one of merit. Ultimately, there will be a fittingness between redeemed persons and their end and, for responsible persons, that fittingness is a form of merit.

Merit is a function of the divine ordination of all things to their ends. Our merit, i.e., that we are brought to our end in a way that accords with our nature, thus manifests the divine goodness (a. 1, ad. 2). Our works do not make God our debtor, since the relation of merit is a function of God's ordering of things. "Rather does he [God] become a debtor to himself, in so far as it is right that what he has ordained should be fulfilled" (a. 1, ad. 3).

Further, merit is not just made possible by this divine ordination. It depends on divine grace moving the self within the meritorious action. "Eternal life is a good which exceeds what is commensurate with created nature" (a. 2c). Thus, no creaturely action, however perfect, can merit eternal life. Only actions within which grace is active can merit eternal life. Grace here does not refer to an external causal relation between God and the self, but to the indwelling of the Spirit. "A man's work is therefore rewarded according to the worth of the grace by which he is made a partaker [*consors*] of the divine nature, and adopted as a son of God to whom the inheritance is due by right of adoption" (a. 3c).[46] There is a sense in which our actions merit eternal life in the strict sense (i.e., condignly), but only in that our actions proceed from the grace of the Holy Spirit, for equality does exist between the Spirit and the Father who rewards (a. 3c). The congruous merit that attaches to our acts as they proceed from our freedom is strictly subordinate. "Thus does the Holy Spirit dwell in a man by grace as the sufficient cause of eternal life, wherefore he is called the earnest of our inheritance in II Cor. 1:22" (a. 3, ad. 3).

The relation of merit requires what Austin Farrer called double agency,[47] that an action can be ascribed both to the human agent and to God acting within the human action. This double agency is not a cooperation where two agents each do part; rather, God is at work moving human action. God (and God alone) can move the human person in this way without violating that person's freedom, for as Creator and Preserver God's relation to the person is, so to speak, an internal one.[48] So, Aquinas can say that God brings the human person to the divinely ordained end of eternal life in a way that does not violate, but affirms the nature of the human as a self-moving rational creature. That self-movement is itself a gift of grace; it is at once a being-moved and a self-moving, but always in that order: the self-moving is dependent on the being-moved.[49] Thus, as moved by grace, a human action can be meritorious both in terms of its being moved by the indwelling Spirit and in terms of its self-movement, but the latter is always dependent on the former.

Finally, the Christological character of merit must not be overlooked. When Aquinas notes that justice in an only relative sense can apply to persons in relation to God, due to the "greatest inequality" between them, his examples of other relations of inequality in which justice might relatively apply are father/child and master/slave, examples taken from Aristotle.[50] As noted above: "A man's work is therefore rewarded according to the worth of the grace by which he is. . . . adopted as a son of God to whom the inheritance is due by right of adoption" (a. 3c) God rewards the faithful as his children and they are children of God in Christ. As Wawrykow puts it, for Thomas

> justice only holds sway when there exists a special community between God and the human person, and this community is itself created by the gift of God. The 'communal' basis of justice is disclosed by Thomas' description of grace in terms of sonship. By grace, God freely elevates people to God's own level, treating them as 'sons' to whom what belongs to the Father can also belong. As the term 'sonship' suggests, the community which lies behind merit is itself Christ-centered. It is through the action of the Son of God that others are enabled to be adopted as God's children.[51]

In summary, merit for Aquinas is a manifestation of God's wise ordination of all things to their ends in a way that affirms their created nature. Humanity is brought in Christ and the Spirit to the gracious end of communion with God. That end is gift, but we are brought to that gift as free and responsible creatures. Our end will fit us as free and responsible creatures as an end that, within the movement of grace, is merited.

The nature of merit for Aquinas helps to clarify what can be—at least to Protestants—a baffling aspect of Catholic teaching on merit. Both Aquinas and Trent[52] teach that while, on the one hand, justification is not merited, neither at the beginning of the Christian life nor eschatologically, on the other hand eternal life is merited. To non-Catholic ears, to say that one merits eternal life, but not justification sounds at best odd. In terms of Aquinas' theology, however, this distinction makes sense.

Aquinas specifies explicitly in Q. 114 what cannot be merited: first grace (a. 5c), justification (a. 5, ad. 1), restoration after a lapse (a. 7), perseverance prior to the heavenly glory (a. 9), and temporal goods other than those that support virtue (a. 10). The sole objects of merit are eternal life (a. 3) and an increase in grace or charity (a. 8). Put differently, the movement of the self into communion with God is not merited. Entrance into it (first grace and justification) is not merited; remaining within it (perseverance) is not merited; returning to it after a lapse (restoration) is not merited. *Within the movement of grace*, however, relations of merit can exist between the entire movement and its end and thus also between moments along the way.[53] "Eternal life" here functions almost as a technical term for the *telos* of the movement of grace. "Eternal life consists in the enjoyment of God [*in Dei fruitione*]" (a. 4c), the enjoyment of God is "the ultimate and principal good of humanity", and thus humanity's ultimate end (II-, q. 23, a. 7c). That grace brings us to this end we never merit; but grace will bring us to this end as ones who merit it.

III. Aquinas, Merit, and the Reformation

How might a Protestant, and more narrowly a Lutheran, reply to Aquinas' presentation? First, many typical Protestant assertions, e.g., that Aquinas or Catholicism teaches that one merits justification or the remission of sins,[54] are now seen to be simply false.[55] Catholic claims about merit are in fact strikingly narrow. Nor did the Reformers object to the concept of meriting rewards from God, an idea explicitly affirmed in the Lutheran Confessions. Article IV of the Apology of the Augsburg Confession, the most extensive discussion of justification in the Lutheran Confessions' states: "We concede that works are truly meritorious, but not for the forgiveness of sins or justification. For they are not pleasing to [God] except in those who are justified on account of faith. Nor are they worthy of eternal life. For just like justification, so also being made alive takes place by faith on account of Christ."[56] The first two sentences of this statement are, as we have seen, also affirmed by Aquinas. The issue is whether one merits eternal life.

By the time Martin Chemnitz came to write his *Examination of the Council of Trent*, the best known and most authoritative Lutheran response to Trent,[57] the narrowness of the controversial issues relating to merit had become clearer. Like the Apology, Chemnitz affirms that Christians do merit rewards from God. "Our own people do not shrink back [*non abhorrent*] from the word 'merit', as it was used also by the fathers. For the rewards are promised by grace and mercy; nevertheless, they are not given to the idle or to those who do evil but to those who labor in the vineyard of the Lord."[58] The controversial issues "between the papalists [*Pontificios*] and us with respect to the teaching about the reward of good works" he notes to be two above all: whether eternal life is merited and whether rewards are given "not from the grace, mercy, and fatherly liberality of the heavenly Father but as a matter of debt, because nothing is lacking in the good works of the regenerate that they should not be judged to have satisfied the divine law fully according to the state of this life and to have truly merited eternal life".[59] Chemnitz sees Trent as answering both questions affirmatively in Chapter 16 of its Decree on Justification. The latter question assumes a contrast between mercy and justice which the Council and Aquinas reject.[60] The question of meriting eternal life hits closer to the mark. The bone of contention seems to lie here.

On closer examination, however, the issue becomes harder to define. The Apology was willing to grant that eternal life is, in a sense, received as a reward.

> If we were to say that eternal life is called a reward, because it is owed to the justified on account of the promise, we would not be speaking unreasonably. For there is a correlation among the gifts with reference to one another, just as Augustine also says: "God crowns his own gifts in us." However, Scripture calls eternal life a reward, not because it is owed on account of works, but because it compensates for afflictions and works, even though it happens for a completely different reason. Just as an inheritance does not come to a son of a family because he performs the duties of a son, nevertheless, it is a reward and compensation for the duties he performs. Therefore, it is enough that the word "reward" is connected to eternal life because eternal life compensates for good works and afflictions.[61]

The difference between this position and that of Aquinas appears to be small, especially if "promise" in the first sentence can be replaced with "divine ordination". The notion of a "correlation among the gifts" appears to be a major step in Aquinas' direction. The question seems to be whether the divine reward and compensation can be said to be a reward but one not owed on account of works.

Chemnitz is close to the Apology. He notes "the explanation of our men" that "eternal life is a reward [*merces*] because it rewards good deeds [*quia compenset benefacta*], even if it is given on account of [*propter*] something else, namely, on account of Christ; as an estate inherited from a father is the reward of an obedient son, even if it happens on account of another cause".[62] Put symbolically, the difference seems to be this: let X stands for the justified Christian in glory, Y stands for eternal life, and Z stand for the good works of the glorified Christian. The difference then is between:

a) X receives Y as a reward and compensation for Z
b) X receives Y as merited by Z.

The difference has become rather thin. Perhaps a different, more oblique approach might help get at underlying issues.

Pesch suggests that in relation to merit, Catholics (Aquinas included) and the Reformers tended to stress different aspects of the concept.[63] Aquinas and the Council of Trent affirm merit as an eschatological concept: eschatologically there will be a true fittingness between eternal life as the end of the movement of grace and the human creature as moved by a grace that does not violate its intrinsic nature as agent. The Reformers, however, feared merit as a practical-ethical concept, as a concept that would underwrite a *quid pro quo* approach to the Christian life. As seen, they were willing when pressed to grant much of the eschatological reality "merit" was meant to describe, but the concept of merit or reward plays a minor role in their positive presentation of salvation. Chemnitz's comprehensive account of the faith, *Loci Theologici*, includes an extensive discussion of justification, within which is included a detailed and spirited discussion of the place of good works in the Christian life. He insists that good works of the justified are, in a carefully defined sense, a necessary part of the Christian life and are themselves pleasing to God.[64] They will be rewarded in this life and the next. At the beginning of the discussion, however, when he elaborates the terms in which good works are to be discussed, he states: "The term 'merit' is used by the fathers and is called *meritum*, that is, a work which is commanded by God, performed by the regenerate in faith, which has promises attached to it either in this life, or the life to come. But because of the misuse of the term and the snares which accompany it, and finally because it is only a word from the unwritten tradition, it is not used by those who are more earnest [*sincerioris*] in their concern for doctrine."[65] The disappearance of the teleological framework within which merit is interpreted in Aquinas accounts for much of the decline in the attention given to the reality Aquinas refers to with the term "merit". But there is also the worry over the "abuses and snares" that seem to go with the term. As Pesch notes, even in Aquinas the term "merit" has a way of determining in a dubious manner the wider discussion of salvation outside the explicit treatise on grace.[66] Here Reformation theology has a "salutary warning" for difficulties to be found even in Aquinas.

What might be the "salutary warning" Reformation theology should hear in the Catholic and Thomist understanding of merit? Let me close with a few points at which Reformation theology might be rightfully pressed.

First, much of the different tone of Lutheran and Catholic or Thomist accounts of merit is rooted in the distinction noted above between existential and sapiential approaches to theology. For Luther, the theologian speaks *coram deo*, before the judgment and mercy of God. In such a situation, faith is self-forgetful; it points away from itself to the glory and forgiveness of God. This self-forgetfulness, this lack of attention to one's own merit, is the common currency of the saints. Often cited in this context is St. Thérèse of Lisieux's "Act of Oblation to Merciful Love" in which she asks that God not count her works, for she wishes to be clothed in God's own justice.[67] Such an attitude is not anathema to Catholic doctrine—witnessed by the fact that this passage from St. Thérèse is quoted at the end of the discussion of merit in *The Catechism of the Catholic Church*.[68] Much of the power of Luther's theology comes from his ability to incorporate the viewpoint of the confessor *coram deo* into all of his theology.

Simply identifying differing perspectives on theology and its relation to the self who speaks in theology is not the end of the task, however. Even if both existential and sapiential approaches to theology are each appropriate and even if much of the difference between Luther and Aquinas on merit lies in their differing modes of theologizing, the question can be asked about the relative strengths and weaknesses of each approach and whether there are problems in Luther's or Aquinas' discussions of merit, even on their own terms. For example, are there aspects of God's work described by Aquinas to which Luther's existential approach either does not or cannot adequately refer? How does the confessor before God praise God's work in herself, whether or not the result of that work be called "merit", if the self is utterly forgetful of self? Even in an existential theology, is a second level of self-forgetfulness needed, in which the self contemplates self, not to mount a claim to its own righteousness, but to praise God's work? Does the praise of God require a sort of God's eye view of the self, so that the self may also be included in the things for which thanks is given to God?

Can a further step be taken? If the greatest gift of grace is that we are made friends of God (John 15:15),[69] then is it impossible, even for the confessor *coram deo*, to call upon God to fulfill the debts which God has taken upon himself in the divine promises? Abraham is also *coram deo* when he bargains with God over how many righteous must there be in Sodom for God to spare the city. Abraham appeals to God's righteousness as a sort of debt God owes to himself: "Far be it from you to do such a thing!" (Gen. 18:25). Is an appeal to God to complete what has been begun, to crown the gifts God has given, inadmissible? Can the confessor *coram deo* call upon God to finish the divine work, to reward the good works the Spirit has wrought, to grant eternal life to those who in Christ and the Spirit are made fit for eternal life? These are questions that the theology of Aquinas presses on the Lutheran, even within the more existential mode of Lutheran theologizing.[70]

A more fundamental question must still be raised. The Lutheran reluctance to speak of merit in relation to something as important as eternal life is not simply practical or ethical. It reflects an understanding of the self in its relation to God that is significantly different from that of Aquinas. For Aquinas, the concept of merit points to God's gracious granting of a place for human action in the scheme of salvation. That action is utterly dependent on grace at every moment. Within the scheme of salvation, however, humanity is permitted to participate in the movement toward the beatific vision. God elevates the human as agent.

How does Lutheran theology respond? Lutherans have agreed that God moves the self in a way appropriate to the self as agent. "God the Lord certainly has one *modus agendi* or way of accomplishing his will in a human being as a rational creature, and another way of accomplishing his will in other, irrational creatures or in a stone or block of wood."[71] The redeemed self cooperates with the Spirit: "As soon as the Holy Spirit has begun his work of rebirth and renewal in us through the Word and the holy Sacraments, it is certain that on the basis of his power we can and should be cooperating [*mitwirken*] with him, though still in great weakness. This occurs not on the basis of our fleshly, natural powers but on the basis of the new powers and gifts which the Holy Spirit initiated in us in conversion."[72]

In recent Lutheran theology, however, any such notion of a cooperation of the justified self has often been rejected vehemently. Gerhard Forde, for example, seemingly rejects all notions that faith is a human action. Hearing and believing "is not an *action* or movement on our part but simply a *passion*, a 'suffering it to be so,' a being slain and raised up."[73] Faith is a being grasped by God's promise, not a grasping of that promise.[74] Eberhard Jüngel is more subtle, but also more difficult to understand. After pages of insistence that we do not cooperate in our justification (an assertion with which Aquinas can agree—justification is an effect of operative, not cooperative grace), Jüngel states in his recent volume on *Justification*: "In faith we comprehend [*vollzieht . . . nach*] the movement of our own justification which has already taken place in Jesus Christ, and it is in that comprehension [*Nachvollzug*] that we also complement [*vollzieht . . . mit*] that comprehension. As those who have been moved, we move."[75] Jüngel goes on, however, to give only a limited picture of the significance of this *Mitvollziehung*, a strong term, in the salvation of the justified. How does it relate to the "creative passivity" which he says is the only possible relation of the self to its justification, a passivity which must be "a very lively, spontaneous and creative inactivity"?[76] What follows in Jüngel's presentation seems to reduce the activity of this passivity to letting God carry out his work in us, but is such a passive non-rejection of what God does the same as a *Mitvollziehung*?

Lutheran theology needs to spell out far more clearly the nature of the human self and its activity, not only in justification, i.e., that relation in which the self stands acceptable before God's judgment, but throughout the Christian life, including the movement in which we are transformed from persons in whom sin rules, to be persons in whom sin is ruled over, and finally to be, in eschatological perfection, persons from whom sin is excluded.[77] For Luther, we participate in that movement already in this life: Christ "does not want us to halt in what has been received, but rather to draw near from day to day so that we may be fully transformed into Christ".[78]

Discussions of justification after the JDDJ need to be open to the questions posed by theologians across the Reformation divide not as challenges to confessional identity but as contributions from fellow participants in a single theological conversation. Even on a topic as controverted as merit, Lutherans (and other Protestants) and Catholics need to hear the question posed by the other. My concern here has been for the questions that Lutheran theology needs to hear in Aquinas' understanding of merit. Aquinas poses for Lutherans the question of how the human self is brought to eschatological glory as self, i.e., as a self-moving and responsible agent. The theologian committed to the Reformation may not wish to adopt Aquinas' (or any other theologian's) understanding of merit. One might finally agree with Pesch that no matter how one may wish to affirm the reality "merit" seeks to describe, the concept "merit" brings with it more problems than it solves.[79] In the new ecumenical situation, however, Aquinas should stand alongside Luther in setting the agenda for both the Lutheran and the Catholic theologian.

NOTES

1   This essay has profited from conversations with Bruce D. Marshall, Joseph Augustine DiNoia, and John Michael McDermott.
2   *WA* 15:184 ("Thomas von Aquin, der born und grundsuppe aller ketzerey, yrthum und ver-tilgung des Evangelii (wie seyne bucher beweysen"). All references to Luther will be to the *Weimar Ausgabe*. When an English translation exists, it will be noted.
3   *Aeterni Patris*, Encyclical on the Restoration of Christian Philosophy, para. 17.
4   Bernhard Lohse, *Martin Luther's Theology: Its Historical and Systematic Development*, ed. Roy A. Harrisville (Minneapolis, MN: Fortress Press, 1999), p. 13.
5   David V. N. Bagchi, *Luther's Earliest Opponents: Catholic Controversialists, 1518–1525*, (Minneapolis, MN: Fortress Press, 1991), p. 17, and Leif Grane, "Die Anfänge von Luthers Auseinandersetzung mit dem Thomismus", *Theologische Literaturzeitung* Vol. 95 (1970), pp. 241–250.
6   See Chapter III, "Luther on the Authority of Thomas" in Denis R. Janz, *Luther on Thomas Aquinas: The Angelic Doctor in the Thought of the Reformer*, Veröffentlichungen des Instituts für Europäische Geschichte Mainz, 140 (Stuttgart: Franz Steiner Verlag, 1989), pp. 82–95. Janz's comprehensive survey of Luther's scattered comments on Thomas is an invaluable aid in understanding Luther's attitude toward Thomas.
7   See references in Janz, *Luther on Aquinas*, p. 5.
8   Otto Hermann Pesch, *Martin Luther, Thomas von Aquin und die reformatorische Kritik an der Scholastik: zur Geschichte und Wirkungsgeschichte eines Missverständnisses mit welt-geschichtlichen Folgen*, Berichte aus den Sitzungen der Joachim Jungius-Gesellschaft der Wissenschaften e.V., Hamburg, Vol. 12, no. 3 (Hamburg; Göttingen: Joachim Jungius-Gesellschaft der Wissenschaften—Vandenhoeck & Ruprecht, 1994), p. 78.
9   Smalcald Articles, II,1,5; in Robert Kolb and Timothy J. Wengert, eds., *The Book of Concord: The Confessions of the Evangelical Lutheran Church*, (Minneapolis, MN: Fortress Press, 2000), p. 301.
10   Janz, *Luther on Aquinas*, p. 56.
11   Janz, *Luther on Aquinas*, p. 114. Pesch contends, however, that while Luther did know Aquinas' work better than earlier scholars had thought, Luther never truly understood Aquinas. See Pesch, *Luther, Thomas, und die reformatorische Kritik*, p. 49.
12   Martin Brecht, *Martin Luther: His Road to Reformation 1483–1521*, trans. James L. Schaaf (Philadelphia: Fortress Press, 1985), 423f.
13   Robert D. Preus, *The Theology of Post-Reformation Lutheranism: A Study of Theological Prole-gomena* (St. Louis, MO: Concordia Publishing House, 1970), p. 36.
14   See Robert P. Scharlemann, *Thomas Aquinas and John Gerhard*, (New Haven, CT: Yale University Press, 1964), pp. 14–22.
15   On Dorsch and his argument, see Winfried Zeller, "Lutherische Orthodoxie und mittelal-terliche Scholastik: Das Thomas-Verständnis des Johann Georg Dorsch", *Theologie und Philosophie* Vol. 41 (1975), pp. 527–546. To my knowledge, no copy of Dorsch's study exists in North America. What is said here on Dorsch is dependent on Zeller's article.
16   Pesch, *Luther, Thomas, und die reformatorische Kritik*, p. 57.
17   Constitution of the Lutheran World Federation, Articles II and V.1, in *From Hong Kong to Winnipeg 1997–2003: The Report of the General Secretary on Behalf of the Council*, (Geneva: Lutheran World Federation, 2003), pp. 161f.
18   On the tradition of the pursuit of an explanatory *Grunddifferenz*, see André Birmelé, "Sinn und Gefahr der Rede von einer Grunddifferenz. Bericht und Reflexionen über eine Kon-sultation und ihr Thema", in *Grundkonsens–Grunddifferenz*, ed. André Birmelé and Harding Meyer (Frankfurt a.M.: Verlag Otto Lembeck, 1992), pp. 181–192.

19 See, for example, Gerhard Forde et al., "A Call for Discussion of the 'Joint Declaration on the Doctrine of Justification'", *Dialog* Vol. 36 (1997), p. 226.

20 Daphne Hampson, *Christian Contradictions: The Structures of Lutheran and Catholic Thought*, (Cambridge: Cambridge University Press, 2001), p. 91. Since Hampson spends much of the book comparing the two systems in relation their varying views of self, revelation, God, salvation, etc., her claim is, taken literally, false by her own demonstration. She must mean something like incomensurable rather than non-comparable.

21 Hampson, *Christian Contradictions*, p. 287. What sets Hampson apart from most of the *Grunddifferenz* tradition is that she is not arguing for the truth of either Lutheranism or Catholicism. For her, they both represent unacceptable options and since they represent the only two options within Christianity on certain fundamental questions, they point to the unacceptability of Christianity.

22 For a more detailed discussion of Hampson's book, see my review in *Christian Century* Vol. 118 (September 12, 2001), pp. 44–46.

23 Hampson, *Christian Contradictions*, p. 242.

24 Hampson, *Christian Contradictions*, p. 245.

25 Otto Hermann Pesch, "Existential and Sapiential Theology—The Theological Confrontation Between Luther and Thomas Aquinas", in *Catholic Scholars Dialogue with Luther*, ed. Jared Wicks (Chicago, IL: Loyola University Press, 1970), pp. 61–81. This essay builds on the final chapter in Otto Hermann Pesch, *Theologie der Rechtfertigung bei Martin Luther und Thomas von Aquin: Versuch eines systematisch—theolgischen Dialogs*, (Mainz: Matthias Grünewald Verlag, 1967).

26 Pesch, "Existential and Sapiential", pp. 76f.

27 I have sought to apply the first/third person distinction to the dispute over the *simul iustus et peccator* in Michael Root, "Beyond the Joint Declaration on the Doctrine of Justification: The Shape of Continuing Discussion on Justification", in *Kirche in ökumenischer Perspektive: Kardinal Walter Kasper zum 70. Geburtstag*, eds. Peter Walter, Klaus Krämer, and George Augustin, (Freiburg: Herder, 2003), pp. 364f.

28 Scharlemann, *Aquinas and Gerhard*, pp. 150f.

29 Aquinas' *Summa Theologiae* will be cited according to various English translations, often altered to bring them closer to the Latin.

30 "Non ille digne Theologus dicitur, qui 'invisibilia' Dei 'per ea, quae facta sunt, intellecta conspicit'" [*WA* I, 354, my translation in text]. The translation of this passage in the American Edition of Luther's Works ("That person does not deserve to be called a theologian who looks upon the invisible things of God as though they were clearly perceptible in those things which have actually happened [Rom 1:20]" *LW* 31:40) inserts a reference to Rom. 1:20, but looses the direct quotation of the Vulgate of Rom. 1:20 that makes up more than half the thesis in the Latin. The direct quotation of Rom. 1:20 makes clear that Luther, at least in this thesis, is criticizing those who believe they can understand the nature of God on the basis of creation. The actual term "theologian of glory" does not appear until thesis 21.

31 Otto Hermann Pesch, *The God Question in Thomas Aquinas and Martin Luther*, trans. Gottfried G. Krodel, (Philadelphia, PA: Fortress Press, 1970), p. 14.

32 Pesch, *Rechtfertigung bei Luther und Thomas*.

33 As Pesch himself notes, see Pesch, *Luther, Thomas, und die reformatorische Kritik*, pp. 61f.

34 The Lutheran World Federation and The Roman Catholic Church, *Joint Declaration on the Doctrine of Justification* (Grand Rapids, MI: Wm. B. Eerdmans Publishing Company, 2000), para. 40.

35 Root, "Beyond the JDDJ", p. 358.

36 The Lutheran World Federation and The Roman Catholic Church, *Joint Declaration*, para. 44.

37 Norman P. Tanner, ed., *Decrees of the Ecumenical Councils* (London: Sheed & Ward, 1990), p. 681.

38 *Justification by Faith*, eds. H. George Anderson, T. Austin Murphy, and Joseph Burgess, Lutherans and Catholics in Dialogue, vol. 7 (Minneapolis, MN: Augsburg Press, 1985), para. 112.

39 Anglican-Roman Catholic International Commission, "Salvation and the Church", in *Growth in Agreement II: Reports and Agreed Statements of Ecumenical Conversations on a World*

Level, 1982–1998, eds. Jeffrey Gros, Harding Meyer, and William G. Rusch (Geneva: WCC Publications, 2000), para. 23–24.

40 Karl Lehmann and Wolfhart Pannenberg, eds., *The Condemnations of the Reformation Era: Do They Still Divide?* trans. Margaret Kohl (Minneapolis, MN: Fortress Press, 1989), p. 66. For a related discussion of the particular canons in Trent on merit, see Otto Hermann Pesch, "The Canons of the Tridentine Decree on Justification: To Whom Did They Apply? To Whom Do They Apply Today?" in *Justification by Faith: Do the Sixteenth Century Condemnations Still Apply?* ed. Karl Lehmann, trans. Michael Root and William G. Rusch, (New York, NY: Continuum, 1997), pp. 190f.

41 The Lutheran World Federation and The Roman Catholic Church, *Joint Declaration*, para. 38–39.

42 For example, on ARCIC, see Alister McGrath, *ARCIC II and Justification: An Evangelical Anglican Assessment of 'Salvation and the Church'*, Latimer Studies, 26 (Oxford: Latimer House, 1987), pp. 45f; on the German condemnations study, see Dietz Lange, ed., *Überholte Verurteilungen? Die Gegensätze in der Lehre von Rechtfertigung, Abendmahl und Amt zwischen dem Konzil von Trient und der Reformation—damals und heute*, (Göttingen: Vandenhoeck & Ruprecht, 1991), pp. 49–51; on the JDDJ, see Forde et al., "A Call for Discussion of the 'Joint Declaration on the Doctrine of Justification'", p. 228.

43 For a comprehensive analysis of what Aquinas said on merit throughout his career, see Joseph Wawrykow, *God's Grace and Human Action: 'Merit' in the Theology of Thomas Aquinas* (Notre Dame, IN: University of Notre Dame Press, 1995). My discussion of Aquinas is indebted to Wawrykow's careful work.

44 *ST.*, q. 114, a. 1c.

45 Wawrykow, *God's Grace*, pp. 182–188.

46 The translation of *consors* as "partaker" preserves the echo of II Pt. 1:4, which in the Vulgate refers to our having been made *divinae consortes naturae*.

47 Austin Farrer, *Faith and Speculation: An Essay in Philosophical Theology*, (New York, NY: New York University Press, 1967), pp. 61–67.

48 On this interiority, see Scharlemann, *Aquinas and Gerhard*, p. 131.

49 See here the admittedly difficult discussion of operative and co-operative grace in *ST* I–II, a. 111, a. 2. My reading of Aquinas on these questions is dependent on Bernard J. F. Lonergan, *Grace and Freedom: Operative Grace in the Thought of St. Thomas Aquinas*, ed. J. Patout Burns (London: Darton, Longman & Todd, 1971).

50 *Nicomachean Ethics*, Book 5, Chap. 6 (1134^b).

51 Wawrykow, *God's Grace*, pp. 203f.

52 Note the precise wording of Canon 32 of the Decree on Justification, which agrees with Aquinas in *ST* I–II, q. 114 that the objects of merit are, within this life, an increase in grace and, eschatologically, eternal life.

53 In I–II, q. 114, a. 8, Aquinas derives the possibility of meriting an increase of grace or charity from the general principle that if merit applies to the term of a movement (eternal life), then it must also apply to the whole progress of that movement (increase in grace or charity along the way).

54 Aquinas, at least in passing, equates justification and the remission of sins (I–II, q. 113, a. 1c). As one does not merit justification, so one does not merit the remission of sins.

55 For example, even Hampson thinks that Trent teaches that, while we do not initially merit justification, we come to merit justification by our later good works. See Hampson, *Christian Contradictions*, p. 212.

56 Kolb and Wengert, *Book of Concord*, p. 171. This citation is from the octavo edition of the Apology, the basis of the German translation included in the original Book of Concord, rather than the slightly earlier quarto edition, which came to replace the octavo edition in many editions of the Book of Concord, including the widely used Tappert translation into English. The quarto edition's statements on merit are similar to those of the octavo edition, but less precise [*The Book of Concord: The Confessions of the Evangelical Lutheran Church*, ed. and trans. Theodore G. Tappert (Philadelphia, PA: Fortress Press, 1959), pp. 162f]. It should be noted that while the Apology is generally ascribed to Melanchthon, Luther and others participated in the revision that produced the octavo edition.

57 The first volume, which includes the discussion of justification, appeared in 1565. Citations will be both to the English translation [Martin Chemnitz, *Examination of the Council of Trent*,

Part I, trans. Fred Kramer (St. Louis, MO: Concordia Publishing House, 1971)] and to the original Latin in the 1861 Preuss edition [Martin Chemnitz, *Examen Concilii Tridentini*, ed. Eduard Preuss (Berlin: G. Schlawitz, 1861)].

58   Chemnitz, *Examination, I*, p. 653; Chemnitz, *Examen*, p. 212.
59   Chemnitz, *Examination, I*, p. 654; Chemnitz, *Examen*, p. 213.
60   Note that Trent's canon 26 on justification states that reward comes "from God through his mercy and the merit of Jesus Christ" (DH 1576). The sense in which Aquinas has a "juridical" understanding of merit is well discussed in Wawrykow, *God's Grace*, pp. 203f.
61   Kolb and Wengert, *Book of Concord*, p. 171.
62   Chemnitz, *Examination, I*, p. 655; Chemnitz, *Examen*, p. 213.
63   Pesch, "Canons of the Tridentine Decree", p. 190.
64   On good works as necessary, see Martin Chemnitz, *Loci Theologici*, ed. Polycarp Leyser (Frankfurt: Sumptibus Haeredum D. Tobiae Mevii, & Elerdi Schumacheri, 1653), Vol. 3, pp. 44–51; English translation, Martin Chemnitz, *Loci Theologici*, trans. J. A. O. Preus (St. Louis, MO: Concordia Publishing House, 1989), pp. 612–619. On good works as pleasing to God; Chemnitz, *Loci Theologici*, Vol. 3, pp. 17–19; English, pp. 581–583.
65   Chemnitz, *Loci Theologici*, Vol. 3, p. 10; English translation, p. 575.
66   Pesch, *Rechtfertigung bei Luther und Thomas*, p. 788.
67   Thérèse of Lisieux, *Story of a Soul: The Autobiography of St. Thérèse of Lisieux*, third edition, trans. John Clarke (Washington, DC: ICS Publications, 1996), p. 277.
68   *Catechism of the Catholic Church*, second edition (Rome: Libreria Editrice Vaticana, 2000), para. 2011.
69   See here Aquinas on the *amor amicitiae*, ST I–II.q. 26, a. 4, and Scharlemann, *Aquinas and Gerhard*, p. 222.
70   Luther himself is willing to say that Abraham "sees that it is impossible for God not to have regard for the righteous; . . . Abraham wanted to compel God to forgive [*cogens Deum ad ignoscendum*]. . . . Abraham reminds God of his duty [*admonet sui offitii*] to spare the righteous and, because of the righteous, even the wicked" WA 43:43; LW 3:234f.
71   Formula of Concord, Solid Declaration, III, 62, in Kolb and Wengert, *Book of Concord*, p. 556.
72   Formula of Concord, Solid Declaration, III, 65, in Kolb and Wengert, *Book of Concord*, p. 556.
73   Gerhard O. Forde, *Justification by Faith—A Matter of Death and Life*, (Philadelphia, PA: Fortress Press, 1982), p. 37.
74   Forde, *Justification by Faith*, p. 22.
75   Eberhard Jüngel, *Justification: The Heart of the Christian Faith: A Theological Study with an Ecumenical Purpose*, trans. Jeffrey F. Cayzer (Edinburgh: T&T Clark, 2001), p. 242; Eberhard Jüngel, *Das Evangelium von der Rechtfertigung des Gottlosen als Zentrum des christlichen Glaubens: Eine theologische Studie in ökumenischer Absicht* (Tübingen: Mohr Siebeck, 1998), pp. 205f.
76   Jüngel, *Justification*, p. 182; Jüngel, *Evangelium der Rechtfertigung*, p. 155.
77   To say that for Luther or Lutheranism there is no such movement or no progress in such a movement, as is said by Forde (Forde, *Justification by Faith*, pp. 25f) or more crudely by Hampson when she is describing Lutheranism (Hampson, *Christian Contradictions*, p. 50) is utterly to misrepresent the Reformation. See, most obviously, Luther in the Large Catechism II, 57: "Because holiness has begun and is growing daily, we await the time when our flesh will be put to death, will be buried with all its uncleanness, and will come forth gloriously and arise to complete and perfect holiness in a new, eternal life. Now, however, we remain only halfway pure and holy." In Kolb and Wengert, *Book of Concord*, p. 438.
78   WA 8:111; LW 32:235.
79   Pesch, "Canons of the Tridentine Decree", p. 198; Otto Hermann Pesch, "Die Lehre vom 'Verdienst' als Problem für Theologie und Verkündigung", in *Dogmatik in Fragment: Gesammelte Studien*, (Mainz: Matthias Grünewald Verlag, 1987), pp. 414–416.

2

EX OCCIDENTE LUX? AQUINAS AND EASTERN ORTHODOX THEOLOGY

BRUCE D. MARSHALL

An ancient saying has it that "the enemy of my enemy is my friend". Whether or not openly invoked, this sentiment frequently fits the conduct of theologians, and not only of warriors and politicians. As early as the four-teenth century, some in the Byzantine church already saw in Thomas Aquinas their chief theological enemy. Protestants too have long seen in Aquinas the most obvious theological embodiment of the errors which jus-tified their separated existence. As Aquinas's standing in Roman Catholicism rose to that of "common doctor" by the late nineteenth century, Protestants and Orthodox alike found yet greater warrant for their opposition to his views. Since Vatican II, however, Roman Catholic theologians have to a sig-nificant extent joined in opposing Aquinas, or at least the "Thomism" which seeks to represent him in each theological generation. Thus Catholic as well as Protestant theology has for some time now made common cause with Orthodoxy against the common doctor. Finding a shared enemy in Aquinas has been a catalyst, and not just a result, of greater ecumenical agreement in theology.

It has perhaps become more common in recent years to regard Augustine as the main western counterpoint to Orthodox teaching, rather than Aquinas. The complaints lodged against both, however, are much the same. And Orthodox theologians over the last hundred years have often zeroed in on Aquinas as the one in whom standard western teaching takes on that form which most needs to be combated. Vladimir Lossky is a case in point, espe-cially on trinitarian issues. Aquinas's trinitarian theology epitomizes those western claims about the Trinity from which, as Lossky sees it, originate not only the separation of the eastern and western churches, but virtually all the

Bruce D. Marshall
Perkins School of Theology, Southern Methodist University, PO Box 750133, Dallas, TX 75275-1033, USA

errors which beset western theology.[1] Sergei Bulgakov is perhaps the main alternative in modern Orthodox theology to the "neo-patristic" (or perhaps more precisely neo-Palamite) view represented by Lossky and many others.[2] Yet despite being far more critical of the church fathers than Lossky, and far more open to Orthodox use of ideas stemming from western philosophy and theology, Bulgakov is at least as stringent in his opposition to Aquinas.[3] This polemic against Aquinas no doubt owes something to the situation of Russian Orthodoxy in the Paris emigration, as a displaced minority in a traditionally Catholic country, whose theological life was dominated at the time by competing neo-Thomistic interpretations of the common doctor. But it led, in any event, to the formation of objections against Aquinas which have become ecumenically commonplace.

The encounter between Aquinas and eastern theology began, of course, with Thomas himself. Aquinas was regularly engaged with the doctrinal issues in dispute between the eastern and western churches, by then divided, above all the *Filioque* and cognate trinitarian matters. Here he vigorously defended western teaching.[4] But he also read widely and sympathetically in the Greek Fathers (albeit in Latin translations), and drew on them extensively in the *Summa theologiae* and other synthetic works (where Pseudo-Dionysius and John of Damascus get the most attention), and also in his biblical commentaries (where John Chrysostom assumes particular importance).[5]

Here, however, I will concentrate on systematic rather than historical questions. I will focus, in fact, on a single problem, though one which appears to lie at the heart of many objections to Aquinas. The worry, in a word, is that the Trinity makes no difference to Aquinas. The economy of salvation, as Aquinas understands it, would be just the same even if God were not the Trinity.

Even here it will be necessary to be selective. I will not go into the claim that Aquinas has a "Nestorian" Christology, and so supposes that the Logos, and *a fortiori* the whole Trinity, are not really engaged with the saving economy. While sometimes directed against western theology in very broad terms, this charge seems especially ill-suited to Aquinas. He gives a remarkably vigorous and explicit account of the ancient conviction that Christ is one: one divine person, who alone is the subject of all that the human being Jesus does and suffers. "If there were another hypostasis in Christ beyond the hypostasis of the Word, it would follow that whatever belongs to this human being would be verified of someone other than the Word—for example, to be born of the Virgin, to suffer, to be crucified, and to be buried". Against this Thomas cites Cyril of Alexandria's fourth anathema against Nestorius, authoritatively approved, as he understands it, by the Council of Ephesus (431).[6] Because Christ is one, conversely, the human being Jesus is truly the subject of all that the Logos is and does: "Because in Christ there is a single supposit, hypostasis, and person . . . we can say that the Son of man created the stars".[7] The unity of Christ is no merely theoretical matter for Aquinas. On it hangs the scandal of the gospel: the preaching of the cross is foolishness to the world, he argues in comment on I Cor. 1:18, "because it includes something which seems impossible according to human wisdom, namely that God dies (*Deus moriatur*), and that the omnipotent becomes subject to the power of the violent". The faithful, however, "see in the cross of Christ the death of God, by which he conquers the devil and the world".[8]

The complaint that Aquinas makes the Trinity remote from human life and history can, however, be reformulated in a more plausible way. The problem has two basic parts. (1) Certainly the Holy Spirit, if not the Son, remains fundamentally absent from the economy of salvation. (2) This profoundly inadequate conception of God's saving work stems from primordial mistakes in the way Aquinas thinks about the persons of the Trinity themselves, and how we are related to them.

To assess the justice of these complaints, I will look at some of Thomas's ideas about deification and grace, and then at some of his claims about the persons of the Trinity, and the way we know them. Many of the criticisms of Aquinas now shared by Orthodox theologians and their friends in the west touch on some genuine element in Aquinas's teaching. Whether they are really fair to Aquinas's views is another matter. But the theologically decisive issue is whether Aquinas offers an account of the disputed questions which does better justice than the views of his critics to matters with which both are concerned.

Deification and Grace

At least since Anselm western theology has been burdened, according to some influential Orthodox theologians of the last century, by an overwhelmingly juridical conception of the human relationship to God. The chief casualty of this flawed outlook is deification: the patristic concept of the divine-human relationship, according to which the outcome of God's saving work in Christ is not simply the payment of ransom or the remission of guilt, but our full conformity to God, a real participation of human beings in the divine nature (cf. II Pet. 1:4). The chief cause of the flaw is forgetfulness of the Holy Spirit, a failure to appreciate the Spirit's unique personal reality and saving action. And the ultimate root of this pneumatological amnesia is the *Filioque*, which inevitably loses "the true notion of the person of the Holy Spirit, by relegating him to the second rank, making of him a kind of helper or vicar of the Son".[9]

Deification, however, clearly has a role in Aquinas's understanding of human beings and their return to God. God's incarnation bestows upon human beings "full participation in divinity, in which the happiness of the human being and the end of human life truly consist. This is conferred upon us by the humanity of Christ". Indeed the motive of the incarnation can be summed up in the ancient adage, "God became a human being in order that the human being might become God".[10] Participation in the divine nature is not, to be sure, the only benefit bestowed on humanity by the saving economy which turns on the incarnation of the Word. Aquinas lists ten *utilitates* which flow from the incarnation, and observes that there must be many more, exceeding the grasp of human beings in their present state.[11] The divine humility enacted in Mary's womb certainly brings not only union with God for fallen creatures, but gifts of exemplary and juridical kinds (assuming that "satisfaction" is a juridical concept).[12] Moreover, explicit references to deification, while not entirely wanting, are rare in Aquinas. Nevertheless the use he does make of these notions ties them closely to central elements in his account of the return of the rational creature to God: grace, adoptive sonship, and the beatific vision.[13] In fact "all of faith's thinking concerns these two things: the divinity of the triune God, and the humanity of Christ. And no wonder. The humanity of Christ is the way by which we attain divinity (*ad Divinitatem pervenitur*)".[14]

The Holy Spirit is the agent directly responsible for this human conformity to God, and it is the Spirit's personal action which links grace, adoption, and the *visio Dei*. The divine light which "belongs to the society of the blessed seeing God [cf. Rev. 21:23] . . . renders them deiform, that is, similar to God".[15] The vision of God in eternity fully actualizes that participation in the divine nature which we already now enjoy by the grace of the Holy Spirit. "The Holy Spirit who indwells a human being by grace is", after all, "the sufficient cause of eternal life". Therefore "the grace of the Holy Spirit which we have in the present life, while it is not equal to glory in its degree of actuality (*in actu*), is nonetheless equal to it in power". For just this reason, Aquinas observes, the indwelling Spirit "is called 'the pledge of our inheritance' [II Cor. 1:22]".[16]

For Aquinas, though, II Peter's talk of sharing in the divine nature links up naturally with Paul's idea that our return to God takes the form of a divine adoption (Rom. 8:15–17, 29–30; Gal. 4:1–7).[17] In this act of adoption we receive, by God's wholly unmerited favor, the full inheritance which belongs by nature to his only-begotten Son—indeed we become so fully the Father's children by the free grace of adoption that we are entitled, just as much as the eternal Son, to have all that is his. To decline this title, whether moved by humility or pride, is to refuse the grace of adoption itself, and so to refuse a share in the divine nature: by the grace of the Holy Spirit "moving us into eternal life . . . human beings, having been made partakers of the divine nature, are adopted as children of God (*in filium Dei*), to whom he owes an inheritance by right of adoption, according to Rom. 8[:17]: 'if children (*filii*), then heirs'".[18]

Since participation in the divine nature takes the specific form of adoption by the Father, deification has an irreducibly trinitarian structure. It is not conformity to an impersonal divine nature, but conformity precisely to the Son. "Adoptive sonship is a participated likeness (*similitudo*) of natural

Sonship".[19] By the Spirit's grace we partake of the divine nature as possessed by the Son in particular. We are conformed specifically to the *filiatio* of Jesus Christ, to the characteristic and relationship eternally constitutive of his personal identity as the Son, in distinction from the Father, the Spirit, and everything else.[20] To become a partaker of the divine nature for Aquinas is thus to take on by grace the Son's unique way of being God, but not his personal identity—we have the full likeness of his Sonship, of his own distinctive way of possessing the divine nature, though we do not, of course, have numerically the same *filiatio*.

Thus the Son is, as Aquinas says, the *exemplar* of our adoptive participation in the divine nature. The Spirit has a different role. He is the *imprimens* of the divine act of adoption, the one who impresses upon us the likeness of the eternal Son become flesh, or, as Aquinas likes to say, the one who "configures" us to the Son.[21] The Spirit's distinctive place in the act of adoption is to serve as direct agent of our conformity to God rather than as the original on which we come to be patterned. The Father's role in the act of adoption is, of course, to do the adopting. He is the *auctor* of our deifying adoption, the one who gives us the entirety of his own inheritance by the gift of the Spirit conforming us to Jesus Christ, the natural heir.[22]

Characteristically for Thomas, however, the matter is more complicated than this. In order to uphold the uniqueness of the incarnation it is necessary, he supposes, to maintain that the outcome or term of God's adoptive "assumption" of human beings is a relationship of the adopted to all three persons of the Trinity, while the outcome of the assumption of human nature in the incarnation is a relationship (namely hypostatic union) of that nature to the Son alone. Assumption "by the grace of adoption . . . is common to the three persons with regard both to its principle [viz., the act which causes it] and to its term".[23] This suggests that the divine act of adoption results in some kind of conformity to the Father and the Spirit, and not only to the Son, though Thomas does not elaborate on what this might be. (There surely is, as we will see momentarily, a sense in which the Spirit conforms us to himself, and not only to the Son. But this has to do with other divine acts, and other outcomes).

This passage need not, however, be taken as a repudiation by Thomas of his own insistence elsewhere that the outcome of adoption is a participation in the Son's *filiatio* in particular, and not only in features (such as the divine *bonitas*, which he mentions here) shared by the three persons in virtue of their common essence. As the act of adoption is common to the three persons, yet undertaken by each in a different way, so (indeed *a fortiori*) the divine essence and goodness common to the three is possessed by each in his own particular way: "the same essence which is paternity in the Father is filiation in the Son".[24] By adoption we therefore participate in the divine nature in a way which conforms to this distinctive—and fixed—pattern of personal possession. Whatever conformity to the Father and the Spirit may result from the act of adoption, it cannot displace that share in the eternal Son's own filial rights in which adoptive sonship chiefly consists.

Evidently Thomas does not think of either the act of adoption or the relations which result from it as "merely appropriated" (in Karl Rahner's phrase) to the divine persons—if this means that the roles or places of the divine persons in either case are interchangeable, and are attributed to one person rather than another only out of a kind of verbal or epistemic fiction. Thomas has a theology of appropriations, of course, but there is nothing "mere" about them.[25]

An Objection: Created Grace

So far Aquinas's theology apparently fails to give grounds for the worry that he has forgotten the Spirit, or reduced salvation to a purely juridical relationship. On the contrary: he insists on the Father's deification of the human creature through adoptive union with the Son, by the personal action of the Spirit. Orthodox theologians (and western critics of Aquinas) have often not noticed this aspect of Thomas's theology. But they might well wonder whether he can be entirely serious about this—whether he can mean by it anything like an Orthodox theologian might normally mean—given the prominence of another concept in his theology: the notion of "created grace".

Grace, Aquinas often says, is a quality (specifically a disposition or habit) created by God in the soul. This "infused" disposition (following Rom. 5:5) is, to be sure, "supernatural". We could not acquire it by our own efforts, and it renders us capable of attitudes and actions beyond our natural ability (like the love of *caritas*, or friendship with God).[26] But, the objection runs, this "grace" remains wholly a created reality, and therefore incapable of sustaining a genuine notion of deification. Interposed between God and the human being, Thomas's idea depersonalizes and reifies grace, and keeps God at a distance. Deprived of direct contact with the persons of the Trinity—and especially with the Holy Spirit, who is supposed to be the immediate agent of deification—we are conformed not to God, but merely to a creature. "Created grace" leaves us not with deification, but with a sort of creaturification.[27]

A. N. Williams proposes radical surgery at this point. Thomas, she observes, uses the term "gratia creata" only infrequently, and then in a sense quite different from that which prompts the worries of Orthodox theologians. From this we may infer that effectively he has no doctrine of grace as a created reality, which may be regarded as an unfortunate invention of later Thomists.[28]

This, however, is to mistake a lexical observation for a conceptual point. Thomas takes it to be "obvious" (*manifestum*) that grace includes not only God's own love for human beings, co-eternal with himself and so not created, but also "the good caused in the creature which follows from God's love". Since uncreated love and creaturely good are linked as cause and effect, "grace" refers primarily to God's own love, but also to the gift which love freely gives—to "what grace puts (*ponit*) in the person".[29] This gift is a form or quality, specifically "the gift of a disposition" (*aliquod habituale donum*), which enables us to seek and love God "with delight and readiness" (*suaviter et prompte*).[30] Since it is a form, the grace which God's love freely imparts to the soul has to be a created reality (*aliquid creatum*).[31] God cannot, either in his essence or (*a fortiori*) in any of his persons, be the form of anything else.[32] If God is to give us the highest gift, "the eternal good of the creature, namely God himself", then he must, it seems, give us the created means to receive him.[33] The grace of God cannot be reduced to this created gift, but neither can it be without the gift. Aquinas's hesitation to speak of "created grace" attests not his denial of this claim, but his high estimate of what the created gift of divine love accomplishes. "Grace is said to be created, in that on account of it human beings are created, that is, established in a new existence—*ex nihilo*, which is to say, not from merits, as Eph. 2:9 teaches: 'created in Christ Jesus for good works'".[34]

Thomas's vigorous defense of the thought that grace has to include a created component poses, however, no obstacle to his affirmation that grace deifies us. Grace deifies not because it lacks any created reality, but because of the kind of created reality grace is. As Aquinas often insists, grace—*gratia gratum faciens*, the created gift which flows from God's unexacted love for the creature and makes us pleasing to him—"conforms" or "conjoins" the soul to God.[35] Were the created gift a kind of adhesive medium interposed between God and the soul, like mortar between bricks, it would join the soul and God only indirectly, rather than by contact, and so any conformity or likeness between the soul and God would be an accident, rather than a result brought about by grace itself. In the knowledge and love wrought by grace, however, "the rational creature . . . touches God himself".[36] Grace, precisely as created gift, does not block direct contact between God and the creature, "rather by grace we are joined to God himself, with nothing created intervening".[37] This immediate contact brings about, moreover, a conformity not only to the divine nature, but to each of the divine three in his personal uniqueness, as we have already observed. "In order for a divine person to be sent to a human being by grace, it is necessary that there be a likening (*assimilatio*) of the human being, by a gift of grace, to the divine person who is sent."[38]

The created gift of grace is a "medium" for Thomas, all right, but evidently not in the sense of an intermediary between God and the human being which keeps the two apart. Rather it is the means by which they are joined. We are not conformed *to* the created habit of grace, touching it instead of God; rather this grace is our conformity itself, the impression the Spirit makes upon us in order that we may touch God.[39] The right simile here is not bricks and mortar, but the ring and the wax. In order to come into contact with sealing wax, a signet ring has to make an impression upon the wax, giving the wax its own shape at every point. Unless the ring creates this impression, there is no contact with the wax, but only distance. The impressed form of the ring is necessary in order to eliminate this distance, and genuinely conform the wax to the ring. But of course the ring itself is not the form of the wax; the ring's impression is. Without the seal of the Spirit, without the created form impressed by the outpoured Spirit, there is no contact of creature with creator—no genuine indwelling of the divine persons, and so no deification.[40]

It is not, however, the metaphysics of form that mainly motivates Aquinas's insistence on "created grace", but the conviction that the indwelling of omnipotence—of the divine persons—has to have an effect on us. So he can make his point about our union with the persons of the Trinity without drawing on the idea of form. The coming of the person of the Word into our human flesh, and of this incarnate Word into our souls, imparts to us divine wisdom, a share in the Son's own knowledge of the Father. This belongs to our inheritance as the Father's adopted children. The wisdom in which the incarnate Word instructs us, however, is not, and cannot be, a merely cognitive grasp. The perception of the Son, and with him of the Father, must be "a kind of experiential knowledge" (*experimentalem quamdam notitiam*), a connatural affinity or likening in which the mind "tastes, as it were", the Son, and so the Father himself. By the incarnate Word's instruction our minds must "break out in love's affection", not because of what our minds are—we too often only know, where we should also love—but because of who the incarnate Son is. He "is not just any sort of word, but one who breathes out Love"—the Holy Spirit. And "just because the Holy Spirit is Love (*Amor*), by the gift of love (*caritas*) the soul is made like the Holy Spirit". By the gift through which the Spirit conforms us to himself, we are fired with love for the Son's instruction, ready to taste the infinite good the adopting Father bestows—his eternal Son, become our flesh.[41]

Aquinas's understanding of the Spirit's work, it appears, not only affirms the deification of rational creatures, but actually sheds light on the subject. By thinking of intimate likeness to God as a conformity, created by the Spirit's touch, to the incarnate Son, Aquinas offers a way of understanding the common faith of east and west: that we human beings have union with the divine persons, and so a real participation in the divine nature, while remaining creatures, rather than members, of the Trinity.[42]

Trinitarian Mission and Personal Identity

Since, as we have seen, Thomas robustly asserts that creatures are immediately united to both the Spirit and the incarnate Son, he and his critics, Orthodox and otherwise, together face two problems of the broadest systematic import. How is it that the persons of the Trinity succeed in giving themselves to us fully, but freely? How, in other words, do they give themselves in such a way that they neither withhold their personal identities from us, nor lose them in the act of the gift? Inseparable from this question about the divine persons and their actions is an epistemic problem. How can we know the very identities of the divine persons—who they are, from all eternity—as we presumably must do if we are to know that just these persons have given themselves to us in time? In terms now current (though I think misleading at best; see below), we need to look at the way Aquinas conceives "the economic Trinity" in its relationship to "the immanent Trinity". In Aquinas's own terms, we need to find a link between the temporal missions of the Spirit and the Son from the Father, on the one hand, and the eternal processions and relations in which the persons of the Trinity have their identities, on the other.

Aquinas and his critics agree that we are united by the action of the Spirit to the persons of the Trinity themselves, and not to created substitutes or *Doppelgänger* of the divine persons. The Spirit, moreover, joins us to each of the persons of the Trinity in such a way that we can know about our union with them. Our deifying adoption can be thought by us; it can become the content of our own true beliefs. Just because we are not joined merely to created effects of the triune God, but to Spirit, Son, and Father, each in his personal uniqueness, it seems that we have to grasp the very identities of the divine persons if we are to know about this union at all. Did our salvation consist only in conformity to effects created by God, we could, at least in principle, know about this saving union without knowing who the God is that brought it about. In that case God would be for us, at least in this life, simply the source of these effects, we would know not who or what. But God has not withheld himself from us in this way. Rather he has given us, even now, a real share in his own tri-personal life. So it must be possible for us to know the identities of the divine persons, and not only to know what effects they have caused.

How, then, can we get a fix on the identities of the divine persons? Given the way the problem arises—that God acts on us in such a way that we have to be able to know who he is in his innermost depths—two alternatives apparently present themselves. Either

(1) the identities of the divine persons just consist in the acts by which they join us to themselves,

or

(2) the identities of the divine persons do not consist in these acts, or any act whose outcome or effect is a creature.

If (1) is correct, then the contents of at least some acts which yield a created effect will belong to who God is; they will be constitutive of his own identity. If (2) is correct, then the contents of no such act will belong to God's identity, and it will therefore be necessary to specify who each of the divine persons is without introducing into his identity any reference to a temporal act.

The considerable attraction of (1) to a good deal of recent theology no doubt lies to a great extent in the directness with which it solves the epistemic problem. The actions of the divine persons are constitutive of their identities; we know their actions, so we know their identities. We have no need to worry that the persons might be different in themselves than they are in their actions toward us. In fact there is no conceptual space in which this worry can even arise. With that the need to link up the temporal actions of the persons with their eternal identities drops away. By failing to include the temporal actions of the divine persons in its account of their identities, a good deal of traditional trinitarian theology created for itself, so the argument goes, a need which it could not meet—a problem which, in the nature of the case, could not be solved. Better to avoid the problem of how to link action to person in God by avoiding the assumption which generates the problem in the first place.

If (1) is correct, then deifying adoption seems like an especially good candidate for an act in which God has his very identity. Adoption presupposes, to be sure, the divine act by which the eternal Son becomes incarnate, and that by which the Holy Spirit is poured out upon all flesh. But the missions of the Son and the Spirit into the world themselves aim, conversely, at our ordered incorporation into the one nature of the three persons. If we follow (1), then, being the *auctor* of adoption belongs to the Father's identity. No adoption, no Father; or, we could say, a Father who did not adopt us would simply be a different person from the Father whose identity we come to know when he makes us his children in the economy of salvation. Similarly, being the *exemplar* of adoption is constitutive of the Son's identity, and being its *imprimens* constitutive of the Spirit's identity (borrowing, for a purpose different from his own, Thomas's way of locating the unique role of each person in the ordered act of adoption).

The difficulty, however, is that the divine act of adoption is contingent. God does not have to make a world at all, let alone enter it so as to unite rational creatures to himself. The triune God would be, and so would have his own identity, even if there were nothing other than God. The triune God has his identity, therefore, apart from any contingent acts he may undertake. So it seems impossible that being the *auctor* of the act of adoption can belong to the Father's identity. Whatever it takes to be the Father, whatever makes this person the Father and no one else, he must possess quite apart from any contingent acts he undertakes. The same goes for the Son as incarnate *exemplar* of our adoption, and for the Spirit as outpoured *imprimens*. The identity of Father, Son, and Spirit apparently cannot consist in any action whose term is a creature (like adoption), and not God himself (like the generation of the

Son or the procession of the Spirit), or in any relation resulting from such an action. Human persons may have their very identities in contingent temporal actions, though even there we need to have some principle of selection by which we distinguish actions which are identity-constituting from those which are not. But it seems impossible that the persons of the Trinity could have their identities in this way. Should the identities of the divine persons consist in actions or relations (as has, in fact, generally been supposed), then these must be non-contingent—actions and relations, that is, which involve no reference to creatures.

At this point defenders of (1) will object that having severed the divine persons from their contingent temporal acts in the fashion just described, it becomes impossible to understand how they could give themselves to us— nothing other than themselves, and nothing less. This is surely the right question to ask, and we will return to it. But it ought to be observed that (1) itself offers no satisfying answer to this question. If being, say, the *auctor* of adoption is constitutive of the Father's identity (that is, if he cannot be the Father without it), then we face two possibilities.

(a) The act of adoption is not contingent, and so not free. In that case our union with his Son in the Spirit cannot be a gift from the Father, nor, *mutatis mutandis*, from the Son or the Spirit. The divine three would indeed join us to themselves, but they would not *give* themselves to us. Rather our union with them would be a result they were compelled to achieve in order not to lose themselves.

(b) The act of adoption is genuinely free and contingent. If being the *auctor* of adoption belongs to the Father's very identity, though, then he becomes a different person by undertaking it than he was before (or to factor out temporal connotations, than he was otherwise). The same goes, once again, for the Son and the Spirit. In that case the divine three give us a gift, all right, but they do not give *themselves* to us. Rather they lose themselves in the very attempt, becoming new and different persons in the effort contingently to give themselves to us. And so they must do, if their contingent saving actions toward us are also identity-constituting for them.

Just here the claim that the economic Trinity and the immanent Trinity are identical—the "axiom" of much modern trinitarian theology—generates a great deal of confusion (while usually associated with Karl Rahner, who formulated it in the fashion now standard, this claim was in play well before him). If we take this axiom at face value, then the immanent Trinity must have all, and only, the same properties as the economic Trinity. Should each be strictly identical with the other, there simply is no distinction between the immanent and the economic Trinity. That is simply what it means for A to be identical with B. In that case the properties of the economic Trinity are the properties of the Trinity, period. And then (1) is, indeed, our only recourse in thinking about the connection between the divine persons and their actions.

Understandably, if inconsistently, many theologians lose their nerve at this point, without really being able to embrace the alternative, namely (2). So they try to find a middle course. Yes, some argue, the economic Trinity is the same as the immanent, but the immanent is not the same as the economic—as though B = A could be true, while A = B was false. Others say that the immanent Trinity is identical with the economic, "setting aside", however, the properties which the triune God takes on by his economic action. But if B = A, we cannot specify A's properties by "setting aside" any of B's.[43] Taken at face value, as in (1), the much-credited identity axiom seems false, but taking it otherwise just generates incoherence.[44]

To be sure, one might take the axiom to mean that the persons of the Trinity are identical in one respect, but not in another. In particular, we could say that the persons themselves are the same "economically" (in relation to the world) as they are "immanently" (were there no world), but their actions are not the same in the two cases. Following this path, of course, amounts to denying that the economic and immanent Trinity are, properly speaking, identical. With that we do not so much interpret the standard axiom as reject it. And thereby we rightly give up the quest for a middle course between (1), which consistently draws a conclusion implied in the axiom, and (2), which rejects that conclusion.

We return, then, to the thought that no temporal act or relation to creatures is part of what it takes to be Father, Son, or Spirit—we return, that is, to (2). In that case, if we are to know who the persons of the Trinity are, we need to be able to isolate some feature or characteristic of each (perhaps several) which is not a temporal action or its outcome. But the very acts by which they join us to themselves (and perhaps other temporal acts as well), while not constitutive of their identities, have to give us an adequate basis upon which to take this step. We need, as it were, to be able to precipitate out those non-contingent features in which the identities of Father, Son, and Spirit consist, and which, by joining us to themselves, they make known to us.

In western theology there is a well-established way to do this. The basic idea, on which there are a number of variants, is that a divine person can be sent into the world only by one from whom he eternally proceeds. In scripture's narrative of salvation, some persons of the Trinity are clearly "sent" by others. This sending, moreover, seems to have a definite pattern to it: the Father sends the Son, and both the Father and the Son send the Spirit; the Spirit sends no divine person, and the Father is never sent. So, for example, the Father sends the Son to be the incarnate *exemplar* of our adoptive sonship, and Father and Son together send the Spirit into our hearts to be the *imprimens* of that adoption.

In this pattern of missions we can perceive the origin of one divine person from another. For how is it that, in God, one person is in a position to send another? It cannot be due to any inherent superiority, "as a master sends a servant". Nor, conversely, can it be a matter of the greater heeding the word of the lesser, "as when an advisor is said to send a king into battle".[45] The only remaining possibility is that one divine person is able to send another because the one he sends originates from him: "In God [mission] implies only a coming forth by way of origin, which takes place in full equality".[46] Thus the missions of the persons display for us the specific order in which one originates from another.[47] The Father sends the Son, who must therefore originate from him, while Father and Son both send the Spirit, who must therefore originate from both. The Father, unsent, must be unoriginate. This order of origin in turn makes available to us the unique identity of each person of the Trinity—the primordial characteristics without which each would not be the one he is.[48]

Like most modern Orthodox theologians, Lossky is concerned to steer well clear of (1). He rejects any suggestion that the creative and redeeming work of the Trinity is other than free and contingent, any confusion of *oikonomia* with *theologia*.[49] At the same time, he is an influential opponent of any trinitarian theology in which "essential unity takes priority over personal diversity".[50] He mistakenly thinks this puts him at odds with Thomas Aquinas. Nonetheless, one might expect a theologian with these twin convictions to embrace, as Aquinas does, some version of the idea that mission displays origin, and origin gives personal identity. Yet Lossky apparently repudiates any thought that the order among the persons of the Trinity exhibited by the economy of salvation gives us access to their inmost personal identities.

In . . . the manifestation of divinity, one can establish the order of the persons, the *taxis*. But one must not, strictly speaking, attribute this to the trinitarian existence in itself, in spite of the "monarchy" and the "causality" of the Father. These do not confer upon him any hypostatic primacy over the other two hypostases, since he is a person only because the Son and the Spirit are also.[51]

On this score Lossky is perhaps not entirely consistent. At times he seems to say that the economic *taxis* or order among the persons does yield knowledge of who they are, and that this knowledge could come in no other way.[52] He even allows that we can "strip away every economic attribution" from the persons of the Trinity, and so "decant" the unique relational characteristics of the three (paternity, filiation, and procession)—as long as the mystery of the Trinity in unity remains intact.[53] This puts him on the road Aquinas wants to travel. But his apparently opposed insistence that we cannot (as it is often put) "read off" the identities of the divine persons from their presence and action in time—not simply that we lack the wit to do it, but that there is no basis in God *for* doing it—has found repeated echoes in recent Orthodox theology.[54]

Lossky has multiple motives here. He does not contest the traditional take on scripture's pattern of temporal missions, where the Father and the Son both send the Holy Spirit, who sends neither. Given this pattern, the principle that a divine person can only be sent in time by another from whom he originates in eternity implies the *Filioque*. Since the late nineteenth century Orthodox theologians have on occasion regarded the *Filioque* as a tolerable (if mistaken) theological opinion. Lossky wholly rejects it, not only as a grave and church-dividing doctrinal error, but as the sure index of an impersonal essentialism chronic in the west, and ruinous of its trinitarian theology.[55] But Lossky also wants to combat an overreaching rationalism which "puts the God of the philosophers and scholars at the heart of the living God".[56] In trinitarian theology this attempt at a conceptual domestication of the divine fails to appreciate that the relations of origin in God (paternity, filiation, and procession) do not constitute the personal identities of Father, Son, and Spirit. Instead they are "signs of the diversity of the persons", which in itself is an "absolute" that finally remains "inexpressible".[57]

For Aquinas, then, the triune God is entirely free to undertake a saving economy which includes temporal missions, or not to. But if there are to be any temporal missions, they will have to follow a fixed pattern prescribed by the relations of origin among the persons of the Trinity. A position like Lossky's agrees that the saving missions of the Son and the Spirit from the Father are free and contingent. But he apparently rejects any necessary relationship between this contingent pattern of temporal missions and the non-contingent order in which the Son and the Spirit proceed eternally from the unoriginate Father.

This is to say, though, that any order of origination among the persons of the Trinity is compatible with any pattern of temporal missions. That the Father begets the Son and that the Spirit proceeds from the Father (as third person rather than second) does not require that the Father can send the Son and Spirit, but cannot be sent by them. Still less does it establish any fixed relationship of possible mission between the Son and the Spirit. And this means that we have no way of knowing, from the pattern of temporal missions which actually comes to pass, what relationships of origin may obtain among the divine persons. Jesus obeys the Father, and undertakes his journey to the cross as a mission offered in love to the Father. But for all we can tell from the relationships exhibited by the history of salvation, Jesus might actually be the Father or the Spirit incarnate, rather than the Son. That Jesus calls the one who sends him "Father", and himself "Son", fails to bridge this gap. Lossky's point, indeed, is precisely that the relationships of fatherhood and sonship on display in the economy of salvation do not require an eternal relationship in which one comes forth from the other. Or so it appears, at any rate, when he pursues the line of thought about the economic *taxis* of the persons which succeeds in generating disagreement with Aquinas.

We might, however, read a position like Lossky's differently, taking our cues at a point where he seems to agree with Aquinas: his suggestion that we can "decant" relational properties of the divine persons from their economic attributions. The idea would be that while the economic pattern of missions does not conform to the order of *origination* among the divine persons, it does reflect relational *properties* unique to each person. This would work better for the Son than the Spirit. In the relationships of fatherhood and sonship which the economy exhibits we can perceive non-contingent relational characteristics which make it appropriate for one person (the Father) to send, and the other (the Son) to be sent. How the mission of the Holy Spirit from both the Father and the Son reflects a characteristic ("procession") which refers to the Father alone remains less clear.

Among Orthodox theologians Dumitru Staniloae takes a different view, and insists on the need for a reliable link between the way the persons are in the economy and the attributes they would have even apart from the economy, in their eternal *theologia*.[58] On this score he makes the influential suggestion (under the guidance of several late Byzantine theologians) that the temporal economy of the persons conforms not, once again, to their order of origin, but to a fixed and non-contingent order in which one "shines forth from" or "manifests" the other. In particular, the Holy Spirit originates from the Father alone, but comes forth eternally to rest on the Son, who rejoices in this gift. As such the Spirit "shines forth" from the Father, manifesting the Father's love for the Son, and equally "shines forth" from the Son, manifesting the Son's love for the Father. The temporal abiding of the Spirit on the Son, and the Spirit's temporal "shining forth" from the Son as well as from the Father, reflect this fixed inner-divine order of abiding and manifestation, without requiring that the Spirit actually originate from the Son. In this way Staniloae tries to establish explicitly what Lossky only hints at: a basis in God for tying the temporal missions of the persons to the eternal order among them, without implying the hated *Filioque*.

Does this approach account for our access to the identity of the divine persons by way of their temporal missions? The strategy is to interpose a middle term between the missions of the persons and their identities which links the two without requiring mission to follow the order of origin. Presumably this third term either gives us identity-constituting features of the divine persons, or it does not. In each case problems arise.

Lossky's version of the strategy seems to take the latter course, especially when he holds that the relational characteristics about which the missions might teach us are "signs" of the personal diversity of the three, rather than features in which their identities actually consist. This simply relocates the problem which leads one to postulate a middle term in the first place. Rather than wondering what the pattern of missions has to do with the identity of the persons, we are now left to wonder what the relational characteristics of fatherhood, sonship, and procession have to do with their identities. As before, the two might vary independently of one another. If paternity, for example, is not in some way constitutive of the Father's identity, then for all we know paternity might actually be a property of the Holy Spirit. In fact Lossky seems to suggest as much when he says that the Father would not be a person without the Son and the Holy Spirit. If the Father's existence as a person, and therefore his personal identity, depends in some way on the Son and the Spirit, then one or both of them presumably has the property of paternity, or something like it, with respect to the Father: *Credo in Patre, qui procedit ex Filio Spirituque.*[59] We could avoid such unwanted results if we had a way of specifying what the Father's identity consists in, and of being sure we were right—that is just the problem we are trying to solve. But since Lossky regards personal identity as finally an "inexpressible" absolute, the problem may simply be insoluble on the terms in which he poses it. In the end, Lossky has considerable difficulty accounting for how the persons of the Trinity give themselves to us so that we actually know who they are, and that they have succeeded in making this supreme gift to us. In fact it seems that on a view of this sort, the divine persons cannot help withholding themselves from us. This seems like a high price to pay for wanting to exclude the *Filioque* a priori.

Staniloae takes the other course. He seems to take the relations of "manifesting" and "being manifested by", and the relation of "shining forth from", as identity-constituting features of the persons to whom they belong.[60] By reflecting these relationships the temporal missions of the divine persons would let us in on their eternal personal identities. Here the difficulty lies in keeping the note of *origin* out of the relationships that the temporal presence of the persons displays to us. For Staniloae the Spirit "shines forth" from the Son and "manifests" the Son to the Father, and the Father to the Son. If "shining forth from the Son" and "manifesting the Son" belong to the Spirit's own identity, then he cannot be without them—no shining forth from the Son, no Holy Spirit.[61] But this means that the being of the Spirit depends on relationships he has to the Son, as the one from whom he shines forth, and the one whom he manifests. And to depend for your being on a relationship to another just is to originate from that person (certainly in God, where there is no question of dependence other than that involving eternal origin). So it looks like the difference between Staniloae's view and Aquinas's, between the Spirit "shining forth" from the Son and "originating" from the Son, is merely verbal. In the Trinity, personal identity seems very deeply bound up with origin. Unlike Lossky, Staniloae apparently accepts this, and thereby succeeds in answering the question of how we can know the eternal identities of the divine persons. But he does so by pretty much agreeing with Aquinas: mission displays origin, and origin gives personal identity.[62]

Objection (1): Does Aquinas have the Pattern of Missions Right?

Contemporary trinitarian theologies often take sharp issue with the view of trinitarian procession and personal identity that we have just been examining in light of standard Orthodox criticisms. They object to this common western triadology (from which, as Aquinas boldly puts it, we can "infallibly infer" the *Filioque*) not by denying that mission displays origin, but by contesting the pattern of missions on which the triadology is based.[63] To suppose that the Holy Spirit is only sent by the Son, and in no way sends or acts upon the Son, is simply to misread scripture's narration of God's saving economy. The Spirit reposes and acts upon Jesus throughout the course of his saving mission: in his conception, his baptism, his journey into the wilderness, his proclamation and ministry, his passion and resurrection. To ignore all this in favor of the Spirit's mission from the Son results in that neglect of the Spirit unhappily characteristic, so the objection goes, of western theology as a whole. It produces artificial clarity about the order of origin among the persons at the expense of the Spirit's equality with the Son in the economy of salvation, and in the triune life itself. We need to acknowledge the fully reciprocal character of the relation between the Son and the Spirit in the economy, and therefore in the order of origin: the Son must be thought of as originating eternally in, or perhaps even from, the Spirit.

We cannot undertake a full treatment of this important question here. Two observations will have to suffice. One concerns Aquinas, the other the logic of the matter.[64]

Contrary to what one might expect, Aquinas insists that the Spirit does send the Son. "Now the Lord God and his Spirit have sent me", Isaiah declares (48:16), and Aquinas applies this typologically to the mission Christ receives from the anointing Spirit to proclaim the gospel (cf. Luke 4:18). There is thus a scripturally mandated sense in which "a divine person is sent by another from whom he does not originate".[65]

Lest this be thought to eliminate the needed connection between order of mission and order of origin, Aquinas observes that the Spirit's capacity to send the Son "is to be referred to the human nature in virtue of which he has been sent".[66] This does not mean that the Spirit somehow sends the human nature rather than the person of the Son. Thomas's consistent rejection of Nestorianism bars this reading, but so do his explicit instructions about how to interpret Christological locutions like *secundum quod homo* and *secundum humanitatem* ("in virtue of being man" or "on account of the human nature"). They do not specify the subject to which a predicate (in this case, "sent by the Holy Spirit") applies, but that in virtue of which it applies to the subject.[67] The Holy Spirit genuinely acts upon the incarnate Son, but only in virtue of his incarnation. So if "to send" means to bring about (or have a distinctive role in bringing about) a created state of affairs which is true of a divine person (such as "proclaims the gospel"), then the Spirit sends the Son. But if "to send" means to determine *that* this state of affairs will be true of a divine person, then only one from whom this person originates can send him. In that sense the Spirit cannot send the Son, but the Son can send the Spirit.[68] Jesus's proclamation of good news to the poor at the Spirit's instigation shows that he is the eternal Son, sent into the world by the Father from whom he originates.

Thus Aquinas strives to save both the scriptural data regarding the sending of the divine persons and the principle that these data, rightly read, disclose to us their eternal origin and identity. Still, one senses the force of the objection that this results in a basically unidirectional reading of the relationship between Christ and the Spirit, a kind of Christological domestication of the scriptural witness to the Spirit's work. This may prompt the thought that the connection between mission, origin, and identity needs to be reconceived. On this score, however, our options are limited.

(1) Assume that the relationship of mission between Christ and the Spirit is mutual or reciprocal rather than unidirectional. This presents us with two possibilities:

(a) We could drop the idea that mission displays origin. The economy exhibits a mutual pattern of mission between the Son and the Spirit, but gives us no basis for deciding which of the two, if either, originates from the other. When it comes to the divine three, however, personal identity apparently depends on origin (though there is controversy as to how). That being the case, leaving origin undecided leaves identity undecided, and so unknown—the pattern of temporal missions fails to disclose the inmost identities of the persons after all. We can try to eliminate the cost of leaving origin undecided by rejecting the dependence of identity upon it. But this implies that the identity of the Son (for example) would be unchanged if he did not originate from the Father. What starts out seeming like laudable epistemic modesty soon exacts a heavy toll.

(b) We could hold on to the principle that mission displays origin. In that case, since the Son and the Spirit send each other, they must originate from each other. But this seems impossible. To originate from another is to depend for your total being on another (in Aquinas's terms, to receive complete *esse* from another). I cannot originate from another who cannot exist unless I do, and, moreover, unless I give him existence—if there be any such, as in God there are. So if the Spirit originates from the Son, then the Son cannot originate from the Spirit, and conversely.

(2) Assume that the scriptural pattern of missions is, at root, unidirectional. This also presents us with two possibilities, depending, once again, on whether we reject or accept the principle that mission displays origin.

(a) We might hold that the Son sends the Spirit, and is not sent by him, but deny that this has any implications for the eternal origin of one from the other. This is the traditional position of Eastern Orthodoxy; we have already considered some of the perplexities to which it gives rise. Similar difficulties would attend the converse suggestion that the Spirit's sending of the Son has no implications regarding origin.

(b) We might, finally, hold that the pattern of contingent temporal missions is unidirectional, and does inform us as to personal origin and identity. In that case we could either (i) give priority in the pattern of mission to the Holy Spirit, sending Christ, or (ii) give priority to Christ, sending the Holy Spirit. The first implies that the Son's origin and identity in some way depend on the Spirit, as trinitarian theologies now sometimes suggest. The second implies that the Spirit's origin and identity depend on the Son. This is Thomas's view, and the one traditional in the west, though with a number of variations.

Seizing either one of the alternatives in (b) will require us to account for the scriptural data which supports the other side. Thomas does this by appealing consistently to the Son's incarnate condition as the reason why the Spirit can genuinely act upon him. He thereby hopes to do justice to the witness of scripture regarding the Spirit's action upon the Son, without allowing this simply to reverse the basic direction of the temporal missions: the Spirit acts upon the Son, but does not *send* the Son in the sense in which he is sent by the Son. If, by contrast, we give priority to the Spirit in the pattern of missions, to what will we appeal in order to account for scripture's witness to the Son's action upon the Spirit—for example, his pouring out of the Spirit on all flesh (cf. Acts 2:33)? We might be able to locate a feature of the Spirit's economic condition which promises to account for this, without surreptitiously turning the Son's action upon the Spirit into a mission in the full sense, which (i) is committed to avoiding (the Spirit's self-effacing kenosis, for example). Then the whole issue of mission and origin will come down to which approach most thoroughly and consistently accounts for the full range of scriptural data.[69]

In any case we cannot settle for a standoff between these two opposed ways of assigning priority in the pattern of missions. That would simply return us to the unhappy alternatives in (1). So while Aquinas's way of accounting for the scriptural witness to the missions of the Son and the Spirit does not seem entirely satisfactory, it is less than clear that there is a coherent alternative which is more satisfactory. So it is surely plausible to pursue Thomas's basic strategy (2.b.ii, in the schema just sketched), and attempt to deal with the complexities of the scriptural witness more effectively than he does.[70]

Objection (2): Could Any of the Three Become Incarnate?

A second objection to Aquinas's way of thinking about the connections between mission, origin, and personal identity in God is that Aquinas himself seems not to believe it. The now commonly alleged proof of this is Aquinas's contention that any of the three divine persons could have become incarnate. That a divine person takes flesh is the work of God's power alone, which is numerically the same for all three persons. Therefore, Aquinas argues, "divine power could have united human nature to the person of Father or of the Holy Spirit, just as it united that nature to the person of the

Son".[71] Here, so the objection goes, Aquinas makes plain a baffling conviction: the persons of the Trinity are completely interchangeable in the economy of salvation. Each could assume the place ascribed to another in the scriptural narrative of redemption, and the narrated economy would remain the same. If Jesus's way from the manger to the cross could transpire unchanged were it the incarnate life of the Father or the Spirit rather than the Son, then the relations among these three displayed by Jesus' life can tell us nothing about their relations of origin. So the persons of the Trinity cannot give themselves to us after all. They might have their identities in particular relations of origin to each other, but we could never know what these relations are from their presence and mission in time.

This is the conclusion, we have argued, to which Lossky is driven. But at least he intends otherwise. Aquinas appears explicitly to embrace a complete disconnection of *theologia* from *oikonomia*, and in so doing reflects the common mind of western theology. We end where we began: the Trinity makes no difference; the economy of salvation would be just the same without it.

Aquinas makes it plain, though, that his theology of trinitarian missions has to interpret his decision regarding this scholastic *topos* on divine power and incarnation, and not conversely. Any divine person could become incarnate. But not just any divine person could be sent by another, and not just any divine person could send another. For Thomas this pattern of missions blocks the inference upon which the objection depends. Any divine person could become incarnate, but *this* incarnation, *this* history of salvation, could come about only by the enfleshment of the Son. Jesus is sent by one divine person, and sends another. If Jesus is himself a divine person he can, therefore, only be the Son. The triune God is free to enact an economy of salvation, or not, an incarnational economy, or not, and an economy of the Son's incarnation, or not. But the economy enacted by Jesus's journey from Bethlehem to Golgotha, Emmaus, and Pentecost requires the incarnation of the Son. The economy of salvation which actually comes to pass would not remain unchanged were another person to become incarnate. It would be unimaginably different.

This follows from the logic of the missions as Aquinas conceives them, but he is in any case quite explicit about it. The Father, since he is unoriginate, cannot be sent.[72] This means that if the Father had become flesh, his incarnation, and the human life he might have led as God incarnate, could not have the character of a mission. The Father could be born of a woman, Thomas observes, but he could not be *sent* into the Virgin's womb, since there is no one who could send him. He is not from another, and "without that incarnation would not rise to the level of a mission (*non sufficeret ad rationem missionis*)".[73] Of course the total existence of the Son of God become our flesh, and not simply his acceptance of it, has the meaning of a mission. An incarnate Father could not set his face toward Jerusalem as a mission from another, could not accept the cross in Gesthemane as an act of obedience to another, could not yield up his life as an offering to another. An incarnate Father could not be the *exemplar* of our adoption, the firstborn among many brothers and sisters.[74] An incarnate Father could not, for Aquinas, be Jesus. "There belong to [the Son] entreaty of the Father, making satisfaction to the Father, and other actions of this kind which exhibit the Father's authority".[75] The Father's authority with regard to the Son is simply his capacity, rooted in relations of origin between the Son and himself, to send the Son while himself remaining unsent.[76] By acting in ways which make plain the authority of another over him, by whom he is sent, Jesus shows that he cannot possibly be the Father.

The same goes, though Aquinas is less concerned to make the point explicitly, for the possibility an incarnate Spirit. A Spirit who became flesh could be sent, unlike an incarnate Father, but he still could not be Jesus. The risen Jesus, after all, sends the Holy Spirit; he pours out the Spirit on all flesh. Jesus therefore has the capacity to send the Spirit, and for Aquinas, as we have seen, this capacity implies origin. For that reason it is irreversible. The Spirit might have become incarnate, but a risen Spirit could not pour out the Son, still less the Father, on all flesh. In fact he would have no one to send. An incarnate Spirit could not do what Jesus does, and so he could not be Jesus, any more than an incarnate Father could.

Counterfactual reflection of the kind Aquinas pursues here aims not to satisfy a merely speculative urge, but to clarify the situation that actually obtains. By showing that any of the divine persons might have become incarnate, Aquinas does not seek to obliterate the possibility of knowing the triune God from the scriptural economy. On the contrary, his argument brings into sharper relief the bond of mission to personal identity, the necessity that any possible economy of salvation take shape in conformity to the non-contingent identities of the divine persons. He seeks to isolate the real reason why the Son alone becomes incarnate: not because this was the only incarnational economy of salvation available to God, but because the economy of salvation we actually have could have been realized in no other way. The argument thus underscores, rather than undermines, the triune God's overwhelming commitment to the particular redemptive design which unfolds in scripture, out of all the possibilities available to him. In the saving economy which Jesus's deeds and words enact, "incarnation is a mission, and this certainly belongs to the Son alone, and not to the Father".[77]

Unde Lux?

Aquinas seems to offer considerable resources for coming to grips with problems Christian theologians—Orthodox, Catholic, and Protestant alike—now commonly regard as fundamental. This suggestion could be extended to a number of areas beyond those discussed here. Rather than regarding him merely as their common enemy, theologians across the denominational spectrum have reason to look to him for light. Not, of course, that Aquinas should become everybody's common doctor. But many might find here a way forward on matters they care about—light from the west. Whether this is likely to happen anytime soon is another question. Official dialogue among the divided confessions has come into very heavy weather, and smooth sailing is nowhere on the horizon. Theology at all levels continues to be done in the service of denominational and other partisan loyalties, and appeals to Aquinas inevitably bring with them a raft of dubious but stubborn associations. Yet the light has its own stubborn way of shining, and the theological mind of seeking it, in spite of everything.

NOTES

1   See "La Procession du Saint-Esprit dans la doctrine trinitaire orthodoxe", in *A l'image et à la ressemblance de Dieu* (Paris: Aubier, 1967), pp. 67–93 (ET "The Procession of the Holy Spirit in Orthodox Trinitarian Doctrine", in John H. Erickson and Thomas E. Bird, eds., *In the Image and Likeness of God* [Crestwood, NY: St. Vladimir's Seminary Press, 1985], pp. 71–96); *Essai sur la théologie mystique de l'église d'orient* (Paris: Aubier, 1944) (ET *The Mystical Theology of the Eastern Church* [London: James Clarke, 1957]), especially chapters 2–5. Unless cited only from an English version, all translations are my own.

2   On this see Paul Valliere, *Modern Russian Theology: Bukharev, Soloviev, Bulgakov: Orthodox Theology in a New Key* (Grand Rapids, MI: Wm. B. Eerdmans Publishing Company, 2000); cf. my review in *Modern Theology* Vol. 19 no. 2 (April, 2003), pp. 305–309.

3   Note, e.g., Bulgakov's criticisms of Aquinas on creation (his view betrays an anthropomorphic conception of God which constitutes "the fundamental defect of Western theology in general and of Thomism in particular"), divine and human agency (Aquinas and Thomism "make determinism the universal principle of ontology"), and the eucharist (transubstantiation as characterized by Aquinas is "a rationalistic, groundless determination that does not have any direct relation to the Christian faith", and as such "an influence that must be completely overcome" in Orthodox theology). The cited passages are, respectively, from *The Bride of the Lamb*, trans. Boris Jakim (Grand Rapids, MI: Wm. B. Eerdmans Publishing Company, 2002), pp. 32, 205; "The Eucharistic Dogma", in *The Holy Grail and the Eucharist*, trans. Boris Jakim (Hudson, NY: Lindisfarne Books, 1997), pp. 79, 69.
    Bulgakov's attitude toward Roman Catholicism hardened considerably after a near embrace of the Catholic Church, during his sojourn in the Crimea from late 1918 to late 1922. Upon his exile from Russia Bulgakov soon came "to reproach himself for having succumbed to the 'bolshevik-catholic' temptation, and for having been prepared to betray Orthodoxy 'at the hour of Golgotha'" (as Bernard Marchadier relates, citing passages from Bulgakov's journals, in the Introduction to his translation of Bulgakov's *Sous les remparts de Chersonèse* [Geneva: Ad Solem, 1999], p. 15. This work, which Bulgakov subsequently withheld from publication, fully details his sympathy for Roman Catholicism during his time in the Crimea.). Bulgakov's attitude toward Anglicanism was much more favorable, to the point of proposing, controversially, limited intercommunion between Orthodox and Anglicans. See "By Jacob's Well", in James Pain and Nicholas Zernov, eds., *A Bulgakov Anthology* (London: SPCK, 1976), pp. 100–113, and Bryn Geffert, "Anglicans and Orthodox between the Wars" (Ph.D. Diss., University of Minnesota, 2003), especially pp. 172–204.

4   Aquinas will argue directly against the teaching of contemporary Byzantine theology, at times sharply. See, e.g., *De Potentia* 10, 4, c, *in fin.*: those—"the Greeks"—who say that "the Holy Spirit is from the Father through the Son, yet not from the Son, do not understand their own words (*propriam vocem ignorant*)", since the one necessarily implies the other (*S.*

Thomae Aquinatis Quaestiones Disputatae, vol. 2, ed P. Bazzi et al. [tenth edition, Turin/Rome: Marietti, 1965], p. 267b). Aquinas's treatise *Contra errores Graecorum*, while it defends (in part II) western teaching on the *Filioque*, papal primacy, the unleavened bread, and purgatory, is mainly an interpretation *in meliorem partem* of a collection of texts from the Greek Fathers (subsequently recognized to be highly defective), to which Aquinas responded at the request of Pope Urban IV. "In it one should not seek an encounter of great breadth between the respective positions of the Greeks and the Latins" (Jean-Pierre Torrell, *Initiation à saint Thomas d'Aquin: Sa personne et son oeuvre* [Fribourg: Editions Universitaires Fribourg Suisse & Paris: Cerf, 1993], p. 180. ET *Saint Thomas Aquinas*, vol. 1: *The Person and His Work*, trans. Robert Royal [Washington, D.C.: Catholic University of America Press, 1996], p. 124).

5   In his commentary on the Gospel of John, for example, Aquinas consistently orients himself by appealing to the interpretations of both Augustine and Chrysostom, usually attempting not to harmonize them, but rather to show that the text admits both meanings (though he occasionally concludes that Chrysostom's interpretation is implausible). This commentary draws heavily on the treatment of John in the earlier *Catena Aurea*, where (in the work as a whole) Aquinas cites 57 Greek Fathers, and only 22 Latin ones (cf. Torrell, *Initiation*, p. 203; ET p. 139).

6   *Summa theologiae* III, 2, 3, c; on the unity of Christ see especially III, 17, 1 (From here on I will cite the *Summa theologiae* by part number only; e.g., III = Tertia pars. I follow the Latin text in the Blackfriars edition, 60 vols. [London: Eyre & Spottiswoode, 1964–73]). For Cyril's anathema in the context of the Council of Ephesus, see DH 255.

7   *Super Evangelium S. Ioannis Lectura*, ed R. Cai (fifth edition, Turin/Rome: Marietti, 1952), (caput) 3, (lectio) 2 (no. 468).

8   *In I Cor.* 1, 3 (no. 47). Raphael Cai, O. P., ed., *S. Thomae Aquinatis Super Epistolas S. Pauli Lectura*, vol. 1 (8th edn, Turin/Rome: Marietti, 1953).

9   Vladimir Lossky, "Rédemption et déification", in *A l'image et à la ressemblance de Dieu*, pp. 95–108; here: p. 101 (ET, p. 103). Cf. Dumitru Staniloae, *Theology and the Church*, trans. Robert Barringer (Crestwood, NY: St. Vladimir's Seminary Press, 1980), pp. 13–15, 107–108.

10   III, 1, 2, c. Aquinas attributes this patristic commonplace to Augustine, though the source turns out to be spurious.

11   III, 1, 2, c.

12   Cf. III, 1, 2, c; ad 2.

13   A. N. Williams gathers the explicit texts on deification in the *Summa theologiae* and takes them as basic to interpreting the whole enterprise of the *Summa*: *The Ground of Union: Deification in Aquinas and Palamas* (New York, NY: Oxford, 1999). The texts themselves have long been noticed; cf. already Henri Rondet, *Gratia Christi: Essai d'histoire du dogme et de théologie dogmatique* (Paris: Beauchesne, 1948), pp. 198–199, 208–209. For a rich collection of passages on deification and cognate ideas from Thomas's biblical commentaries, with running annotations, see Luc-Thomas Somme, *Thomas d'Aquin, La divinisation dans le Christ* (Geneva: Ad Solem, 1998). Giles Constable locates the notion of deification in the complex discussion of likeness to Christ in the medieval west; see "The Ideal of the Imitation of Christ", in *Three Studies in Medieval Religious and Social Thought* (Cambridge: Cambridge University Press, 1995), pp. 143–248; on Aquinas see especially pp. 237–238, 245.

14   *Compendium theologiae* I, 2 (no. 3). Raymund Verardo, ed., *S. Thomae Aquinatis Opuscula Theologica*, vol. 1 (Turin/Rome: Marietti, 1954), p. 14a.

15   I, 12, 5, c; cf. ad 3; 6, c.

16   All from I–II, 114, 3, ad 3.

17   Aquinas's theology of adoptive sonship has generated an extensive modern literature. For a recent presentation of many pertinent texts in Thomas, plus an account of the modern debate, see Luc-Thomas Somme, *Fils adoptifs de Dieu par Jésus Christ* (Paris: Vrin, 1997).

18   I–II, 114, 3, c.

19   III, 23, 4, c. "Adoptive sonship is in a certain way a likeness of eternal Sonship" (23, 2, ad 3; cf. 23, 1, ad 2; 24, 3, c).

20   On taking the relation of *filiatio* as a property or characteristic constitutive of the Son as a particular person, cf. I, 30, 2, ad 1 (it is one of the relational properties in God which are "quasi personas constituentes"; 32, 3, c drops the "quasi"). Since "whatever has accidental existence in created realities has substantial existence when carried over into God" (28, 2,

c), the relation of *filiatio* and the property of possessing it must alike be thought of as them-selves having substantial existence. Thus "subsistent Sonship is the person of the Son" (30, 2, c; cf. 41, 6, c). Thomas's idea that the divine persons are constituted by opposed rela-tions, which must be thought of as subsistent, is often taken to be *the* scholastic under-standing of the trinitarian persons. But this idea was in fact extensively contested in the Middle Ages (see below, note 48).

21 See *De Potentia* 10, 4, c (*Quaestiones Disputatae*, vol. 2, p. 267a); *Super Ioannem*, 14, 6 (no. 1957).

22 On Father, Son, and Spirit as, respectively, *auctor*, *exemplar*, and *imprimens* in the divine act of adoption, cf. III, 23, 2, ad 3.

23 III, 3, 4, ad 3.

24 I, 42, 6, ad 3; cf. 42, 4, ad 2. For similar remarks regarding the Spirit, cf. 30, 2, ad 4; 37, 1, ad 4.

25 On this see Bruce D. Marshall, "What Does the Spirit Have to Do?", in Matthew Levering, ed., *Reading John With St. Thomas Aquinas*, (Washington, DC: Catholic University of America Press, forthcoming); idem, *Trinity and Truth* (Cambridge: Cambridge University Press, 2000), pp. 251–256. The objection that the places of the divine persons turn out (fatally) to be interchangeable arises in a different way with regard to Thomas's contention that any of the three might have become incarnate. On this see below, pp. 41–3.

26 See, e.g., I–II, 109, 3, c.

27 So Lossky, e.g., argues that for Orthodox theology "the power of love communicated to the soul by the Holy Spirit, while distinct from the divine hypostasis of the Spirit", cannot be, as it is for Aquinas, "a created effect, an accidental quality whose existence depends on our created substance. Rather it is an uncreated gift, a divine and deifying energy in which we really participate in the nature of the Holy Trinity" (*Théologie mystique*, pp. 210–211; ET, pp. 213–214). Lossky rejects with equal insistence, though for different reasons, the standard western alternative to Aquinas, namely Lombard's view that "the power of love" in us is *not* a created gift, but the person of the Holy Spirit himself. Bulgakov is equally antago-nistic to the notion of created grace; cf. *Bride of the Lamb*, pp. 298–300.

28 Cf. *Ground of Union*, pp. 84–89.

29 All from I–II, 110, 1, c. For Aquinas any divine act is, on account of God's simplicity, co-eternal with himself and identical with his own being (although we cannot avoid thinking of them as distinct; cf. I, 19, 2, ad 1). But this does not mean that the *effect* of every act, the gift that follows from it, is the same as the divine being. On the contrary, the term of any free (and so contingent) divine act is not God, either as essence or person, but some created reality. Even the hypostatic union is "a created reality" (*aliquid creatum*; III, 2, 7, sc), while the person of the Word, and the free divine decision to unite a human nature to him, are not. Conversely, even the will to create a world is identical with the divine being, but this does not, of course, mean that the creature who results from that will is identical with the divine being. So it is with grace. Considered as "the eternal love of God itself", grace is identical with God's own being. Considered as "a certain supernatural reality in the human being which flows forth" from God's love, grace is not identical with God's own being (I–II, 110, 1, c).

30 I–II, 110, 2, c.

31 Cf. I–II, 110, 1, ob 2, on which more in note 33. *Caritas* too, the disposition to love God with the intimacy of friendship which flows from grace as *habituale donum*, has to be "a created reality in the soul" (II–II, 23, 2, sc).

32 "It is not possible that God in any way enter into composition with another, either as a formal principle or as a material principle" (I, 3, 8, c).

33 I–II, 110, 1, c. Thomas's reply (I–II, 110, 1, ad 2) to the objector who denies (ob 2) that grace is "a created reality in the soul", and so a "medium between God and the soul", does not, as Williams oddly suggests (*Ground of Union*, p. 88), implicitly agree with the objector that grace is not really a created medium. The point is rather that God gives (new) life to the soul not by being its form (which is impossible), but by being the efficient cause—the creator—of a form it would otherwise lack.

34 I–II, 110, 2, ad 3. As texts like this indicate, Aquinas denies that grace, even as created dis-position, "depends on our created substance", rather than on the love of God which alone can cause it (against the suggestion of Lossky and others; cf. above, note 27). It should be

observed that if Aquinas only rarely speaks of "created" grace, he never speaks expressly of "uncreated" grace. Both members of this lexical pair become pivotal only in later reflection on the topic (for some of the history here, see Gérard Philips, *L'union personnelle avec le Dieu vivant: Essai sur l'origine et le sens de la grâce créée* [second edition, Leuven: Peeters, 1989]). But just as Aquinas has his own way of talking about what "created grace" typically refers to, so also "uncreated grace": "by the word 'grace' it is sometimes possible to signify something uncreated, either God's acceptance [of us], or the uncreated gift which is the Holy Spirit". *In* II *Sent.* 26, 1, 1, c (P. Mandonnet, O. P. & M. F. Moos, O. P., eds., *S. Thomae Aquinatis Scriptum Super Libros Sententiarum*, 4 vols [Paris: Lethielleux, 1929–1947]).

35 "By grace the soul is conformed to God" (I, 43, 5, ad 2). Thomas here speaks of the conformity wrought by the missions of the Son and the Spirit. They dwell in us "only by way of sanctifying grace (*per gratiam gratum facientem*)" (I, 43, 3, sc), but sanctifying grace is precisely that "by which the human being himself is conjoined to God" (I–II, 111, 1, c).

36 I, 43, 3, c.

37 *In* I *Sent.* 14, 3, c. The context makes it clear that Thomas is talking about the created gift, and not only the divine love from which it springs: because grace joins us to God immediately, it is also "necessary that grace come forth from God into us without any intermediary".

38 I, 43, 5, ad 2. On conformity to the indwelling Father, though without any mission (a point to which we will return), cf. 5, c.

39 For this reason the attainment of life's final aim does not eliminate the need for a created disposition which joins us to God, but perfects it. The created light of glory "is not required for the vision of God in the manner of a likeness in which God is seen, but rather in the manner of a certain perfection of the intellect, strengthening it to see God . . . It is not a medium *in* which God is seen, but rather a medium *by* which (*sub quo*) God is seen. Therefore it does not take away the immediacy of the vision of God" (I, 12, 5, ad 2).

40 On the argument of the last two paragraphs see also Bruce D. Marshall, "Action and Person: Do Palamas and Aquinas Agree about the Spirit?", *St. Vladimir's Theological Quarterly* Vol. 39 no. 4 (1995), pp. 379–408; here, pp. 386–392.

41 All, once again, from I, 43, 5, ad 2. On faith's knowledge as rooted in a "connaturality" with the triune God by grace, cf. Bruce D. Marshall, "*Quod Scit Una Uetula*: Aquinas on the Nature of Theology", in Joseph Wawrykow and Rik Van Nieuwenhove, eds., *Aquinas as Theologian* (Notre Dame, IN: University of Notre Dame Press, 2004).

42 In western theology a strong notion of deification is not confined to Aquinas, or to Roman Catholic theology more generally. For example, Luther also makes much of the idea (if not the word), though he articulates it in another way than Aquinas, against the background of quite different concerns. Cf. Bruce D. Marshall, "Justification as Declaration and Deification", *International Journal of Systematic Theology* Vol. 4 no. 1 (2002), pp. 3–28.

43 The language in this case is Rahner's; cf. "Der dreifaltige Gott als transzendenter Urgrund der Heilsgeschichte", in Johannes Feiner & Magnus Löhrer, eds., *Mysterium Salutis*, vol. 2: *Die Heilsgeschichte vor Christus* (Einsiedeln: Benziger Verlag, 1967), pp. 317–401; here: p. 383. ET *The Trinity*, trans. Joseph Donceel, second edition (New York, NY: Crossroads, 1997), p. 101.

44 On why a distinction between the immanent and the economic Trinity is more an obstacle than an aid to understanding the actions of the Trinity and the identity of the divine persons, see my essay, "The Trinity", in Gareth Jones, ed., *The Blackwell Companion to Modern Theology* (Oxford: Blackwell, 2003).

45 I, 43, 1, c.

46 I, 43, 1, ad 1.

47 Aquinas stresses, in his version of this argument, that the missions do not simply point to the eternal processions, as though these were the remote background of the missions. Rather the processions themselves are given with the missions, present in the missions as their necessary basis: "A mission includes an eternal procession, and adds something to it, namely a temporal effect" (I, 43, 2, ad 3).

48 Though in the medieval discussion there is considerable controversy about how origin yields identity: over whether the identities of the divine persons consist in opposed relations which result from origin (as Aquinas and the Dominicans after him held; cf. above, note 20), or in the mode of origination itself (as Bonaventure suggests, and as Scotus held,

along with many theologians of the late thirteenth and fourteenth centuries, especially the Franciscans). For a useful brief sketch of the differences between these approaches, with references to further literature, see Russell L. Friedman, "Gabriel Biel and Later Medieval Trinitarian Theology", in Russell L. Friedman and Lauge O. Nielsen, eds., *The Medieval Heritage in Early Modern Metaphysics and Modal Theory, 1400–1700* (Dordrecht: Kluwer, 2003), pp. 99–120.

49   "L'apophase et la théologie trinitaire", in *A l'image et à la ressemblance de Dieu*, pp. 7–23; cf. pp. 8–9 (ET, p. 15).
50   "La Procession du Saint-Esprit", (above, note 1), p. 84 (ET, p. 88).
51   "La Procession du Saint-Esprit", p. 89 (ET, pp. 92–93).
52   "We cannot know God outside the economy in which he reveals himself". "L'apophase et la théologie trinitaire", p. 9 (ET, p. 15).
53   "L'apophase et la théologie trinitaire", p. 17 (ET, p.24).
54   Not least in connection with a desire, which Lossky shares, to be faithful to the legacy of Gregory Palamas. Orthodox interpreters regularly read Palamas as blocking any move from economy to theology, from the economic manifestation of the persons in their common energies to their properly personal existence in the unreachable divine essence (cf., e.g., John Meyendorff, *A Study of Gregory Palamas*, trans. George Lawrence [second edition, New York, NY: St. Vladimir's Seminary Press, 1998], p. 232). Dorothea Wendebourg in particular has taken this to mean that for Palamas and his modern heirs the persons themselves are simply absent from the economy of salvation; only the impersonal divine energies are actually given and present (cf. *Geist oder Energie: Zur Frage der innergöttlichen Verankerung des christlichen Lebens in der byzantinischen Theologie* [Munich: Chr. Kaiser Verlag, 1980]). One can see why Palamas sometimes gives rise to this worry, but it probably goes too far; see my essay, "Action and Person", (above, note 40), pp. 385–386. Wendebourg's thesis has generated considerable debate; cf. the comments in Reinhard Flogaus, *Theosis bei Palamas und Luther* (Göttingen: Vandenhoeck & Ruprecht, 1997), pp. 72–75, 212–215, and A. N. Williams, *Ground of Union*, pp. 139–142.
55   I will not attempt to go into the *Filioque* here. For a detailed survey of Aquinas's main texts on the topic, see Gilles Emery, "The Procession of the Holy Spirit *a Filio* According to St. Thomas Aquinas", in idem, *Trinity in Aquinas* (Ypsilanti, MI: Sapientia Press, 2003), pp. 209–269. For discussions of some of the main systematic issues, including the objection that the *Filioque* suppresses the "personal diversity" of the three hypostases, see my essays, "The Defense of the *Filioque* in Classical Lutheran Theology: An Ecumenical Appreciation", *Neue Zeitschrift für systematische Theologie und Religionsphilosophie* Vol. 44 no. 2 (2002), pp. 154–173 (with references to literature on the history of the controversy, and on the extensive modern ecumenical discussion), and "Action and Person", especially pp. 401–408. The suggestion in the latter essay that trinitarian theology can reach pretty much the same results with or without the *Filioque* now strikes me as excessively optimistic. It is difficult to finesse this issue, especially on Thomistic grounds.
56   "La Procession du Saint-Esprit", p. 84 (ET, p. 88).
57   "La Procession du Saint-Esprit", p. 75; cf. p. 84 (ET, pp. 79, 87).
58   "In this [economic] revelation of itself the Trinity also draws our attention to certain premises about the intrinsic relations between the divine Persons. The theological teaching on the inner reality of the Holy Trinity is based on these indications and on the bond which joins the eternal relations between the divine Persons together with their saving activity". Dumitru Staniloae, "The Holy Trinity: Structure of Supreme Love", *Theology and the Church* (above, note 9), pp. 73–108; here: p. 75. See also "Trinitarian Relations and the Life of the Church", idem, pp. 11–44, and Staniloae's dogmatics, in English as *The Experience of God*, vol. 1, trans. Ioan Ionita and Robert Barringer (Brookline, MA: Holy Cross Orthodox Press, 1994), pp. 245–280.
59   The western Middle Ages extensively debated the question of how the Son can proceed from the Father, and the Holy Spirit from both, without the Son and the Spirit adding anything to the Father's being. It was generally perceived that this would be an undesirable result, since it would make the Father in some way originate with respect to the Son or the Spirit. The issue comes up with particular force in connection with the question of how the Holy Spirit can be, as person, the love of the Father and the Son for one another, without adding something to the Father and the Son which they would otherwise lack. In Aquinas

see, e.g., I, 37, 1–2; 39, 7, ad 2. John of Damascus had already seen the problem clearly: "if the Father does not have something, then neither does the Son or the Holy Spirit". *De Fide Orthodoxa* I, 8 (John of Damascus, *Writings*, trans. Frederic H. Chase [New York: Fathers of the Church, 1958], p. 184 [translation altered]).

60   "Byzantine theologians tried to show that on the one hand a relationship of origin between Son and Holy Spirit was not necessary, and that on the other hand there *did* exist a certain relationship which distinguished Son and Holy Spirit as persons". *Theology and Church*, p. 15 (italics in original).

61   "It is in this sense that we are to understand the statement that the Spirit is 'through the Son', that is, the Spirit shines forth 'because of the fact that the Son exists, and for the sake of the Son'". *Theology and Church*, p. 98.

62   The upshot of this argument might seem to be that the *Filioque* is unavoidable. Aquinas certainly sees it this way, but the issue is more complicated than so far appears. The Franciscan tradition in medieval trinitarian theology (see Friedman's essay, above, note 48) generally accepts the principles that mission displays origin, and that identity is origin-dependent (indeed they have a stronger view of the latter point than Aquinas). But against Aquinas they reject the thought that proceeding from the Son as well as the Father is identity-constituting for the Spirit. Whether this coheres with their acceptance of the idea that the Spirit's place in the scriptural pattern of missions (and so his sending by the Son) has to display his origin is another matter; here a good deal of historical research yet needs to be done.

63   The quoted phrase is from *De Potentia* 10, 4, ad 14 (*Quaestiones Disputatae*, vol. 2, p. 269b).

64   The suggestion that Aquinas neglects the distinctive economic role of the Spirit fails to find any support in the texts; on this see my essay "What Does the Spirit Have to Do?" (above, note 25). The present question, though, is whether he ties the Spirit's mission in a plausible way to an account of the Spirit's place in the trinitarian order of origin.

65   I, 43, 8, sc & c.

66   I, 43, 8, c. Cf. *De Potentia* 10, 4, ad 14: "That the Son is said to be sent by the Holy Spirit is to be understood as applying to the Son on account of his human nature".

67   See, e.g., III, 16, 10–12, and Bruce D. Marshall, *Christology in Conflict* (Oxford: Blackwell, 1987), pp. 184–185.

68   This I take to be the sense of Thomas's distinction between "principium personae" and "principium effectus" (I, 43, 8, c) in the concept of mission.

69   Coping with the scriptural data is not simply a matter of adding up the number of passages which favor each side. Considerations like relative simplicity and conceptual coherence count for an interpretation of the scriptural pattern of missions. So Aquinas argues, for example, that any interpretation which has the Son proceeding from the Spirit is conceptually implausible, since it effectively turns the Spirit into the Father: "It cannot be inferred that the Son is from the Holy Spirit . . . because it would follow that the Holy Spirit would be the Father, since to be the Father is nothing other than to have the Son proceeding from him" (*De Potentia* 10, 4, ad 21). Orthodox theologians, to be sure, have often made a cognate objection against the *Filioque*: it turns the *Son* into the Father, since a divine person can originate only from the Father. But this too, Aquinas argues, is conceptually incoherent. Being the origin of the Spirit is not opposed to any person-constituting feature of either the Father or the Son. On the contrary: "To be the origin (*principium*) of the Holy Spirit does not belong to the Father *as* Father, that is, by reason of paternity. In this way he is related only to the Son. Otherwise it would follow that the Holy Spirit would actually be the Son" (*De Potentia* 10, 4, c [*Quaestiones Disputatae*, vol. 2, p. 266a]). Of course this implicates further conceptual claims, in particular the notion that the persons are constituted by pairs of opposed relations (see above, notes 20 and 48), and ultimately the question of how to account coherently for the unity of the triune God.

70   Among theologians who have followed this course, see especially Matthias Joseph Scheeben, *Die Mysterien des Christentums* §§22–31 (Joseph Höfer, ed., *Gesammelte Schriften*, vol. 2 [third edition, Freiburg: Herder, 1958; first published 1865]; ET *The Mysteries of Christianity*, trans. Cyril Vollert [St. Louis: Herder, 1946], pp. 126–180), and Herman Schell, *Das Wirken des dreieinigen Gottes* (Mainz: Verlag von Franz Kirchheim, 1885), the better part of which (pp. 141–622) is devoted to pursuit of this strategy.

71   III, 3, 5, c.

72 Cf. I, 43, 4.
73 III, 3, 5, ad 3.
74 The Trinity could still carry out the act of adoption, but the roles of the persons in this act would remain fixed by characteristics tied, as we have seen, to origin (cf. III, 3, 5, ad 2; 3, 8, c, and above, notes 19, 22). The divine act of adoption would thus look utterly different to us than it actually does. That our adoption has the lucidity it possesses in scripture's economy is part of what Aquinas means by talking about the "appropriateness" (*convenientia*) of the Son's incarnation, in contrast to any other possibility.
75 *In III Sent.* 1, 2, 2, c (no. 95).
76 "We note in the Father's authority with respect to him the fact that [the Son] is from another" (*In III Sent.* 1, 2, 2, c [no. 95]).
77 *Super Ioannem* 8, 3 (no. 1192).

3

THOMAS AQUINAS AND JUDAISM

HENK SCHOOT AND PIM VALKENBERG

Introduction

Writing on Thomas Aquinas and Judaism is a delicate matter. No Christian theologian in the twenty-first century can escape an awareness of recent and remote atrocities, also in the name of Christianity, committed against the Jews; namely, the Shoah. It lays a heavy burden on those from a Christian perspective who now want to reflect on Jews and Judaism. Since this particular awareness is quite recent, we cannot of course expect Thomas Aquinas to share in our modern sense of delicacy. But if we want to be able to determine whether he can be helpful today in dialogue between Christians and Jews, we should first of all try to understand the basic character-istics of Aquinas's theological approach to Judaism generally. In the interests of making this a manageable task, we will have to leave aside a number of Aquinas's otherwise interesting political and practical contributions on how to deal with Jews, as for instance his letter to a countess of Flanders regard-ing the matter of governing the Jews under her rule. We will also need to set to one side the many occasions where Aquinas mainly repeats the traditions concerning Judaism and Jews that he inherited from the Christian *adversus Iudaeos* tradition. Following Jeremy Cohen's distinction between Aquinas's political and traditional side, where he largely echoes the rather tolerant Augustinian tradition, and his theological side, where he more or less mirrors the aggressiveness of a new mission to the Jews by the mendicant friars,[1] we concentrate on the latter because that is, perhaps surprisingly, where Aquinas's insight is most helpful to us. Before turning directly here, however, it is necessary to begin with a short survey of the contemporary

W. G. B. M. Valkenberg
Dept. of Theology and Religious Studies, Catholic University of Nijmegen, P. O. Box 9103, 6500 HD Nijmegen, The Netherlands
H. J. M. Schoot
Catholic Theological University of Utrecht (KTU), Heidelberglaan 2, 3584 CS Utrecht, The Netherlands

debate as to whether the mendicant friars represented a new approach to Judaism and Jews in the Christian theological tradition. Next, we will concentrate on three aspects of Aquinas's theological approach to Judaism: his characterisation of Judaism as a form of disbelief; his christocentric reading of the Old Testament; and finally his treatment of circumcision as a sacrament administered to Christ. In conclusion, we will indicate some elements in the very structure of Aquinas's theology that might help us develop a new theology of the relationship between Christians and Jews. What is particularly relevant here is Aquinas's understanding of salvation history, where God's incarnation in Christ decisively determines the relation between Old and New Testament analogous to the relation between the human and the divine nature in Christ.

1. The Mendicant Friars: A New Approach to Jews and Judaism in the Middle Ages?

In the beginning of the thirteenth century, a new type of cleric entered the ecclesiastical scene. The Franciscan and Dominican mendicant friars would have enormous impact on the life of church and society. The basic characteristic of this new type of religious is that it combines in a novel synthesis the two types of clergy already known, i.e. monks and diocesan priests. The former were bound to a certain place, their monastery, whereas the latter were bound to a certain task, i.e. the basic care of souls. The mendicants, as they are called because of their dependence on alms, were neither; neither bound to place nor to (parish) ministry, they were free to devote themselves to the mission they chose to pursue.

This freedom was exercised in a society that is often regarded, centuries later by modern interpreters, as unified and homogeneous, even totalitarian. One does not need to have a romantic soul to admit that this is still a prevalent view of the later Middle Ages. Europe in the West was Christian, and almost no other outlook was heard of let alone encouraged to seek social embodiment. However, there were notable exceptions. In the Iberian peninsula, for example, Jews lived side by side with Muslims and Christians, sometimes serving Muslim rulers and, especially after the twelfth century Christian *reconquista*, Christian rulers. In both instances Jews mostly lived in prosperity and relative freedom. Some heretical upsurges were known in a few regions, especially in what now is called southern France and northern Spain: the Cathars.

The zeal of St. Dominic, who preached to these heretics, was handed down to his followers, who became famously devoted to teaching and preaching. Some of these Dominicans would concentrate on teaching theology to students, as Thomas Aquinas did. Others would focus on preaching to those who did share the faith, or those who did not, or even those who no longer did. The last two categories were minorities, to be sure. But preaching to such minorities suggests that to the extent that Christendom increased its strength, adverse pressures on 'otherness' increased as well.

The preaching friars needed the teaching friars in many respects. They were dependent upon them for the knowledge of languages, most importantly Hebrew and Arabic. In the course of the thirteenth century such knowledge spread rapidly. No longer confined only to the monastery of St. Victor in Paris, where Hebrew was read, and no longer restricted to the monastery of Cluny, where knowledge of Arabic was disseminated, Dominicans founded an increasing number of teaching houses (*studia*) where friars learnt the language they would need in order to preach to their various constituencies.[2] Some would also begin reading Hebrew and Arabic sources, introduce these sources into their theology, and use this knowledge when asked to pass judgement on e.g. the Talmud.

There is no argument among scholars about the reality of these new developments, although there is clearly considerable dispute over their meaning and significance. By and large, the newly formed orders of mendicant friars were less reliant on traditional views and given instead to new and different modes of inquiry reflecting their own distinctive outlooks and interests. No longer did they simply condemn the Talmud outright and have it burned, but they actually made concerted efforts to read these books, with a view to finding new ways to persuade Jews to cross over to Christianity. Jewish sources were thus employed to fashion arguments that could serve their missionizing efforts. This missionary strategy was new and explains the transition from forbidding and burning to reading and employing the Talmud. But does it bespeak a fundamental change in attitude towards Jews, a revolution in theology, as Cohen maintains? Or does it manifest yet another, albeit more subtle, version of received Christian intolerance, as Hood argues?[3]

Christian theology seems to develop in the direction that contemporary Judaism can no longer be regarded as the legitimate heir of the God-given Torah and the people who received it. For from the thirties to the seventies of the thirteenth century a view on rabbinic Judaism arises that is more and more hostile to it. Up till now Jews were tolerated in Western Christian Europe, largely for three theological reasons, two of which originate in Augustine's writings. Augustine considered the presence of Jews in his society as beneficial, and therefore they should be treated in a friendly manner. According to Augustine, the fact that Jews had to live in the *diaspora* after the temple was destroyed, was valuable and useful proof of their divine punishment for not accepting the Messiah, corroborating the truthfulness of Christian faith in Christ. Moreover, Jewish independent adherence to the Torah and the Prophets constitutes proof of the authenticity of these scriptures that Christians consider important for verifying their faith in Christ, whose coming was foretold in these very scriptures. A third theological reason for tolerating Jews was that the Apostle Paul was convinced of the eventual conversion of all Jews to Christ, when Christ comes again.

Of course, other reasons, notably of a non-theological nature, may be given as well—e.g. reasons of an economic or a sociological nature. But with the great exception of the pogroms in connection to the first crusade, at the end of the eleventh century, Jews lived their lives relatively calmly and prosperously in the Christian west, for Christian theology had been largely in accordance with such a situation. This does not of course entail that the Christian position regarding Jews was right. Jews were considered slaves by Christians, for example, who could not be in command of Christian servants; moreover, Jews mostly were not allowed to possess land. Many Jews were forced into livelihoods of shop-keeping, craftsmanship and the lending of money, despite their former influential role, for instance, in the development of the Iberian peninsula and in international trade. With the rise of pre-capitalist society and the closed shops that guilds constituted, the roles of Jews in Christian societies were more and more limited to money-lending, interest and pawn-broking. That these financial activities were forbidden for Christians (and Muslims), and most importantly the huge tariffs involved, partly accounts for the negative popular image Jews enjoyed.

The friars exacerbated the economic and political pressure felt by Jews during this time. Apparently they considered the abiding presence of Jewish communities to be a challenge for Christian society. Their growing knowledge of the rabbinical tradition, made it clear to them that the rabbinical tradition, as they discovered it in the Talmud, had developed in opposition to Christian views and interpretations. Here they encountered stories they considered to be fables—e.g., stories about how to avoid the angel of death or accounts of demons, but also sexual tales deemed inadmissible, involving Noah and Cham, or Samson. Here they also encountered anthropomorphic language about God they considered blasphemous—God roaring like a lion three times at night, or playing with Leviathan are but two examples. Most disturbing of all, they encountered liberal interpretations of commandments in the Torah, mockery of Jesus Christ, and the proffered admissibility of lying to and cheating of Gentiles.

Despite their small minority status, Jews were able to arouse enormous indignation. For these 'outsiders by choice' (Hood) were frequently suspected of cooperating with Christian heretics in trying to have people forswear their religion. Not only did they aid and abet Christian heretics, they were considered to be heretics themselves. Their Judaism was no longer faithful to the Torah and their religious cult (e.g. Sabbath, circumcision, dietary laws) was, since the coming of the Messiah, no longer legitimate. To the contrary, that observance constituted, in the eyes of some, disloyalty to the Torah. All kinds of nasty accusations were spread about Jews crucifying Christian children, or desecrating hosts. Books were burned; Jews were subjected to forced baptism or expelled.

This development of the Christian attitude towards Jews, from Nicholas Donin in the 1230s, through the famous disputation of Barcelona between

Rabbi Nachmanides and Dominican friar Pablo Cristiani in 1263, to Friar Raymundo Martini in the 1270s, when he published the major medieval sourcebook of anti-Judaism, his *Pugio Fidei* (*Dagger of Faith*), is to a large extent a mendicant affair. So it seems likely that Thomas Aquinas is somehow involved in it; how was he?

The picture that emerges from the studies of this topic paints Aquinas as objective, sober and positive: a moderate conservative who is traditional to the extent that he explicitly recommends granting the Jews the rights that they have according to canon law.[4] He is opposed to forced baptism, but is rather tough on usury.[5] Aquinas does not consider himself an expert in political matters concerning Jews.[6] He contributes in no way to the hysterical folktales that circulate at the time about crimes Jews allegedly commit. Aquinas, as the scholar he is, reads Jewish authors, in translation, and defends the Christian faith also in light of Jewish considerations, and does so in a manner that is detached, respectful and firm.[7] Aquinas's major involvement in the Dominican mission among the Jews is his preparation of the *Summa contra Gentiles*. This work, which is more of a combination of philosophical and dogmatic theology than a work of sheer apologetics, seems to be written at the request of Aquinas's former Master General and the genius of the Dominican mission, Raymundus de Peñaforte.[8] It is the only book Aquinas has written in which he refers to the 'Talmut', and in particular to a condemned proposition in it, which says that sometimes God sins and is cleansed from sin (I, q. 95). Two years before Aquinas arrived in Paris as a student the Talmud was burned there; Pablo Cristiani preached in Paris in 1269, when Aquinas was resident in the city; Raymundo Martini employed large parts of the *Summa contra Gentiles* in his *Pugio Fidei*; but the exact nature of Aquinas's relationship with these events and persons, both of whom are chief 'employees' in Raymundus de Peñaforte's mission, is unknown to us now. Theologically, it is quite clear that not only any anti-Jewish verbal abuse is absent from his works, but Aquinas also never explicitly harboured the theory of post-biblical Judaism as heretical.[9] But it is true of course that for Thomas Aquinas the person and message of Jesus Christ is central to his outlook on Church and Society, and even dominates his historical philosophy.[10] Christ is the pivotal point of history, which translates into visions on how Christ was present in Jewish scriptures that for Christians form the Old Testament, on the status of the (old) law and its precepts in regard of the new one, and on contemporary Jewish belief, to which we will turn now.

2. Judaism as a Form of Disbelief

From a Christian point of view, the relation between Christianity and Judaism is special. On the one hand, Judaism has to be viewed as a religion of its own with its own history that continues after the coming of Christ. In order to do justice to the otherness of Judaism, Christian theologians have to consider it as a different religion with its own sources, its own history and its own characteristics. But, on the other hand, since the Christian church acknowledges the Hebrew scriptures as testimony of the covenant between God and His people, Judaism belongs to Christian identity as well. This double perspective implies that a Christian who wants to do justice to Judaism as a religious phenomenon should approach this religion both as different and as familiar. Generally speaking, theologians are inclined to view Judaism from the perspective of Christian identity only, and therefore they have difficulty in doing justice to Judaism in its otherness. A clear example of this has been given in the previous section: Christian theologians in the thirteenth century wanted to ban the Talmud because for them it symbolised a heretical tradition of interpretation of the Old Testament. Or they used the Talmud against the Jews in order to show that it confirmed that the Messiah had come in the person of Jesus of Nazareth. In both cases, the Talmud was judged from the inner perspective of Christianity. In the same manner, Aquinas feels free to interpret the Old Testament from a christocentric point of view, as we will show in the next section; but first, we need to ask ourselves if we can find traces in Aquinas of respect for the otherness of Judaism. Once again, we have to be aware that this is a modern question, and therefore we should expect Aquinas to provide either an awkward answer to it or no answer at all.[11] In point of fact, the way that Aquinas shows respect for the otherness of Judaism is to consider Judaism as a form of disbelief.

One of the areas in which the difference between the worldview of a Christian in the Middle Ages and a Christian in modern, pluralistic society is very much apparent, is precisely the assessment of people of other faiths.[12] In the Middle Ages, the general idea was that most of the people were Christians, and that those who did not follow the lead of the Church did so out of stubbornness. Theologians contemplated the marginal case of the *nutritus in silva* (someone who is left in the woods, and grows up without knowledge of Christian faith) but the general thought was that practically everybody could know that they were to be saved by Christ. It goes without saying that this is a worldview radically different from our own. At that time, however, no one seemed to bother very much about other peoples and cultures: to most of the civilians, these 'others' were either indifferent or threatening. The famous axiom *Extra Ecclesiam nulla salus* (there is no salvation outside the Church) fit in with this mentality very well.[13]

Aquinas seems to share this mentality when he deals with disbelief as a vice contrary to the theological virtue of faith (*Summa theologiae* II-II, qq. 10–16). For him, *infidelitas* is disbelief rather than unbelief: a rejection of what should be believed rather than a lack of assent.[14] Someone who does not believe willingly denies the truth of Christian faith, and thus commits a sin excluding him or her from salvation. Even those who, through no fault of their own, have heard nothing about the faith, are condemned, albeit because of other sins. Disbelievers are not different people believing different things;

they are people who simply depart from the truth.[15] There is no place for real difference: the others are deviators, either because they resist the faith before it has been accepted (such is the case of the pagans), or because they resist it after having accepted it—either in the mode of a prefiguration (such is the case of the Jews), or in the mode of the truth itself (as is the case with heretics).[16] In other words, Jews and pagans deviate from the ultimate end of their lives because they refuse to assent to Christ; heretics, on the other hand, do assent to Christ but not in a correct way.[17] In a certain sense, the heretics are the worst, because they once knew the fullness of faith and yet resisted it.[18] They are therefore not to be tolerated in the least: because they corrupt the faith, they deserve capital punishment, even as forgers are condemned to death by the civil authorities. When the Church is convinced that heretics will not change their minds, she will excommunicate them and hand them over to the civil judges in order to be put to death.[19]

It seems that Aquinas gives us an awkward answer indeed. He seems to be unable to do justice to the otherness of Judaism as a different religion, since the difference between the two religions is immediately identified with the theological difference between true faith and disbelief. On the one hand, the disbelief of the Jews is not as bad as heresy, since they did not accept the truth of Christian faith; on the other hand, their disbelief is not as complete as the heathens, insofar as the latter did not expect Christ at all. There is, however, a sense in which Aquinas does value the otherness of Judaism properly, viz. his insistence that Jews do not belong to the spiritual authority of the Church.[20] Therefore, the children of Jews must not be baptised against the will of their parents. On this issue, Aquinas suggests that he defends the usual practice of the Church against a then recent urge to baptise Jewish children.[21] Aquinas gives two reasons why he is so unresponsive to the idea of forced baptism of Jewish children: first, this new practice is detrimental to the faith, since these children do not know what they believe when they are baptised. And therefore, they might easily be persuaded by their parents to renounce what they unwittingly embraced. But it goes against natural justice as well, since parents are responsible for their children until they reach the age of reason. Therefore, the Church would violate the parental rights of the Jews if she would allow this practice.[22] Moreover, the process of faith should always be voluntary. And therefore, Jews cannot be compelled to believe as long as they stay outside the spiritual authority of the Church. Therefore, the famous word of the Gospel: *compelle intrare*, that is: "make them come in" (Luke 14: 23) does not apply to the Jews because they cannot be coerced to accept the Christian faith.[23] In the same manner, the Church should tolerate the rites of the Jews, because as figures of faith they are a certain witness to the truth.[24]

In this context, Aquinas has also something to say about inter-religious dialogue between Christians and Jews. The Church cannot forbid the communion of the faithful with Jews, because she has no right to pass spiritual

judgement on them. But the Church forbids, under penalty of excommuni-
cation, any communication with heretics or apostates. As regards the persons
who want to communicate with Jews or pagans, they may do so if they have
a firm faith, so that the communication will lead to the conversion of disbelievers or unbelievers rather than to the turning away from faith by the
believers. If, however, one is not that firmly grounded in faith, communication with disbelievers and unbelievers should be forbidden, because the
probability of downfall from faith is to be feared in such instances.[25]

3. The Interpretation of the Hebrew Scriptures

Judging from the previous section, it is possible to say some good things
about the way in which Thomas Aquinas deals with the otherness of Judaism.
At least, he demonstrates an awareness of the fact that the Church does not
have any spiritual authority over Jews, which means that their natural rights
as Jews should be honoured and not violated. But this is only the other side
of the fact that Jews are outside of the Church in its role as instrument of salvation. It is not yet a positive valuation of Judaism as such. Something of the
latter is hinted at, however, when Aquinas claims that Jews are, theologically
speaking, in a certain sense already inside the Church, since the Jews are an
integral part of the Church's identity. If one is to learn more from Aquinas on
the theological importance of Jews and Judaism, one must gain a better grasp
of the way in which Judaism is 'internal' to Christian identity.

From the point of theological identity, the relations between Christians and
Jews are determined by what they have in common. Again, Aquinas classi-
fies the Jews, in a middle position between heathens and Muslims on the
one hand and heretics on the other. Because Christians share no common
Scripture with heathens and Muslims, they should, according to Aquinas,
only use reason when disputing with them. With Jews, however, Christians
have the Old Testament in common, and with heretics Christians share both
the New and the Old Testament. Whereas the common ground determines
the mode of conversation,[26] the issues that divide both religions determine
its content. Historically speaking, from the Christian point of view, the
person of Christ as Saviour of humankind has always been the most important issue in this conversation. It is therefore necessary to look at Aquinas's
christological interpretation of the Old Testament if we really want to appreciate his theological approach to Judaism.

Many things can be said about the manner in which Thomas Aquinas
deals with the Old Testament in his theology. It could be very interesting,
for instance, to give an analysis of the way in which he engages the Old Law
as one of the biblical parts of his *Summa theologiae*.[27] But in our opinion, the
most important clue for understanding Thomas's theological approach to the
Old Testament is his christocentrism. By this we mean that Christ is, for him,
the centre of the history of salvation, and that both the New and the Old

Testament refer primarily to Christ. Of course, on this point Aquinas follows the way in which the Christian tradition from the very beginning has interpreted its Scriptures with Christ in mind. But he does this in quite a distinct manner, as we will show with reference to his commentary on the Psalms.[28]

In the prologue to Aquinas's commentary on the Psalms, which is roughly contemporaneous to the third part of his *Summa theologiae*, he states that Christ and his members form the subject matter of this book. "Everything that pertains to faith in the incarnation is treated thus clearly in the Psalms that they seem to be a Gospel instead of a prophecy."[29] Aquinas corroborates this christological interpretation of the Psalms by refuting the approach of Theodore of Mopsuetia, who contends that nothing is expressly said about Christ in the prophecies, but that some words were applied to him later on. Quite the contrary, Aquinas says, the Spirit as the author of Scripture has ordered the words of the Psalms in such a way that some of these words have as their principal meaning that they are signs of things to come.[30] Some words refer to historical facts in the life of David, the human author of the Psalms, and may be interpreted as referring to Christ as well; but some other words refer mainly to Christ. This gives a certain inconsistency to Aquinas's interpretation of the Psalms: in some cases, the christological interpretation belongs to the literal sense of the Psalm; in other cases, it belongs to the spiritual sense.[31] This inconsistency is caused by the fact that Aquinas takes seriously the Jewish way of interpreting Scripture by applying it to new situations, as the first followers of Jesus did in their testimonies. In fact, the way in which Aquinas interprets the Psalms christologically is guided by the quotations from the Psalms in the New Testament. Although his christological interpretation of the Psalms seems to be problematic in the eyes of a modern theologian who wants to respect the otherness of the Jewish Scriptures, the way in which Aquinas accounts for his method of interpretation shows his continuity with the first Christian (and therefore Jewish) interpretations of their (Jewish) Scriptures.[32]

On the one hand, Aquinas refers to the person of Christ very frequently in his commentary on the Psalms: some five hundred times, which appears to accord with the christological emphasis in his prologue. On the other hand, he does not seize every opportunity to give a christological explanation.[33] Some of the Psalms do not afford any occasion to engage in christological interpretations, except perhaps that Aquinas interprets the words *in finem* in the title of some Psalms as a reference to Christ who is the way towards the destination of our Christian life.[34] In some cases, the words of the Psalms may have different meanings, so that a literal interpretation, with its reference to historical circumstances, may be followed by a spiritual (or mystical, or allegorical) interpretation in which those very same words are interpreted as referring to Christ. But in some other Psalms, the main reference is to Christ alone, while the historical reference is only figuratively invoked. With reference to Ps. 2:2: "The kings of the earth stand ready, and

the rulers conspire together against the Lord and his anointed king",
Aquinas remarks: "This is said of Christ, the anointed one, under the likeness of David".[35] But he gives his source immediately: Acts 4:25 where Peter
and John and other followers of Christ quote Ps. 2:2. In this manner, many
Psalms may be read at the historical level, where they refer to the history of
David; at the allegorical level, where they refer to Christ; and at the moral
level, where they refer to the Church.[36] In their literal meaning, a good
number of the Psalms refer to David, even as they refer to Christ in their
mystical sense; but the 'modern' implication that the literal sense must be
the true sense, is turned around by Aquinas: the mystical sense leads to the
true interpretation that refers to the mystery of Christ, according to the
words of St. Paul in Romans 10:18 (quoting Ps. 19:4).[37] Aquinas's practice
reflects the usual Christian approach of Judaism and the Old Testament:
what has been said in the Old Law figuratively is now revealed in Christ in
truth. This means that although the christological interpretation is an interpretation *secundum mysterium* and not a literal one, it is nonetheless the true
interpretation according to the authors of the New Testament.

Introducing the next Psalm, Aquinas gives a similar idea of his christocentric approach: "Although some of the things in this Psalm literally refer
to David, they belong to Christ properly and truly. According to mystery,
they also belong to the Church and a just man."[38] At these places, the christological interpretation is at one and the same time a possible interpretation
but also the only true and proper interpretation. All of which is to say that
Aquinas's christocentrism does not erase other possible interpretations, since
they are juxtaposed and often preceded by words such as "these words could
be explained in the following way . . .".[39] The juxtaposition of plural possible readings and one true reading creates a tension that is characteristic
for the Christian approach to the Old Testament.[40]

At some places, however, Aquinas seems to indicate that the christological interpretation is the only possibility, so that the *littera* of the text refers
to the history of Christ. In these cases, the christological sense that modern
theologians would accept as at most a figural sense, is in Aquinas's opinion,
the literal sense of the Psalm. Again, Aquinas appeals to the authority of the
Apostles, viz. Peter who says that David spoke about Christ (Acts 2:25).[41] On
the same authority, Aquinas says that the words of Ps. 40:7, "In the beginning of the book, it has been written about me that my desire is to do thy
will", refer to Christ, since the Apostle in Hebrews 10:7 quotes these verses.[42]
Even stronger is the authority of Christ himself who applied the beginning
of Psalm 22 (and therefore the whole Psalm) to his own person in Matthew
27:46. For that reason, the literal meaning of this Psalm refers to Christ.
Finally, Aquinas refers to the authority of Christ in his explanation of
Ps. 41:9: "Even the friend whom I trusted, who ate at my table, exults over
my misfortune", as follows: "Since Christ Himself according to John 14:18
used this word concerning Judas, we will explain this as referring to Christ."[43]

These instances make clear how New Testament texts are determinative for Aquinas in his interpretation of the Old Testament. Whereas most phrases in the Psalms refer to the history of David, and may sometimes be applied to Christ in a spiritual manner, some phrases from the Psalms that are quoted in the New Testament must be taken to refer to Christ truly, since Christ is the truth of God.

It has to be kept in mind, though, that these explicit christological explanations are, in a certain sense, exceptional in Aquinas's commentary. In large parts of this text, he mainly uses the Old Testament in order to interpret texts from the Old Testament: *Scriptura sui ipsius interpres*. A quick survey of Aquinas's commentary on the Psalms reveals that the number of quotations from the Old Testament, mainly from the Psalms, is twice as great as the number of quotations from the New Testament.[44]

4. Circumcision as a Sacrament Administered to Christ

It is said sometimes, that in the course of its history Christianity has completely forgotten about the Jewishness of Jesus. Mockingly, scholars say that Christ was more the first Christian than a son of Jewish descent. Some even intimate that had the church valued the descent of its founder more correctly history would have taken a different turn:

> Would there have been such anti-Semitism, would there have been so many pogroms, would there have been an Auschwitz, if every Christian church and every Christian home had focused its devotion (. . .) on icons of Christ not only as Pantocrator but as *Rabbi Jeshua bar-Joseph*, Rabbi Jesus of Nazareth, the Son of David, in the context of the history of a suffering Israel and a suffering humanity?[45]

There can be no question but that Jesus should be viewed as a Rabbi, as a Jewish teacher and prophet, and that the awareness of this among Christians has been, by and large, quite bleak. Against this background it is rather remarkable to see that Aquinas is quite explicit on this subject. In his first large theological work he even calls Christ the *Frater Iudaeorum*, and he does so in the context of questions regarding the reasons why Christ was circumcised.[46] The account of Christ's circumcision is given in Luke 2:21: "When the eighth day came and the child was to be circumcised, they gave him the name Jesus, the name the angel had given him before his conception." Gabriel had told Mary that her son would be named Jesus, and so it was done during his circumcision.

Aquinas is the first in Western theology to develop on such a large scale a theology of the mysteries of life and passion of Christ. Having reflected upon the incarnation and the relation between divinity and humanity in Christ, he continues by considering all major 'historical' events of his life, from conception to resurrection. The discussion centres around what he calls 'convenience': given these facts, why was it done thus? What reasons could there have been? And why was it not done otherwise? This applies to Christ's circumcision too. Did Christ need to be circumcised? In the *Summa Theologiae* one can detect Aquinas's major questions: was circumcision not prescribed to Abraham in order to remember God's promise which is, however, now fulfilled with the birth of Christ? What Christ does entails an example for Christians, but Christians are not supposed to have their children or themselves circumcised? And Aquinas's third question is most telling of all: circumcision is meant to do away with original sin, but Christ did not have any. So why was it necessary that Christ be circumcised? The last question is a sequel to the traditional confession that he who is supposed to cleanse from sin, is clean himself.

Aquinas's last point is quite telling, since it apparently assumes that the doctrine of original sin was a Jewish doctrine as well, and even more, that circumcision had been an effective means to do away with this sin. It brings to attention the general way in which Aquinas considers the relationship between the commandments given before or in the Torah, which Aquinas called the Old Law, and the new dispensation. We will turn to this shortly, but first we need to pay attention to Aquinas's answer to the questions concerning Christ's circumcision. In the *Summa Theologiae* Aquinas gives seven reasons for the convenience of this circumcision, before he answers the three questions mentioned above. Christ was circumcised (1) in order to testify to the reality of his human body in front of those who were to doubt it; (2) to approve of the circumcision of old instituted by God; (3) to prove himself to be a member of Abraham's family, the one who received the commandment of circumcision as a sign of his faith in Christ; (4) to prevent Jews from having an excuse, were he not circumcised; (5) to give us an example of the virtue of obedience it was done on the eighth day, according to the law; (6) to show that he did not reject this ordinary remedy for the cleansing of sin; and lastly (7) to free people from the burden of the law by himself carrying it.[47]

It is quite clear how positive Aquinas is regarding this instance of what he calls "sacrament of the old law".[48] To him it is the most important sacrament of the old law, because it has such a great and important effect, i.e. cleansing from original sin. Christ's personal history approves of this ritual, and he employs it in carrying out his salvific mission. In answering the three questions, Aquinas understands Christ's circumcision as a prefiguration of his passion, being the final and true realisation of God's promise of which the general circumcision was also a sign. Christ thereby shows himself faithfully obedient to the law. Being buried with Christ by baptism means for Christians a kind of spiritual circumcision, by which they take leave of a life of the flesh. Old Testament circumcision removes original sin and is a sign of Christian spiritual circumcision. It is not just a sign of future removal of sin, it is not only valued as a prefiguration of the Christian dispensation, but it really removes original sin even before the passion of Christ.

In the course of his authorship Aquinas has changed his views on the sacramentality of circumcision. In the treatise on the sacraments of the *Tertia Pars* of the *Summa Theologiae*, which astonishingly contains a separate question on circumcision, in between baptism and exorcism (q. 70), Aquinas retracts his former vision on this, and to avoid misunderstanding he does so twice; apparently we are dealing with an important issue.[49] Having explained the efficacy of the sacraments of the new law in general, Aquinas here treats the question whether the sacraments of the old law cause any grace. In general Aquinas distinguishes between the conferring of justifying grace, which he denies to "the sacraments of the old law", and the signification of faith in Christ through which the fathers of old indeed were justified.[50] The sacraments of the old law cannot be said to cause grace by themselves, but only inasmuch as they prefigure Christ. To Aquinas the sacrament of circumcision, however, seemed at first to be the exception to the rule. Some, he notes, say that circumcision does not bestow any grace, but only lifts sin. This cannot be, for humans are only justified from sin through grace. Therefore others have said that the grace bestowed by "the sacraments of the old law" only removes the guilt. Aquinas rejects this as well. He then mentions the view that he himself used to subscribe to but which he now retracts: the grace conferred is positive in the sense that it makes one worthy for eternal life, but it cannot suppress the desire which persuades one to sin. This, Aquinas says, proves to be not true for anyone looking into the matter attentively. For a minimum of grace is capable of resisting any desire whatsoever and of meriting eternal life. And so, in the end, the exception is normalised and does not exist any more. Circumcision confers grace inasmuch as it is a sign of Abraham's faith in the future baptism of Christ. It really 'works', but not in and by itself, but through the mediation of belief in Christ's future baptism.

Through circumcision Abraham differentiated himself as a believer from the non-believers, moving out from his homeland and his family, on the promise of God that in and through his offspring, which is Christ, all nations of the earth would be blessed. This makes circumcision the sacrament of faith and gives it a profound similarity with the sacrament of baptism, which is also a sacrament of faith (*ST* III, q. 70, a. 1–2). Aquinas repeats his overview of possible views on the gracious efficacy of circumcision in his separate question on circumcision in particular. He states explicitly that the grace that circumcision grants has all the usual effects. Baptism does so by the act of baptism itself, *ex opere operato*, and circumcision because of the signification of Christ's passion (*ST* III, q. 70, a. 4).

Now, Richard Schenk has shown in a thorough and penetrating study that Aquinas developed his opinion on the basis of Bonaventure's exposition, very much like another theologian of the time, Robert Kilwardby did.[51] But Aquinas and Kilwardby develop in quite opposite directions. Whereas Aquinas chooses to reduce the literal efficacy of this sacrament in order to save the fullness of grace it confers, Kilwardby takes the alternative possibility and allows for all sacraments of the old law to have gracious effects in and by themselves. At first sight, and this is Schenk's interpretation, it seems that Kilwardby operates more in line with modern respect for the authentic singularity of Jewish religious rites.[52] But on the other hand one cannot deny that in Aquinas's theological maturing process the centrality of the Mystery of the Incarnation grows and grows, and that in his theological project it is quite a logical tack to derive the effectiveness of sacraments of the old law from their prefiguration of Christ. One could moreover argue that Aquinas's unwillingness to distinguish between full Christian grace and partial Jewish grace might be of importance to his attitude toward Jews as well.

Aquinas's treatment of the sacrament of circumcision, and more particularly his treatment of the circumcision of Christ, shows him a theologian steeped in tradition, on top of which he makes his own final decisions. In doing so he fully acknowledges the importance of circumcision in the days from Abraham to Christ, admitting the bestowal of full grace through it. Making his way through life, Aquinas comes to appreciate also that there is no grace but through Christ alone, and this is the reason why he is so eager to correct his former views on circumcision. But when reflecting upon the circumcision of Christ, Aquinas fully acknowledges the Jewish lineage of Jesus, which forms part of the reason why Christ was circumcised in the first place. Christ was circumcised and baptised. He was baptised in order to start the new law, but he was circumcised in order to confirm and fulfill the old law.[53] Circumcision of course is connected to naming the one circumcised, as is baptism, and naming is of paramount importance to both the Jewish understanding of religion and Aquinas's interpretation of it. The name Jesus, God saves, constitutes the program of his life and mission, and connects him to God. Nothing is more central to him than that, and inside the centrality of that mission his circumcision is placed. To Jesus' identity belongs his Jewishness, according to Aquinas, and he says so explicitly: *Frater Iudaeorum.*

5. Perspectives

There are several instances in which Aquinas directly addresses the Judaism of his age. He treats social and political issues, and issues like mandatory baptism. More interesting, however, is what we can encounter on the level of the very structure of Aquinas's theological authorship. For Aquinas, as the systematic theologian he is, works often through establishing connections between the various tracts of theology. And thus he connects, employing the word *mysterium*, the context of interpreting the Old Testament with the theology of the hypostatic union in Christ. The new covenant is founded on what Christians call the old covenant, the sacred Jewish scriptures. The Old Testament is said to prefigure the New Testament, and we have seen above the ways Aquinas, as many theologians of his day and the authors of the New Testament themselves before him, thinks about Christ when interpreting the Old Testament. Christ himself is present in the Old Testament, sometimes as its literal meaning, sometimes as its spiritual meaning. This presence is *secundum mysterium*, according to mystery. And of course, the same word *mysterium* is used for the union of divinity and humanity in the one person of Christ, the hypostatic union. As shown elsewhere, Aquinas employs the word *mysterium* analogously, intimating a relationship between Christ's hidden presence in the Old Testament and God's hidden presence in Christ.[54] The exact nature of this relationship is not elucidated by Aquinas. It belongs, however, to the deep structure of his way of doing theology. And so we are entitled to ask whether the one might be helpful in approaching the other, whether Aquinas's account of the hypostatic union might help us develop his perspectives on the relationship between Old and New Testament, and ultimately between Judaism and Christianity.

This rather formal, structural tack might surprise some. There are, however, fundamental reasons why this need not be. For Aquinas's interpretation of the theology of the hypostatic union is to a large degree a formal one. Aquinas does not so much take the doctrine of the two natures of Christ as a description of his personhood, as he employs it as an ontological background for reflecting upon the person and work of Christ. He does not think that one should develop the theory of two natures into a 'greek' biography of Jesus of Nazareth, so to say. Instead the theory of Christ's two natures helps in interpreting what the Gospels say about him. So, a somewhat formal interpretation should not surprise.

But there is more to it, because medieval symbolism referred to the divine word as its primary analogate. Holy Scripture, as well as all books and words in general, indeed eventually nature itself, are expressions of the Logos, of the Word of God. The Word of God expresses itself in all that God creates. And even more so: Holy Scripture *is* the Word of God, the Torah *is* the Word of God. But the same is said of the person of Christ: he *is* the Word of God. This brings the Torah and Christ under the same consideration: both can be said to be the Word of God, yet both are not exclusively identified as such. For the Torah consists of human language, and Christ is human 'as well'. Both the Torah and Christ fit into medieval symbolism, because of their ultimate way of symbolising the divine.

So there is an analogy between the Torah and the person of Christ. To speak of analogy implies at least two things: a similarity against the background of an even larger dissimilarity, and the need for special naming, special signification. Both should be kept in mind when reading the following.

Aquinas's approach to the hypostatic union relies heavily on the teachings of the councils of Chalcedon and Constantinople II. Chalcedon (451) teaches a mostly negative view on the relationship between divinity and humanity in Christ. Both natures are, on the one hand, unmixed and unchanged and, on the other, undivided and inseparable. Humanity is not thereby absorbed by divinity; the divine and the human are not competitive nor is the one endangering the integrity of the other. On the contrary, it is precisely because of his divinity that Christ can come so close to humanity as to have humanity exist in his person; both do not belong to the same level. On the other hand, we are not allowed to think of Christ as essentially a duality, as a composite of two different substantial natures accidentally united. No, this unity is a real one, albeit inexplicably real. In developing these views on the hypostatic union, Aquinas is engaged in a kind of theology which is fundamental in character. It constitutes a second order reflection on the concrete history of Jesus of Nazareth, and is not meant to be a biographical sketch. It attempts rather to approach the mystery that God is the author of Jesus's words and acts in a way that is even more radical than the way God is the author of all creatures. In the end the contours of an apophatic christology emerge, which accounts for the impossibility of comprehending God's hidden presence in Christ as well as its salvific efficacy for humanity.

It might be fruitful to pursue the experiment to attribute what is said about the hypostatic union to the relationship between Old and New Testament. They should not be mixed, for they have their own independent meaning and authenticity. They should not be changed, as was sometimes done in the Middle Ages, in order to have the text more evidently signify Christ. Christ's presence in the Old Testament constitutes an identity of meaning which is unheard of, and will never be completely unravelled. And thus such meanings should not be divided or separated, for that would result in a detrimental dualism, in strife and competition, in robbery and hatred.

It is not difficult to translate this approach of the relationship between Old and New Testament to the relationship between Judaism and Christianity. It respects the legitimacy of Rabbinical interpretation of the Tenakh, even as it respects the legitimacy of the Christian interpretation of the Old Testament. Both may go together, because of Christ's acknowledgement and observance of the 'old law', and also because of Christ's fulfillment of it. They may also be congruent because of Paul's interpretation of the non-withdrawal by God of his eternal promise made to the Jewish people (Rom 11:28–29). To be sure, the covenant may be called 'old', but that does not mean that it is ended. To interpret the *diaspora* of the Jewish people as punishment for the crucifixion of Christ is something Aquinas is not likely to subscribe to, even though he considers Judaism under the heading of 'disbelief'. He will not, however, consider Rabbinical Judaism as heretical, and was perhaps inspired not to do so because of this fundamental aspect of his overall theological authorship: the principle of non-competition between God and creation, as taught by fundamental christology, and translated into biblical theology.[55]

More than in Aquinas's age, our own era is very sensitive to the tension that exists between Judaism and Christianity, for reasons indicated at the outset. But in a very fundamental sense Aquinas was well aware of this tension, and all the more remarkable it is that he does not belong to those among his brothers who wanted to lift that tension. In the relationship between Christianity and Judaism there is, so to speak, no room left for either Nestorianism or for Monophysitism; i.e., for a duality which only admits of accidental union or for a unity which absorbs the typical features of one or both 'constituents'. Aquinas might teach us that it is good theology to try to uphold the tension, instead of doing away with it to the detriment of both Christianity and Judaism.

As we mentioned above, the central word in this theological approach is *mysterium*. Aquinas links the mystery of divine presence in the Old Testament to the mystery of the hypostatic union in Christ. Now, the Latin word for this originally Greek expression is the word *sacramentum*. Christian authors employ it to refer to the specific sacred signs that mediate God's grace. And so, the mystery of divine presence in the sacraments is carried into the analogy as well. In recent days the word sacrament is used not only to refer to a specific ritual—for example, the Jewish ritual of circumcision—but to Judaism as such. Walter Cardinal Kasper states that "Judaism is as a sacrament of every otherness that as such the Church must learn to discern, recognise and celebrate".[56] Kasper's utterance is striking and deserves much more study and comment than can be offered here. But the attribution to Judaism of (something like) the very reality which is most precious to the Church is remarkable indeed. Aquinas would certainly have been struck by this approach. And yet, the preceding argument has shown a possible continuity with the very essence of his thought. Moreover, one even has to acknowledge that this uncollapsable tension, this togetherness which seems to be impossible, accords with the very idea of a relation between Judaism and Christianity that cannot be figured out completely. It constitutes a genuine mystery, being both incomprehensible and yet at the same time saving and historical. The relation between Judaism and Christianity, seen with the eyes of Christian faith and reflected upon by Christian theology, is indeed beyond comprehension. It 'just' needs to be discerned, recognised and celebrated, which—we admit—implies a program for ages.

NOTES

1   See Jeremy Cohen, *Living Letters of the Law: Ideas of the Jew in Medieval Christianity*, (Berkeley, CA: University of California Press, 1999).
2   Cf. M. M. Mulchaney, *"First the bow is bent in study . . .": Dominican education before 1350*, (Toronto, Canada: Pontifical Institute of Mediaeval Studies, 1998).
3   Jeremy Cohen, *The Friars and the Jews: The Evolution of Medieval Anti-Judaism*, (Ithaca and London, Cornell University Press, 1982). John Y. B. Hood, *Aquinas and the Jews*, (Philadelphia, PA: University of Pennsylvania Press, 1995). For a moderate position on the role of the Mendicants cf. Robert Chazan, *Daggers of Faith: thirteenth-century Christian missionizing and Jewish response*, (Berkeley, CA: University of California Press, 1988).
4   Canon law provided for both a certain protection and a certain segregation and oppression of Jews. For example, forced baptism was forbidden by the Pope (Callixtus II, 1119–1124,

Sicut Iudaeis, later included in the *Decretales* of Gregory IX, 1234), as in fact were all crimes against the Jews. However, the protection accorded Jews under these decretals carried an important qualification, namely, as long as Jews did not conspire against Christianity.

5   According to the major thesis of John Hood, in his *Aquinas and the Jews*. Hood finds Thomas's uncompromising stance on the illegitimacy of usury something that would be abused, a few decennia later, as a pretext by rulers who were interested in confiscating Jewish property.

6   Cf. his *Epistola ad ducissam Brabantiae*, also improperly called *De regimine Iudaeorum*.

7   Cf. his *De Rationibus Fidei ad cantorem Antiochenum*.

8   For an elaborate discussion of background and motives see Jean-Pierre Torrell, *Initiation à Saint Thomas d'Aquin. Sa personne et son oeuvre*, (Fribourg: Editions Universitaires, 1993/(2nd revised and augmented edition, 2002), pp. 153–156 and Rolf Schönberger, *Thomas von Aquin's 'Summa contra Gentiles'*, (Darmstadt: Wissenschaftliche Buchgesellschaft, 2001).

9   According to both Cohen and Hood, however, one can make a case for a conjectural interpretation of Aquinas as *implicitly* considering post-biblical Judaism as heretical: See John Hood, op. cit., p. 108; Jeremy Cohen, *Living Letters of the Law, Ideas of the Jew in Medieval Christianity*, (Berkeley, CA: University of California Press, 1999), pp. 364–389.

10   Cf. Henk J. M. Schoot, *Christ the 'Name' of God: Thomas Aquinas on Naming Christ*, (Louvain: Peeters, 1993) and Matthew Levering, *Christ's Fulfilment of Torah and Temple: Salvation According to Thomas Aquinas*, (Notre Dame, IN: University of Notre Dame Press, 2002).

11   For a similar approach, see Paul J. M. van Tongeren, "Thomas Aquinas on Forgiveness and Tolerance", in *Tibi Soli Peccavi: Thomas Aquinas on Guilt and Forgiveness* (Publications of the Thomas Instituut te Utrecht, n.s., vol. III), Henk J. M. Schoot (ed.), (Leuven: Peeters, 1996), pp. 59–73.

12   Otto H. Pesch, *Thomas von Aquin: Grenze und Größe mittelalterlicher Theologie*, (Mainz: Matthias-Grünewald-Verlag, 1988), pp. 52–65.

13   Francis A. Sullivan, S. J., *Salvation Outside the Church? Tracing the History of the Catholic Response*, (Mahwah, NJ: Paulist Press, 1992).

14   See the explanatory note in *St. Thomas Aquinas, Summa theologiae, volume 32: consequences of Faith (2a 2ae.8–16)*. Latin text, English translation, introduction, notes and glossary by Thomas Gilby O. P., (Cambridge: Blackfriars, 1975), pp. 38–39.

15   *Summa theologiae (STh)* II-II, q.10 a.1.

16   *STh* II-II q.10 a.5.

17   *STh* II-II q.11 a.1.

18   *STh* II-II q.10 a.6.

19   *STh* II-II q.11 a.3: *utrum haeretici sint tolerandi*. Gilby (*op. cit.*, p. 89) makes the dry remark that one can only appreciate this article "when its historical period is kept in mind".

20   According to the principle *de his qui foris sunt*, Christians should not intervene in the practice of Jewish religion; cp. I Cor. 5: 12–13.

21   *STh* II-II q.10 a.12: "*Et ideo periculosum videtur hanc assertionem de novo inducere, ut praeter consuetudinem in Ecclesia hactenus observatam, Judaeorum filii invitis parentibus baptizentur*".

22   *STh* II-II q.10 a.12 arg.s.c.

23   *STh* II-II q.10 a.8 ad 2um.

24   *STh* II-II q.10 a.11.

25   *STh* II-II q.10 a.9.

26   See *Summa contra Gentiles* I, c.2. Also Pim Valkenberg, "How to Talk to Strangers: Aquinas and Interreligious Dialogue in the Middle Ages", in *Jaarboek 1997 Thomas Instituut te Utrecht*, vol. 17, pp. 9–47.

27   For the biblical character of *STh* I-II q.98–105, see Jean-Pierre Torrell, *Initiation*, p. 228.

28   Since there is, as yet, no critical edition of the commentary on the Psalms, we follow the Vivès edition: *Doct. Ang. D. Thomae Aquinatis Opera Omnia, vol. 18: in Psalmos Davidis Expositio*, studio St. Fretté (Paris, 1889), pp. 228–556. The references to this commentary, however, do not indicate page numbers but the number of the Psalm and the number of the *lectio* in Aquinas's commentary on this psalm.

29   "*Omnia enim quae ad fidem* [in the Vivès-edition: *finem*] *Incarnationis pertinent, sic dilucide traduntur in hoc opere, ut fere videatur evangelium et non prophetia*", prol.

30   "*Prophetiae autem aliquando dicuntur de rebus quae tunc temporis erant, sed non principaliter dicuntur de eis, sed inquantum figura sunt futurorum: et ideo Spiritus sanctus ordinavit quod*

quando talia dicuntur, inserantur quaedam quae excedunt conditionem illius res gestae, ut animus elevetur ad figuratum", prol. See also *in Ps.* 21, lect. 1.

31 Cf. Pim Valkenberg, *Words of the Living God: Place and Function of Holy Scripture in the Theology of St. Thomas Aquinas*, (Leuven: Peeters 2000), p. 183.

32 See Pierre Grelot, *Le mystère du Christ dans les Psaumes*, (Paris: Desclée, 1998).

33 See Thomas F. Ryan, *Thomas Aquinas as Reader of the Psalms*, (Notre Dame, IN: University of Notre Dame Press, 2000), pp. 14–16, 61–64 and 107–112.

34 See, among others, *in Psalmos* 4 lect. 1: Christ is the end of the Law; ps. 5 lect. 1; ps. 39, lect. 1; ps. 40, lect. 1, and the prologue to the *tertia pars* of the *Summa theologiae*.

35 *"Mystice haec dicta sunt sub similitudine David de Christo"*, *in Ps.* 2, lect. 1; cf. Grelot, *op. cit.*, p. 52.

36 See Aquinas's commentary on the third Psalm, lect. 1 and 5. Also, ps. 7, lect. 3; ps. 10, lect. 1; ps. 26 lect. 12.

37 *In Ps.* 18, lect. 1: *"Psalmus iste secundum veritatem exponitur de Christo, quia Apostolus de hoc auctoritatem ad mysterium Christi Rom. X inducit"*.

38 *In Ps.* 19, lect. 1.

39 See, for instance, *in Ps.* 17, lect. 1: *"Et quia per David significatur Christus, omnia ista referri possunt ad Christum, vel secundum caput, vel secundum corpus, scilicet Ecclesiam"*. Also, *In Ps.* 34, lect. 1: *"Mystice pertinet ad Christum verum David: et secundum mysticam explicationem est secundus Psalmus eorum qui prolixe loquuntur de passione Christi . . . hic ergo Psalmus, sive legatur ex persona David, sive Christi, vel cujuscumque duo facit"*. This juxtaposition of possible explanations is one of the characteristics of Aquinas's exegetical works as opposed to his systematic-theological works, see Pim Valkenberg, *op. cit.*, pp. 187f.

40 See, for instance, *in Ps.* 27, lect. 1 (*. . . non figurali, sed vero David, scilicet Christo . . .*), and the rest of the Psalm, where the christological explanation is one of the possibilities (*. . . de Christo autem potest exponi . . .*).

41 *In Ps.* 15, lect. 1.

42 *In Ps.* 39, lect. 4; *"Haec verba forte vellet aliquis exponere de David . . . sed quia Apostolus exponit de Christo, et nos etiam exponamus de eo"*.

43 *In Ps.* 40, lect. 6: *"Et quia ipse Christus, Joan XIII istud verbum introducit de Juda, ideo nos de Christo hic exponamus"*.

44 Ryan, *op. cit.*, p. 173 n. 22 gives a comparison with the number of quotations from both Testaments in the *tertia pars* of the *Summa theologiae*.

45 Jaroslav Pelikan, *Jesus Through the Centuries: His Place in the History of Culture*, (New Haven, CT: Yale University Press, 1985/1999), p. 20.

46 *In IV Libri Sententiarum* IV, d.1, q. 2, a.2, qua. 2.

47 The first four Aquinas derives from Epiphane, the last three from Bede. Jean-Pierre Torrell makes this point in *Le Christ en ses Mystères la vie et l'oeuvre de Jésus selon saint Thomas d'Aquin*, t.1 (Paris: Desclée, 1999), p. 181.

48 Aquinas distinguishes three major components in the Old Law: moral precepts, ritual or ceremonial precepts and judicial precepts. The second category mentioned is subdivided in four parts: sacrifices, sacred things (e.g., tabernacle, vessels), sacraments and customs (e.g., dietary, clothing). Sacraments concern the institution for divine service of the people or of ministers through consecration. The most general sacrament is the rite of circumcision, through which one is admitted to the observance of the law. Other sacraments are the consecration of the priest, eating of the paschal meal, offering of ritual sacrifices and eating of bread in the temple, and (priestly and common) purification rites. All of these sacraments have rational causes, both literal and figurative; literally they derive their signification from the function they have in the divine service at that time; figuratively they have their signification inasmuch as they signify Christ. Cf. *STh* I–II, qq. 99–105, esp. q. 102,4.

49 *STh* III, q. 62,6 ad 3 and 70,4. Cf. *In Rom.* IV, l. 2. Aquinas's former views are contained in *In IV Libri Sententiarum IV*, d.1, q. 2, a.4, qua. 3.

50 This is carried by the distinction between final and efficient causes. A final cause may have moving power even before it occurs, and thus faith in "something that is hoped for" is said to move the one who believes. An efficient cause cannot do this, and yet that would be needed for something which proceeds through a non-mental exterior use of something, which applies to sacraments; e.g., before passion and resurrection of Christ purification rites cannot have efficacy in themselves; this can only happen afterwards. This same ratio-

nale also applies to the sacrament of penance. Aquinas's analysis of causality here is important, since it reminds one of an important divergence in interpreting the efficacy of sacraments in general in the thirteenth century: namely, the question whether or not the sacraments realise what they signify *ex opere operato.*

51   Richard Schenk, "Covenant Initiation: Thomas Aquinas and Robert Kilwardby on the Sacrament of Circumcision", in: Carlos-Josaphat Pinto de Oliveira OP (ed.), *Ordo Sapientiae et Amoris. Image et Message de Saint Thomas d'Aquin à travers les récentes études historiques, herméneutiques et docrinales,* Hommage au professeur Jean-Pierre Torrell OP à l'occasion de son 65ᵉ anniversaire (Fribourg, Suisse: Editions universitaires, 1993), pp. 555–593.

52   Schenk mentions that beginning with William of Auvergne, halfway through the thirteenth century, some theologians would look for an immanent Jewish sense for the ritual regulations, instead of always construing them as prefiguring Christ in some way or other. The rule of circumcision on the eighth day, for example, does not primarily point to the day of the resurrection of Christ, but to the point in time where the infant would no longer be too fragile and would not yet be of an age when pain would be felt. To William the immanent Jewish meaning of circumcision was the second meaning he had found in Maimonides: remembrance of the covenant with this one and only God, what he calls 'spiritual chastity', *op. cit.* p. 561.

53   "*Christus non solum debebat implere ea quae sunt legis veteris, sed etiam inchoare ea quae sunt novae. Et ideo non solum voluit circumcidi, sed etiam baptizari*", *STh* III, q. 39,1 ad 2.

54   Schoot, *op. cit.,* chapters 1 and 6.

55   David Burrell employs Chalcedon's formula to approach the uniqueness of Jerusalem. See "Jerusalem after Jesus", in *The Cambridge Companion to Jesus,* Markus Bockmuehl (ed.), (Cambridge: Cambridge University Press, 2001), pp. 250–264, here p. 252 and p. 257.

56   Walter Cardinal Kasper, President of the Pontifical Commission for Religious Relations with the Jews, "Address on the 37th Anniversary of *Nostra Aetate*", October 28, 2002.

4

THOMAS AQUINAS AND ISLAM

DAVID B. BURRELL, C.S.C.

The work of Thomas Aquinas may be distinguished from that of many of his contemporaries by his attention to the writings of Moses Maimonides (1135–1204), a Jew, and Ibn Sina [Avicenna] (1980–1037), a Muslim. His contemporaries, especially in Paris, were responsive to the work of another Muslim, Ibn Rushd [Averroës] (1126–1198), for his rendition of the philosophical achievements of Aristotle, but Aquinas' relation to Averroës and to those who took their lead from him was far more ambivalent. Aquinas respected "Rabbi Moses" and Avicenna as fellow travelers in an arduous intellectual attempt to reconcile the horizons of philosophers of ancient Greece, notably Aristotle, with those reflecting a revelation originating in ancient Israel, articulated initially in the divinely inspired writings of Moses. So while Aquinas would consult "the commentator" [Averroës] on matters of interpretation of the texts of Aristotle, that very aphorism suggests the limits of his reliance on the philosophical writings of Averroës, the *qadi* from Cordova. With Maimonides and Avicenna his relationship was more akin to that among interlocutors, and especially so with "Rabbi Moses", whose extended dialectical conversations with his student Joseph in his *Guide of the Perplexed* closely matched Aquinas' own project: that of using philosophical inquiry to articulate one's received faith, and in the process extending the horizons of that inquiry to include topics unsuspected by those bereft of divine revelation.

We may wonder at Aquinas' welcoming assistance from Jewish and Muslim quarters, especially when we reflect on the character of his times: the popular response to the call to arms of the crusades as well as a nearly universal impression on the part of Christians that the new covenant had effectively eclipsed the old. Aquinas may have shared these sentiments, for all we know, yet his overriding concern in reaching out to other thinkers was

David Burrell
C.S.C., University of Notre Dame, 327 Malloy Hall, Notre Dame IN 46556, USA and Tantur Ecumenical Institute, P.O. Box 19556, 91194 Jerusalem, Israel

always to learn from them in his search for the truth of the matters at hand. In this respect, he epitomized the medieval respect for learning with its conviction that "truth was where one found it". So he was more inclined to examine the arguments of thinkers than their faith, trusting in the image of the creator in us all to search out those traces of the divine handiwork, a theological premise that will prove useful in guiding our explorations into Aquinas' reliance on Islamic thinkers, and better than attributing to him an ecumenical or interfaith perspective *avant la lettre*. Yet it would not be untoward for us to note how other thinkers attempting to employ the inherited philosophy to elaborate their faith-perspective were for that very reason helpful to Aquinas in his vocational task.

It is worth speculating whether the perspective of Aquinas and his contemporaries was not less Eurocentric than our own. What we call "the west" was indeed geopolitically surrounded by Islam, which sat astride the lucrative trade routes to "the east". Moreover, the cultural heritage embodied in notable achievements in medicine, mathematics, astronomy, and well as the logical, philosophical commentary, translation, and original work in metaphysics begun in tenth-century Baghdad, represented a legacy coveted by western medieval thinkers.[1] Marshall Hodgson has called the culture that informed this epoch and extended from India to Andalusia "the Islamicate", intending thereby to include within its scope Jewish thinkers like Maimonides who enjoyed the protected status of *dhimmi* and contributed to Muslim civilization.[2] Christians like John of Damascus enjoyed a similar status, reserved by Qur'anic authority for "people of the book", yet the divisions in Christendom saw to it that thinkers in Paris were better acquainted with Muslim and Jewish thinkers than with their co-religionist in Islamic regions.

Aquinas' own geographic and social origins could well have predisposed him to a closer relationship with thinkers representative of the Islamicate than his contemporaries could be presumed to have had, in Paris at least. For his provenance from Aquino in the region of Naples, itself part of the kingdom of Sicily, reflected a face of Europe turned to the Islamicate, as evidenced in the first translations commissioned from Arabic: "Latin, Muslim, and Jewish culture mingled freely in Sicily in a unique way that was peculiarly Sicilian."[3] Moreover, in his later years, when his Dominican province asked him to direct a theological *studium*, Aquinas expressly chose Naples (over Rome or Orvieto) for its location, and that for intellectual reasons: "there was a vitality about Naples that was absent from Rome or any other city in the Roman province".[4] So it might be surmised that these dimensions of his own personal history led him to be more open to thinkers from the Islamicate than his co-workers from Cologne or Paris might have been. In any case, the number and centrality of the citations from Avicenna and Moses Maimonides leave no doubt as to their place in his intellectual development. By styling that place as one of interlocutor, I have tried to finesse the vague historical category of *influence* in favor of one more familiar to philosophers and theologians of every age, and especially those consciously working in a tradition of inquiry, who treasure what they learn as a result of contending with their predecessors' arguments, even when their interlocutors lie beyond the reach of actual conversation.

Towards an Interfaith, Intercultural Environment

The mentoring of Georges Anawati, O.P., at the Institut Dominicain d'Etudes Orientales in Cairo, with the assistance of the Dominican host community there, succeeded in opening my perspectives to see how much Aquinas' classical synthesis of Christian philosophical theology was already an interfaith achievement.[5] Indeed, were it not for the "Eurocentric" perspectives of western medieval scholarship, his numerous and strategic citations of "Rabbi Moses" Maimonides, of Avicenna [Ibn Sina] and of "the Commentator" Averroës [Ibn Rushd] should have suggested that conclusion long ago. For me, the privilege of working in the foyer created by scholars in Cairo may have offered the Mediterranean perspective needed to appreciate the way in which Aquinas' intellectual inquiry bridged the divide initially posed by alien faiths, allowing him to discover and exploit cognate strategies for explicating shared perspectives on creation, providence, and often parallel trajectories towards the goal of human fulfillment. Louis Gardet has shown how Aquinas' debt to the Islamic thinkers whom he knew directly lay largely in the area of conceptual strategies: "Rather than an encounter between Christian and Islamic worlds, the work of Thomas Aquinas bears witness to an encounter between Christian thought and an Islamic philosophy of Hellenistic inspiration, with a few forays into *kalâm*."[6] Yet it took the extensive work of Louis Gardet and Georges Anawati, epitomized in their ground-breaking *Introduction à la Théologie Musulmane* in 1948 to call *our* attention to the ease with which Aquinas negotiated the thought world of Islam.[7]

Besides the major philosophers noted, Aquinas' main source for Islamic religious thought was Moses Maimonides' *Guide of the Perplexed*, from which he profited in Latin translation.[8] So it seems he knew next to nothing about the relation between "the philosophers" [*falâsifa*] and the religious thinkers whom we identify with *kalâm* (or "dialectical theology") and whom Aquinas' translations led him to classify as "those speaking [*kalam*] with regard to Islamic law" [*loquentes in lege Maurorum*]. He cited them mainly as witnesses for a view of the created universe which removed any authentic causality from it, and so our having the requisite knowledge of natural things by that *scientia* which Aquinas (following Aristotle) demanded. And since Aquinas' primary goal was to show how *theologia* could be a *scientia* within the perspective afforded by a creator, a conclusion of that sort was clearly to be avoided. The philosophers would also require correction in the direction of free creation of the universe, yet Aquinas had no inclination to identify their works with Islamic teaching, even though he had no access to al-Ghazali's critique of them nor to Averroës' rejoinder. This strengthens Gardet's contention that his was not a cultural dialogue; he never attempted to use his interlocutors to explore their Islamic background, but rather regarded them as fellow inquirers into issues metaphysical and theological. What may astound us is the way his ease of access to their works and their conceptual strategies combined with an apparent insouciance regarding the faith tradition which those same works should invariably manifest. Yet that would be quite understandable were he to regard their faith as utterly alien, yet recognize their stellar intellectual capacities for what they were: a common humanity and intellectual acumen would unite what an alien faith could easily divide.

What seemed to have given Aquinas such access to the works of thinkers from the Islamicate, including Maimonides, was their synchrony regarding the oneness of God. This primordial revelation of the Hebrew scriptures and the Qur'an crowns Aquinas' presentation of the doctrine of God in the initial section of his *Summa Theologiae*, where the apparently unsurprising query— whether God is one? (1.11)—caps the eight previous questions detailing how we might use our intellectual tools to identify God uniquely. As the placement of this question, together with its internal development, reveals, it is asking much more than whether there be but one god. The "oneness of God" elaborated there is closer to what the rabbis and imams celebrate as the signal revelation of God to Moses and to Muhammad, respectively. Moreover, the presence of Jews and Muslims to Aquinas' consciousness may well have directed him to accentuate the oneness of the divinity at the outset of the *Summa* which he constructed for purposes of improved pedagogy. An additional motivation, closer to prevailing Dominican concerns, would have been the specter of Manichean dualism stemming from the mission against Albigensians which had fairly defined Dominic's earliest preaching.[9] With regard to the presence of Judaism and Islam, however, it is worth reminding ourselves that the novel revelation of Islam only reinforced the original Jewish insistence that God is one, which had figured trenchantly in the early elaboration of Christian doctrine. Why else can we surmise that it took four centuries to clarify the central teaching of Christianity about Jesus (Chalcedon, 451) out of which a full-blown trinitarian doctrine emerged?[10] In this respect, then, Aquinas could be said to be beginning at the beginning when he sets out to underscore the oneness of God in the opening questions of the *Summa*. Yet that strategy also served to link his treatment with the tenet of faith central to both Jews and Muslims, allowing him to appreciate the contributions of a Maimonides or an Ibn Sina as confirming an inquiry shared.

As Louis Gardet observed, however, it was primarily in the domain of conceptual strategies that Aquinas mined his Islamic predecessors. Yet as he did with Aristotle, we shall find him appropriating them to his use, where his use is more determined by the perspectives of scripture and Catholic teaching than simple philosophical coherence. For while Aquinas was scrupulous about proper argument—"lest weak arguments seem to give plausibility to the other side of the debate"—his sensitivity to what Robert Sokolowski has dubbed "the distinction" of creator from creation dominated his project of showing how *theologia* could be a *scientia* within the perspective afforded by a creator.[11] For whereas Plato had suggested some facsimile of a creator, Aristotle had presumed an eternal universe in a way that ruled out any question of origins. So the work of Moses Maimonides would prove especially fruitful, while that of Avicenna required extensive modification, though his central distinction between *essence* and *existence* would prove utterly strategic, as we shall see.[12]

Resolving a Standing Aporia of Aristotle

The most complete map of these conceptual alternations has been provided by Edward Booth, in his *Aristotelian Aporetic Ontology in Islamic and Christian Writers*.[13] The *aporia* in question can be made evident quite easily: Aristotle insisted that the existing individual offered the paradigm for substance—*that which is*, yet every time we characterize a substance we do so by using a formula. The structure of that formula (or definition) is meant to display the matter-form composition of substance, yet in such a way as to express the species and not the individual. So individuals end up being nothing more than instantiations of species, and the primacy of "first substance" gives way to what seems to be the subject of any discourse: "second substance". Tracing this recurrent *aporia* through the subsequent commentary tradition yields little progress in resolving it, and even offers some explanation why the earliest interpretation of Aristotle's *Metaphysics* tended in a Neoplatonic direction. Indeed, subsequent presentations of portions of Plotinus' *Enneads* as the "Theology of Aristotle", and of selections from Proclus as the *Liber de causis* (thought by many to represent a development of Aristotle), confirmed that direction.[14] One had to wait until the sixth century for John Philoponus to recover something of the more properly Aristotelian synthesis of Alexander of Aphrodisia (late second century), yet the urge to syncretism favored the earlier Neoplatonic readings into the golden age of Islamic philosophers. Al-Kindi, as a believer, "found the categories of Proclus, modified in a monotheistic sense, very suited to express his religious sense of dependence of the world on God" (p. 90), while al-Farabi went on to develop the emanation scheme which furnished the hallmark of classical Islamic philosophy.

Yet the translation of Aristotelian texts by the early thirteenth century led medieval thinkers like Albert to grapple directly with that *aporia*. He resolved it in a "logico-emanationist" direction, however, relying on Boethius' "identification of universal with individual" (p. 175) to develop "structures [which] seemed to make the ultimate individual, logically (and emanation-ally) conceived, identical with the individual, physically conceived" (p. 192). A resolution of this sort effectively turned "*Metaphysics* VII, which is really a record of metaphysical uncertainty, [into] a subject for systematic and ratio-nal exposition" (pp. 195–196). So with regard to the recurring *aporia*, one would have to class Albert with the commentators, seeking to resolve a dialectically fruitful tension into a logically acceptable teaching. Booth credits pseudo-Dionysius' treatise on the *Divine Names*, which he had studied "attentively" with Albert, with directing Aquinas away from Albert by showing that "*esse* could not be limited to a single radiation or formality amongst many from the divine first cause" (p. 204). His final chapter recounts how Aquinas attained "the superior viewpoint of *esse*, [and so was] capable of appreciating the individual according to any and every aspect, [thereby] liberating Aristotelian ontology from is aporetic hesitance" (p. 263). Which is to say that Aquinas only succeeded in resolving the original *aporia* of individual/formula for substance by raising the entire discussion to a new level: the presence of the One as creator, bestowing *esse* to each individual, retained proper Aristotelian respect for formal structures while offering such immediacy to the creator/creature relation that the status of individuals as paradigms for substance was clearly vindicated.

A recent masterful study, *Substantiality and Participation in Thomas Aquinas*, by Rudi teVelde, shows how pseudo-Dionysius' way of employing the lan-guage of *esse* allowed Aquinas to move beyond the accepted Platonic view of a plurality of forms by stipulating that "the perfection of being [*esse*] vir-tually includes every other perfection".[15] This form of analysis could main-tain "that God possesses the fullness of perfection in virtue of his being alone" (p. 256), since *esse* could not be a form like other forms, and identi-fying God's as *esse subsistens* not only distinguishes the creator from every-thing else (that is, all creatures), but shows why such a one might freely allow its essence to be participated in its act of creating. Only God can create, Aquinas insists, for "producing existence absolutely, not merely of this thing or of that sort of thing, belongs to the meaning of creation. . . . [And] among all effects the most universal is existence itself, which should accordingly be the proper effect of the most universal cause, which is God" (*ST* 1.45.5). The atmosphere here is thoroughly Neoplatonic, though appropriately "cor-rected", as we have seen, by Dionysius. So the final resolution of Aristotle's standing *aporia*, itself a legacy from his own formation under Plato, will require an adroit set of Platonic strategies, notably an account of creation by way of *esse* which will bring *participation* as its inevitable corollary. Now it will be an Islamic transformation of Proclus, translated from Arabic into Latin as the *Liber de Causis*, which will offer Aquinas the strategies required to articulate the creator as *cause of being*.

Critical Assistance in Articulating a Cause of Being

As his commentary on this seminal text (which he recognized to be an Islamic adaptation of Proclus) displays, however, the Neoplatonic scheme it followed and propagated could hardly on the face of it expound a free creator. So Aquinas' re-directing of the Arabic text, *Kitâb al-khaîr* [*Book of the Pure Good*], will prove to be as significant (or more) as the particular re-casting of Proclus by the anonymous Muslim writer. Yet the fact remains that Aquinas did fasten on this work as key to his endeavor to incorporate a free creator into the Hellenic heritage, just as he insisted on employing the term "emanation" for creation, even after removing and gutting the scheme of necessary emanation enthusiastically adopted by the Islamic thinkers, al-Farabi and Ibn Sina, ostensibly to articulate the revelation of a unitary creator of the universe. That same scheme, trenchantly attacked by al-Ghazali and Moses Maimonides in the name of revelation as impugning a free creator and so rendering revelation itself incredible, was rejected by Aquinas for mediating the act of creation.[16] So another way to cast our net is to ask why Aquinas still felt that *emanation* offered the best metaphor for the *sui generis* activity of creation, even of a free creator.

The need for a fresh perspective becomes evident once we remind ourselves that Aquinas realized full well that none of Aristotle's four causes could describe the act of creating, notwithstanding his celebratory identification of Aristotle's *prime mover* with the liturgical formula: "*quod est Deus per omnia saecula saeculorum*" (closing his commentary on the *Physics*). Indeed, his occasional use of "efficient cause" to identify the creator of all is manifestly "loose" or "improper", and only intended to contrast this causality with others even less apt. For Aristotle's *efficient cause* always presupposes a subject upon which to work. So Aquinas needed a conception of *causality* not available from Aristotle, yet intimated (as we shall see) in the *Liber de causis*; indeed, a *cause-of-being*. Furthermore, one of the crucial arguments opposing free creation to necessary emanation had been that the axiomatic model used to propose it (and make it *necessary*) failed to distinguish the originator from all that originated from it, since an axiom differs from other premises only by its prominent place in the deductive order. Yet "the distinction" of creator from creation proves notoriously difficult to articulate, as Robert Sokolowski has shown so ably in his *God of Faith and Reason*.[17] Indeed, customary western attempts to separate creatures from the creator falsify the relation as effectively as some "eastern" attempts to collapse them. Fear of pantheism has moved western thinkers to parse the *distinction* as a *separation*, yet I shall argue that this strategy has diluted the specific assertions of Jewish-Christian-Muslim faith in a creator, so demoting the creator to "the biggest things around" and promoting a secular ethos.[18]

Yet affirming that shared faith in a free creator will entail philosophical effort, and watching Aquinas adapt the *Liber de causis* to that end might encourage us to similar efforts. Allow me first to identify those who have helped me to the point of appreciating what the *Liber de causis* must have meant for Aquinas, and how we might be enabled to make similar intellectual moves ourselves. I have already mentioned Sokolowski's careful and extended inquiry into "the distinction" of creator from creation, to articulate its *sui generis* character. A trenchant remark by Bernard McGinn at our conference on "God and Creation" (in which Sokolowski participated) alerted me to the partial and polemical way in which I was then (1989) opposing free creation to emanation, while Sara Grant's exploring Shankara's use of nonduality to probe "the distinction" which Aquinas proposed began to dispel my fears of pantheism.[19] Still more recently, and doubtless in conjunction with John Milbank and Catherine Pickstock's "radically orthodox" proposals for reading the Christian tradition (including Aquinas), I have become fascinated with two thinkers thus far relatively marginal to philosophical theology: Scottus Eriugena and Meister Eckhart.[20] Their affinity with Neoplatonic vehicles of thought to help articulate "the distinction" *not* as a *separation* has led me to find them to be better guides to what Aquinas was trying to articulate in a "cause-of-being" (and hence "the distinction") than what has often passed as canonical Thomist interpretation. And the inquiry into Aquinas' use of the *Liber de causis* will, I hope, indicate why this is the case.

Let us begin by posing a question which I have hitherto been content simply to deconstruct: how is it that the One, whose proper effect is things' very being, effects that? Given the precision of Aquinas—there can be no *process* whereby things come to be—it is easy to deconstruct: there is no *how*; coming to be takes no time, creation involves no *change* (in Aristotle's sense) from one thing to another, requiring a substratum. But is there then no way at all to articulate what happens in the infinite shift from nothing to something? We could, as I have, simply reiterate Aquinas' insistence that the "proper effect of a creator is the to-be of things", but that tells us very little indeed; and should we parse it as "bestowing being on things", that way of speaking (we shall see) falsifies the relation as well. Here is where the *Liber de causis*, as Aquinas adapts it, may well lend a hand: think of creating as an ordering—a salient feature of the emanation scheme, for things come to be according to their kind, whether we are following Genesis or Aristotle! *Existing*, of course, is not a kind, but whatever is, is inanimate, animate, or intelligent, in the sense that something may simply exist, or exist as a living being, or as an understanding being. Now this fact of categorization (or levels of *formal cause* [Aristotle]) elicits two opposing pictures. One is additive: being + self-motion + intentional; and hence subtractive as well: taking away intelligence will yield vegetative, removing that yields simple inanimate being. The other retains the sense of modes of existing, regarding them as ascending levels as well, but relates these levels not additively but virtually. That is, the being of inanimate things is regarded as restricted, those capable of growth and/or of self-motion more ample, and those also endowed with understanding and intention yet more fully realizing the reaches of being.

Both pictures are present in the *Liber de causis* as well as in Aquinas, yet the effort to incorporate a free creator into the scheme of categorization will inevitably privilege the *virtual* picture. The tension surfaces quite dramatically (for those who can unveil drama in ontology!) when Aquinas proposes to identify the creator God uniquely as the One whose very essence is to-be. This succinct formula offers *simpleness* as the "formal feature" securing "the distinction" by singling out God in the only way possible—without turning God into god, the "biggest thing around", and so effectively eclipsing God's divinity as well as "the distinction".[21] Yet we must meet the *prima facie* objection that what is simple is ontologically "lower" than what is composed or complex, much as animate things are more complex than inanimate. He does this by reversing the picture itself, proposing that the One whose essence is to-be (and so can cause all else to be) should not be conceived as "mere being" but as the fullness of being, so that *simpleness* here denotes plenitude rather than a lack.[22]

But how can we execute such an about-face? What makes one see (as in Wittgenstein's duck/rabbit example) that the virtual picture of levels of being must take precedence over the additive? I suspect that the effort to incorporate and properly articulate a creator into one's metaphysics will decide it, but there are supporting arguments as well. The most telling, I believe, is one derived from Aristotle's argument to the unity of substantial forms, captured in the maxim: the being of living things is to live.[23] Indeed, contrary to the *prima facie* sense of the *Liber de causis*, the levels of being are not separable or subtractible. Take away *life* from a living thing and *it* remains inanimate for a very short while; indeed, what is left begins to decompose into elements and is soon no longer identifiable as one thing. This fact supports the virtual picture: being expresses itself in different ways. Moreover, if "higher levels" were simply added, what would make the resultant being one sort of thing? This is what Aristotle meant by the "unity of substantial form". Moreover, a closer reading of the *Liber de causis* reveals just such a picture. The bestowal of being [*esse*] by the first cause is an orderly bestowal, yielding an inherent order structuring each existing thing so that higher levels are implicit in lower. Indeed, were this not the case, were being not an abundant source expressing itself in different ways, then *existing* would have to be pictured (as many do) as something added to a potential thing, as in "actualizing a possible state of affairs". But that picture is doubly redundant, for it presumes (1) "potential things", that is, an order or structure present before something exists; and (2) that *existing* is a feature (or "accident") which can be added to a non-existing "thing". These two incoherencies are in fact one, but it is instructive to see how *existing* must be construed as a feature once one adopts "possible things".

Ironically enough, so-called "existential" readings of Aquinas, by their description of *esse* as "act of existing", can unwittingly turn *esse* [to-be] into a feature. It is true, of course, that by identifying *esse* as *act* Aquinas expressly intended to eliminate that move, suggested by Avicenna's terminology of *existing* as an "accident ['arad]". Yet his own expression of "receiving *esse*" could subvert his own intentions as well.[24] So how can we escape these traps? The *Liber de causis* offers a way: to see creation as the orderly bestowal of things' being, which adopts the metaphor of *emanation* and sees *existing* as a participation in being by virtue of the One whose very essence is to-be, and so alone can make things participate in being. And as a way of spelling out the metaphor of *participation*, we are invited to see it as an order inherent in each thing. So *existing* is no more something *added to* a thing than learning is something acquired, like a degree after one's name. The degree is acquired, of course, as a step in credentialing, but *learning* (as Socrates insisted) is really *recollection*, as we utilize others to hone the faculties already present in our being intentional persons. What comes with our mode of being is an ordered set of capacities, which stand to be perfected and need help to do so, but when perfected are so from within. Moreover, these capacities in intentional beings *desire* their perfection, that is (in *Liber de causis* terms) they are so shaped from within as to strive to return to their proper good, their source. Such is the power of a creation-centered picture of *being*: *virtual* (not additive), and *directional* towards its source. This picture is completed in fully intentional (or free) agents, whose freedom can be expressed as a "hunger for the good" and so best seen as a response rather than an initiative.[25] Such a picture underscores the antinomies which Socrates had already exposed in the alternative view of freedom as "doing what I want to do", which can so easily mean slavery to multiple desires; and also express Nietzsche's model of self-creation as exactly what one must undertake without a creator.

The fullness of the act of existing is displayed in its order, much as the efficacy of any of our actions is assured by the ordering it displays towards its goal. We focus authentically, not by eliminating all but one feature, but by aligning all the relevant features in a proper order, so that the effect is orchestrated. Notice that we cannot escape metaphors here, for there is no given ordering. Revelation assists by allowing us to name "the Good". And further by providing us with some strategies of ordering—the Torah, the example of Jesus, the Qur'an—yet here again, discernment is always needed, and traditions can subvert as well as elaborate a given revelation or way. The urpattern derives from creation, as conceived by the *Liber de causis*: orderly emanation from the One so that the intentional portion of creation desires to return to its source. Moreover, such an order is not imposed but inherent, as *existing* is not an added feature but an inherent gift. This is seen most fully, according to Aquinas, when we can appreciate this source as freely bestowing what it truly is. That is, its manner of being is triune, so that in creating, it freely communicates the manner in which it naturally communicates.[26]

Before concluding this elucidation of creator as "cause of being", let us return to the original question: how is it that the One, whose proper effect is things' very being, effects that? The "first cause infuses all things with a single infusion, for it infuses things under the aspect [*sub rationem*] of the good" (123 [110]). Aquinas concurs, reminding us that it had already been shown that "the first cause acts through its being, . . . hence it does not act through any additional relation or disposition through which it would be adapted to and mixed with things" (123–124 [111]). Moreover, "because the first cause acts through its being, it must rule things in one manner, for it rules things according to the way it acts" (134 [111]). The following Proposition 21 links this "sufficiency of God to rule" (125 [112]) with divine simpleness: "since God is simple in the first and greatest degree as having his whole goodness in a oneness that is most perfect" (126 [113]). Hence Proposition 23 can assert: "what is essentially act and goodness, namely, God, essentially and originally communicates his goodness to things" (1342 [118]). With such a One there can be no anxiety about "control"; indeed, the simile which the proposition on divine rule elicits is that "it is proper for a ruler to lead those that are ruled to their appropriate end, which is the good" (ibid.). For to "infuse things under the aspect of the good" is precisely to bring all things to be in a certain order, inherent in their very existing, so there is nothing "external" about divine providence, no imposition—neither "inasmuch as it establishes things, which is called creation; [nor] inasmuch as it rules things already established" (137 [122]). Indeed, the initial diversity comes from the first cause, who "produces the diverse grades of things for the completion of the universe. But in the action of ruling, . . . the diversity of reception is according to the diversity of the recipients" (137 [123]). Yet since the original order comes from the One, the One in ruling will "effortlessly" adapt itself to the order established in creating. Another way of putting all this, and one which should dissolve most conundra regarding "divine action", is to remind oneself that the creator, in acting, acts always as creator; and this proposition elucidates Aquinas' contention that *creating* and *conserving* are the same action, differing only in that conserving presupposes things present.

Yet since the manner of that action will ever escape us, for its very simplicity belies any *manner* at all—no "relation or disposition", the best we can do is to remind ourselves that it ever acts by constituting the order which inheres in each existing thing, in the measure that it is. (And since essence measures *esse*, it is pointless to oppose essence to existing in things that are.) Yet since "order" is a consummately analogous term, we can never be sure we have detected the originating divine order in things, though our conviction that there is one, inscribed in their very being and our intentional attitudes towards them, will continue to fuel our inquiry. Crude classifications—inanimate, animate, intentional—can be supplemented by refined mathematical structures and symmetries (as in DNA), yet each stage of analytic tool will be serving our innate desire to unveil the activity present in these infused "goodnesses" (130 [116]) which constitute our universe. And to grasp something of that constitutive ordering is to come closer to its sources, "because every knowing substance, insofar as it has being more perfectly, knows both the first cause and the infusion of its goodness more perfectly, and the more it receives and knows this the more it takes delight in it, it follows that the closer something is to the first cause the more it takes delight in it" (138 [123]). All is not light or delight, of course, because in truth we cannot, ourselves, hope to *know* "the first cause and the infusion of goodness". Indeed, "the most important thing we can know about the first cause is that it surpasses all our knowledge and power of expression" (46 [43]), for "our intellect can grasp only that which has a quiddity participating in 'to-be' [while] the quiddity of God is 'to-be itself'" (52 [17]). Indeed, that is why Aquinas can concur that "the first cause is above being inasmuch as it is itself infinite 'to-be'" (51 [47]). Yet since "what belongs to higher things are present in lower things according to some kind of participation" (30 [17]), we can be said to share, as beings, in this inaccessible One.

Reflecting on Aquinas' particular task, we can fairly say that he was concerned to show how *theologia* could be a *scientia*—with neither of those terms translatable into their current modern language cognates. To accomplish this task he received help from thinkers in the Jewish and Muslim traditions: from Maimonides, the very strategy itself; and from the *Liber de causis*, a philosophical focus on faith in divine unity [*tawhîd*]. Yet as we have noted, he managed as well to exploit the resources of his own tradition, notably in assimilating creation to processions within a triune God. We are placed to appreciate and to develop other features of his thought, as Eckhart did, underscoring the *sui generis* relation which creation is, and search for metaphors to elucidate it, like *nonduality*. In this way, we can use his subtle appropriation of the *Liber de causis* to carry out similar adaptations of our own. For me, this has meant coming full circle to appreciate the mode of reflection enshrined in *emanation* to illuminate the uniqueness of the creation-relation, in full realization that we shall never adequately articulate it. Yet we can reach for metaphors, as Aquinas did in appropriating the *Liber de causis*, or as Sara Grant did in expounding Shankara's *nonduality*, in a vein reminiscent of Meister Eckhart. And should some be put off by the apparently disembodied "intellectuality" of all this, they need only recall Pierre Hadot's reminders that such rarified modes of thought can only be executed in a milieu shaped by sustained and rigorous "spiritual exercises".[27] Such is the inherent *telos* of philosophical theology, as it strains, in the persons of its practitioners, to align itself with the goodnesses infused in things, the divinely ordained order of being.

Cultural Exchange Enriching Conceptual Strategies

In the wake of John Paul II's exploratory encyclical *Fides et ratio* (1998), one of my confreres, then serving as rector of a Catholic seminary in Africa, was invited to Rome for a global consultation on the complex relations between faith and reason. His African perspective emboldened him to add culture to the diptych to form the triad: reason, culture, and faith. When I heard this, I was initially impressed by his unwitting insertion of Charles Sanders Peirce into the discussion: any polarity is ever in danger of becoming just that, so a third will invariably be needed. Beyond that general recommendation, however, these observations regarding Aquinas' extraordinarily fruitful use of conceptual strategies adapted from Islamic inquiries confirms his recommendation. For despite his frequentation of Paris as a venue for teaching and scholarship, Aquinas' Mediterranean roots drew him to encounter "an Islamic philosophy of Hellenistic inspiration", as Louis Gardet has put it, to determine how much of that might be put at the service of Christian thought in general as well as his specific task of showing how *theologia* could be a *scientia*. It was cultural difference which fertilized his prescient metaphysical elaboration of Jewish, Christian, and Muslim faith in a free creator—something which each averred but had articulated in different ways. Moreover, it may have been the dominant role which creation must play in Islam that motivated Islamic thinkers to develop this article of faith. For while it can be said that the "coming down" of the Qur'an to humankind via the Prophet parallels the covenant of God with Israel and the incarnation of the Word in Jesus, what the Qur'an asserts—in countless ways—is the origin of all things in the One (God), to the point where their central religious thinker, al-Ghazali, will insist that "the meaning of faith in divine unity [*tawhîd*] is that there is no agent but God most high".[28] That is, in the absence of either covenant or incarnation, the creating activity of the one God is central for Islam, though in practice it is the verses [*ayât*] of the Qur'an which alert human beings to recognize the things in this world as signs [*ayât*] of the presence of its creator.

Such features of the Islamic worldview, as Louis Gardet has noted, utterly escaped Aquinas, whose sense of unity-in-difference among human inquirers must nonetheless have encouraged him to adopt and adapt thought-forms which flourished in the world of Islam. We are better placed, of course, to appreciate that world as a culture counterpoised to our own, as we are better informed about the myriad differences. Ironically enough, however, that does not easily translate into our willingness to learn form cultures different from ours—especially when it is a matter of adopting or adapting new conceptual strategies. Yet the touted ideal of pluralism, as well as current attention (in the francophone world) to *difference*, should predispose us to opening to diverse ways of thought and expression, notably in "essentially contested" matters like those germane to philosophical inquiry. Yet the fact is that "pluralism" is better commended than observed among philosophical practitioners in western academe itself, so what would motivate inquirers who tend to shun difference within a culture to venture beyond it? Nothing short of what Alasdair MacIntyre has called an "epistemological crisis", which is exactly what Aquinas encountered in the celebrated *aporia* bequeathed from Aristotle.[29] Yet the inertia endemic to academic subfields can easily obscure the edges of any epistemological crisis, nor is the inadequacy of current categories to meet the demands of a particular inquiry necessarily evident. One may have a pervasive sense of inadequacy, but until a prescient diagnostician emerges, usually armed with a fresh scheme, these will not be felt as "crises".

The best contemporary example of this situation is itself controversial: Samuel Huntington's proposal to analyze international relations by the pregnant metaphor of a "clash of civilizations". Himself an acknowledged leader in the field of international relations, his initial proposal (in *Foreign Affairs* [1993]) intended to challenge the model of statecraft prevailing in the discipline by introducing cultural factors hitherto considered quite irrelevant for constructing explanatory models. That proved upsetting enough to practitioners of the trade, as distinguished contributors to a subsequent issue of *Foreign Affairs* demonstrated palpable resistance to learning such new languages. Huntington's arguments for adopting a new paradigm were persuasive enough: religious convictions and other cultural practices have clearly been more effective markers of personal identity than citizenship; social mores a more effective molder of attitudes than laws.[30] Yet these will be far less susceptible of quantitative analysis than survey research of stated attitudes. So entire subdisciplines would be challenged for their relevancy should these factors be accepted as relevant. Moreover, Huntington's own presentation of this fresh paradigm for analysis proved especially faulty in its structure, which predictably imported preoccupations from settled ways of analysis. One could begin with the title, "clash of civilizations", where the dominance of *clash* bespoke the overriding preoccupations of statecraft politics so accurately summarized by Hegel's "every state needs an enemy". Moreover, "civilizations" appeared on stage with many of the trappings of states: identifiable entities with geographical borders, without a hint of the porous and shifting character of cultural constructions. All of this, of course, is perfectly understandable, as those who attempt to offer a fresh paradigm for inquiry will inevitably exhibit traces of their settled methods.

More telling, however have been the examples offered to show how this new analysis might proceed, where countless *obiter dicta* presumed a superior evaluation of "western civilization", with its forms of thought and analysis, redolent of nineteenth-century colonizing attitudes—"Orientalism" *redivivus*. Indeed, Edward Said's screed describing those manners of presenting and analyzing others which he collated to exhibit a set of features "Orientalism" continues to pose an articulate challenge to anyone seeking to understand someone or something different. However starkly and polemically his depictions may be drawn, it is difficult at once to escape their point or to negotiate successfully so formidable a task.[31] Moreover, successful passage seems notably blocked by political and economic hegemony. Besides the relative absence of motivation on the part of "haves" to come to know "have-nots"—as these conventional descriptors show all too well, everything conspires for the "haves" to present themselves as the veritable paradigm of human being. Bernard Lewis' own screed, composed in response to 11 September 2001—*What Went Wrong?*—admits of two antithetical readings: with us? or with them?—but the presumptions operative in the book's "argument" nowhere suggest the first option.[32] Something must have gone wrong with them! The direction of his polemic utterly obscures the fact that western liberal society appears to have reached at least an "epistemological crisis", as public space recedes more and more, income disparity becomes obscene, and raising children with integrity more daunting than ever. Yet jeremiads of this sort are common coin to self-styled radicals and conservatives alike.

So it might behoove western thinkers to attend to an alternative like the one proposed by President Mohammad Khatami of Iran in addressing the United Nations General Assembly on 21 September 1998, where he called for a "dialogue among civilizations". Admittedly presented as a counter-response to Huntington, the journal *Global Dialogue* devoted its Winter 2001 issue to the subject, inviting participants from Europe, America, and central as well as west Asia. They struggle with how one may try to understand others in a way that does not obliterate their difference, and the results manifest how the effort demands that we leave the presumed certainties of our native perspective to solicit assistance from those same others in our inquiry. Epistemological issues abound: can we simply presume the analytic categories we usually employ to be adequate to understanding realities that systematically elude our considerations? Or must we rather presume that anything which eludes our considerations cannot be real, so that the first option cannot be a real one? Put this starkly, which is a philosopher's wont, it would be difficult to accept either horn of the dilemma. The way out, of course, is to be open—as cultures have ever been, though not without protest—to adopting and adapting unfamiliar forms of thought and analysis to meet a situation that keeps presenting itself as intractable.

In a characteristically penetrating essay in this issue of *Global Dialogue*, Fred Dallmayr uses Hans-Georg Gadamer to delineate the sort of epistemological strategies needed for "civilisational dialogue".[33] In the process he notes how much western civilization owes to his Graeco-Roman and to its Judeo-Christian components, anticipating Remi Brague's recent twist on that dual legacy, detailing its refraction through Rome: *Eccentric Culture: A Theory of Western Civilization*.[34] So interculturality seems rather to be the norm than the exception. Yet where the cultures are in fact in conflict, carrying it off will require, as Chaim and Rivka Gordon have underscored, actively confronting the injustice which dominant cultures continue to visit on others, and which short-circuit the very dialogue which Khatami counsels.[35] Yet confrontation will be fruitless if it leads by accusation; it must take the form of a "joint quest for justice". Only then can there be a "genuine dialogue between persons from different spiritual heritages [that] can add substantially to the breadth and depth of the mode of existence of those involved in dialogue".[36] These seasoned observations of Chaim and Rivka Gordon reveal the underside of our "ecumenical" age, where we can find ourselves carrying on a "dialogue" abstracted from the devastating effects wrought in the name of our respective religious faiths. It is this specific form of "bad faith" which their directions mean to expose and re-direct. Yet as we mentioned at the outset, the times in which Aquinas lived were more characterized by separation and relative ignorance of one another's faith-life. The single exception reflects the situation of Christians in Islamic lands, and is reflected in his extended response to a query by the "Cantor of Antioch" to respond to standard Muslim objections to Christian doctrine.

Antioch, like Andalusia, sported regular disputations between Muslims and Christian interlocutors, which itself offers a fascinating perspective on Islamic culture. Yet Aquinas' response—"Reasons for the Faith against Muslim Objections"—shows little or no appetite for disputation, but simply takes the opportunity to offer a succinct resumé of Christian doctrine regarding those points which the Cantor identifies for him as neuralgic for Muslims: that Christ is the "Son of God", that he was crucified, that Christians eat his body, and that merit must give way to "divine decree" or "predestination".[37] Apparently composed in 1264, in the wake of a work designed to give the "reasons for faith," the *Summa contra gentiles* (SCG), Aquinas summarizes much of his treatment there in response to the specific queries of the Cantor. He is not responding directly to a Muslim interlocutor, as he has already professed his ignorance of the particulars of the Muslim faith in the just completed *Summa* (SCG 1.2), but rather trying to equip the Cantor with a set of strategies for an informed response: that is, one which takes the opportunity of the objections to plumb more deeply what we already believe as Christians.[38] By adopting this tack, Aquinas shows himself to be responding as we have described his overall strategy with respect to other faiths: we can learn from their questions better ways to elucidate our own set of beliefs. This confirms Bernard Lonergan's assessment of Aquinas' theological *élan*: a continual searching for the truth of matters revealed.[39]

Concluding Reflections

Ours is a very different world from Aquinas', yet his ability to see the presence of interlocutors from other faiths as a spur to understanding of his own tradition offers us a model which deftly eschews intellectual colonizing, and

displays the way in which every living tradition grows by carefully responding to challenges from without. Yet what must animate that approach is a
lively confidence in the truth of one's own tradition, together with the realization that such a truth will continue to outstrip any standing articulation
of it. So one seeking the truth of matters revealed will always have something to learn from others; the polar opposite (again from Lonergan) is to
need certitude. Yet a proper phenomenology of a living religious faith will
be able to identify needs of that sort as obstructions to the internal development of the faith itself, exposed so neatly in Kierkegaard's ridiculing of
anyone intent on "defending the faith".[40] We have explored in detail the
appropriation which Aquinas made of a set of philosophical strategies trans-
mitted to him by an Islamic rendition of a Neoplatonic text, the *Liber de causis*
[*Kitab al Khair Mahd*], as he sought to articulate the faith assertion—central
to Jews, Christians, and Muslims alike—of a free creator, in properly metaphysical terms as the "cause of being". The deft way in which he adapts this
(already adapted) text of Proclus displays how he executed his calling to
show that *theologia* could be a *scientia*: not by reducing itself, Procrustean-
fashion, into Hellenic categories, but by employing them in a way that
respects their logical power yet allows them to illuminate, rather than
pretend to explain, matters which will resist explanation in simply human
terms.[41] No wonder his synthesis of Christian doctrine, once shown to be the
intercultural, interfaith achievement it is, has proven to be normative for subsequent generations as well.

NOTES

1 Joel Kraemer *Humanism in the Renaissance of Islam* (Leiden: E. J. Brill, 1986), *Philosophy in the Renaissance of Islam* (Leiden: E. J. Brill, 1986).
2 Marshall Hodgson, *The Venture of Islam* (3 vols.) (Chicago, IL: University of Chicago Press, 1961).
3 James Weisheipl, O.P., *Friar Thomas D'Aquino: His Life, Thought, and Works* (Washington, DC: Catholic University of America Press, 1983) p. 15.
4 *Ibid.*, p. 296.
5 *Knowing the Unknowable God: Ibn-Sina, Maimonides, Aquinas* (Notre Dame, IN: University of Notre Dame Press, 1986); *Freedom and Creation in Three Traditions* (Notre Dame, IN: University of Notre Dame Press, 1993); "Aquinas and Islamic and Jewish Thinkers", in Norman Kretzmann and Eleonore Stump, eds., *Cambridge Companion to Aquinas* (Cambridge: Cambridge University Press, 1993), pp. 60–84.
6 Louis Gardet, "La connaissance que Thomas d'Aquin put avoir du monde islamique", in G. Verbeke and D. Verhelst, eds., *Aquinas and the Problems of His Time* (Leuven University Press/The Hague: Martinus Nijhoff, 1976), pp. 139–149; citation at p. 149.
7 Paris: J. Vrin, 1948, 1970, 1981.
8 Two scholars, independently of each other, undertook to translate the *Guide* into Latin soon after its composition: Samuel Ibn Tibbon and Jehudah al-Harizi. Ibn Tibbon checked his work with Maimonides to produce a quite literal rendering, while al-Harizi wrote in a supe-rior style. Most likely Aquinas had access to al-Harizi. See my "Aquinas' Debt to Mai-monides", in Ruth Link-Salinger et al. eds., *A Straight Path: Studies in Medieval Philosophy and Culture* (Washington, DC: Catholic University of America Press, 1989), pp. 37–48.
9 John Inglis, "Emanation in Historical Context: Aquinas and the Dominican Response to the Cathars", *Dionysius* Vol. 17 (1999), pp. 95–128.

10   Thomas Wienandy: *Does God Change?: the Word's Becoming in the Incarnation* (Still River, MA: St. Bede's Press, 1985).

11   Robert Sokolowski, *The God of Faith and Reason* (Notre Dame, IN: University of Notre Dame Press, 1982 and Washington, DC: Catholic University of America Press, 1995); the reference is to Aquinas, *On the Eternity of the World*, trans. Cyril Vollert (Milwaukee, WI: Marquette University Press, 1964) *ad fin*.

12   *Knowing the Unknowable God* (see note 5); "Essence Avicenna and Greek Philosophy", *MIDEO* [= *Mélanges de l'Institut Dominicain d'Etudes Orientales* (Cairo)] Vol. 17 (1986), pp. 53–66.

13   Cambridge University Press, 1983.

14   See Peter Adamson, *The Arabic Plotinus: A Philosophical Study of the "Theology of Aristotle"* (London: Duckworth, 2003), and the treatment by Cristina d'Ancona Costa in her *La Casa della Sapienza* (Milano: Geuriin, 1996).

15   Rudi teVelde, *Substantiality and Participation in Thomas Aquinas* (Leiden: E. J. Brill, 1995), p. 256.

16   See my *Knowing the Unknowable God* (Notre Dame, IN: University of Notre Dame Press, 1986).

17   Robert Sokolowski, *God of Faith and Reason* (Notre Dame, IN: University of Notre Dame Press, 1982 and Washington, DC: Catholic University of America Press, 1995).

18   See my "Creation, Metaphysics, and Ethics", *Faith and Philosophy* Vol. 18 (2001), pp. 204–221.

19   See her study, *Towards an Alternative Theology*, which comprises the Teape lectures given at Cambridge and Bristol in 1989, with the subtitle: "Confessions of a Non-dualist Christian" (Bangalore: Asia Trading Corporation, 1991 and Notre Dame, IN: University of Notre Dame Press, 2002).

20   See John Milbank and Catherine Pickstock, *Truth in Aquinas* (London and New York: Routledge, 2000), along with the insightful introduction to Eckhart by Deidre Carabine, *John Scottus Eriugena* (Oxford and New York: Oxford University Press, 2000), and Bernard McGinn's masterful study, *The Mystical Thought of Meister Eckhart, the Man from whom God Hid Nothing* (New York: Crossroad, 2001).

21   See my *Aquinas: God and Action* (London: Routledge and Notre Dame, IN: University of Notre Dame Press, 1979).

22   Aquinas, *Summa Theologiae* 1.3.; see Rudi teVelde, *Substantiality and Participation in Thomas Aquinas* (Leiden: E. J. Brill, 1995), pp. 266–279.

23   Aristotle: *De anima*, Bk II, ch. 4, 415b12–13; Aquinas: *Com on De anima*, lib. 2, ch. 7, lines 172–187 (pp. 97–98 of Lenonine); paragraph 319 of the Marietti-Pirotta edition.

24   See my "Essence and Existence: Avicenna and Greek Philosophy", in *MIDEO* [= *Mélanges de l'Institut Dominicain d'Etudes Orientales* (Cairo)] Vol. 17 (1986), pp. 53–66.

25   See my "Freedom and Creation in the Abrahamic Traditions", *International Philosophical Quarterly* Vol. 40 (2000), pp. 161–171; and the development by Eleonore Stump, "Intellect, Will, and the Principle of Alternate Possibilities", in Michael Beatty, ed., *Christian Theism and the Problems of Philosophy* (Notre Dame, IN: University of Notre Dame Press, 1990), pp. 254–285; amplified in Eleonore Stump, *Aquinas* (New York: Routledge, 2003), pp. 177–206.

26   *ST* 1.32.1.3.

27   Pierre Hadot, *Philosophy as a Way of Life: Spiritual Exercises from Socrates to Foucault*, essays edited by Arnold Davidson (Chicago, IL: University of Chicago Press, 1995).

28   Al-Ghazali, *Book of Faith in Divine Unity and Trust in Divine Providence*, trans. David Burrell (Louisville, KY: Fons Vitae, 2002), p. 42.

29   Alasdair MacIntyre, "Epistemological Crises, Dramatic Narratives, and Philosophy of Science", *The Monist* Vol. 60 (1977), pp. 453–472.

30   The original article in *Foreign Affairs* (1993), pp. 23–49, was subsequently expanded into a book: *The Clash of Civilizations and the Remaking of World Order* (New York, NY: Simon and Schuster, 1996).

31   *Orientalism* (New York, NY: Pantheon, 1978), and see Norman Daniel's equally articulate review: "Edward Said and the Orientalists", in *MIDEO* [= *Mélanges de l'Institut Dominicain d'Etudes Orientales* (Cairo)] Vol. 15 (1982), pp. 211–221.

32   Bernard Lewis, *What Went Wrong?* (New York and Oxford: Oxford University Press, 2002).

33   "A Gadamerian Perspective on Civilisational Dialogue", *Global Dialogue* Vol. 3 (2001), pp. 64–75.

34 Translated by Samuel Lester (South Bend, IN: St. Augustine's Press, 2002).
35 Haim and Rivka Gordon, eds., *Israel/Palestine: The Quest for Dialogue* (Maryknoll, NY: Orbis Books, 1991).
36 Haim Gordon, "Lessons in Dialogue: The Israeli-Palestinian Experience", *Global Dialogue* Vol. 3 (2001), pp. 76–83, at pp. 79, 81.
37 *De rationibus fidei* (*Opera omnia*, Leonine ed. Vol. 40 B [Romae, 1969]), with Preface by H.-F. Dondaine; English translation by Joseph Kenny, O.P., *Islamocristiana* Vol. 22 (1996), pp. 31–52; French translation by Gilles Emery, O.P., *Saint Thomas d'Aquin: Les raisons de la foi* (Paris: Cerf, 1999).
38 For a thorough treatment of the background for Aquinas' observations regarding Islam in *SCG* 1.6, as they reflect, while sometimes modifying, "habitual themes of the Muslim-Christian polemic", see Simone Van Reit, "La *Somme contre Gentiles* et la polémique islamo-chrétienne", in *Aquinas and the Problems of His Time* (note 6). In my analysis of *De rationibus fidei*, I have been assisted by a study of Christopher Wells, to appear in a volume of papers from the "Light Conference" in Oxford in 2002. For extensive background concerning Muslim–Christian exchanges around Aquinas' time, see Gabriel Reynolds, "St. Thomas' Islamic Challenge: Reflections on the Antiochene Question", *Islam and Christian Muslim Relations* 12 (2001), pp. 161–189.
39 Bernard Lonergan, *Method in Theology* (New York, NY: Herder and Herder, 1972).
40 Søren Kierkegaard, *Sickness unto Death*, trans. Howard and Edna Hong (Princeton NJ: Princeton University Press, 1980): "Now we see how extraordinarily stupid . . . it is to defend Christianity, . . . how it connives even if unconsciously, with offense by making Christianity some poor, miserable thing that in the end has to be rescued by a champion" (87).
41 For a detailed literary exploration of this prowess of Aquinas, see Olivier-Thomas Venard, O.P., *Littérature et théologie: Une saison en enfer* Vol. 1: Thomas d'Aquin Poète et Théologien (Geneva: Ad Solem, 2002).

5

AQUINAS MEETS THE BUDDHISTS: PROLEGOMENON TO AN AUTHENTICALLY THOMAS-IST BASIS FOR DIALOGUE

PAUL WILLIAMS

Thomas, of course, did not know any Buddhists. Nor (as far as I am aware) had he ever heard of Buddhism. It is difficult to know what he would have made of a *religion* that denied the existence of God. Nevertheless we can be quite sure how he would have responded if he had met Buddhists learned enough in their own religion to discuss it with him intelligently. We should not expect to find Thomas respectfully asking the Buddhists for meditation instruction, seeking to incorporate Buddhist meditation into his own Christian way of life. Why would he need religious practices so obviously unnecessary to Christ and his immediate apostles? We should not expect to find Thomas seeking common ground with Buddhists in the interests of a supposed tolerance, modifying key Christian positions in the light of Buddhism, and apologising for the traditionally exclusive nature of Christian claims. Both Thomas and his Buddhist friends believe in the absolute objectivity of truth, and for both knowing that truth in the deepest possible way saves— it sets one free. This is why both Buddhism and Christianity are (as I am sure you do not need reminding) missionary religions.[1] And, as we shall see, Christianity and Buddhism differ as radically as possible in what that truth is and where it lies. So we would not find Thomas suggesting that once we get to the essential core (perhaps through inner meditative experience) really Buddhism and Christianity are not that dissimilar. Therefore the issue of God as understood by Christ and Christian tradition through the Holy Spirit and expressed in uttered truth claims ("dogmas") can be set to one side as not really central to their dialogue. And we would not find Thomas then joining

Paul M. Williams
University of Bristol, Centre for Buddhist Studies, Theology and Religious Studies, 3 Woodland Road, Bristol BS8 1TB, UK

with Buddhists to sit in silent meditation. How can one sit with others in silence and not seek to help them find the truth that they so obviously seek? Sitting with Buddhists in silent meditation would *de facto* show a lack of charity, and perhaps also a lack of clarity about where truth lies. Christ sent out His disciples to preach the Good News, not to sit with pagans in silence.

Rather, Thomas would have listened to the Buddhists with respect. As an enthusiast for Aristotle, not to mention Muslim and Jewish philosophy, Thomas certainly did not think he had nothing to learn from non-Christians. He would have questioned his Buddhist friends, carefully seeking to understand their position and arguments in detail before responding. And he would have replied as a Christian, in charity seeking in accordance with Christ's mission to His disciples to show the Buddhists that their arguments against the existence of God were faulty and their own final fulfilment lay in Christ. In other words, Thomas would have respectfully sought to convert the Buddhists to Christianity in the most effective way possible. And if he could not persuade them to commit themselves to Christ at least he could protect others from their dangerous influence by showing that Buddhist arguments do not entail the falsehood of Christian claims.

So I cannot here rehearse Thomas Aquinas's actual response to Buddhism. What I can do is go straight to the point that would have been deemed central to both Thomas and his Buddhist friends, not seeking to put it to one side in the interests of "tolerance" and "peaceful coexistence". That is the issue of God. There are those who think the issue of God should not be central to dialogue between Christians and Buddhists because it is confrontational. Their position would be incomprehensible to Thomas. God, particularly as revealed in Christ through Sacred Scripture, is what Christianity is all about (see e.g. *Summa Contra Gentiles* 1:2–3). If we put that to one side there is nothing left on which to dialogue. No wonder all that remains is sitting in silence. There are also those who think that the issue of God in Christian-Buddhist dialogue is a misleading one since perhaps the Christians and Buddhists do not differ as radically as first appears. That is what I wish to consider in this paper. I want to show that there can be no question that with reference to God what Thomas accepts, the Buddhist denies. And I want to consider this issue not in abstract, but with reference to the Buddhist refutation of God in some central doctrinal texts. I shall mainly use the *Bodhicaryāvatāra* ("Introduction to the Conduct that Leads to Enlightenment") by Śāntideva (seventh/eighth centuries CE), but I shall also refer to the *Madhyamakāvatāra* ("Introduction [or 'Supplement'] to the Middling") of Candrakīrti (sixth century CE). These texts are not particularly original in their treatment of the refutation of God. I could have chosen any of many other Buddhist works that refute God. But I have chosen these because of their importance to Buddhists particularly in Tibet, because I am very familiar with them and their commentaries, and because they are Mahāyāna texts.[2] Some consider that while traditions of Buddhism originating earlier like Theravāda may be unsympathetic to the existence of God, this is different with Mahāyāna Buddhism. That is simply not true. If anything there are more refutations of God in Mahāyāna texts than elsewhere. In addition the *Madhyamakāvatāra* and the *Bodhicaryāvatāra* are absolutely central works in the particular tradition of Buddhism espoused by the Dalai Lama. The *Madhyamakāvatāra* is the official textbook for philosophical matters in his dGe lugs pa (pronounced: Gelukpa) school, and the Dalai Lama has published commentaries to the *Bodhicaryāvatāra*. Indeed this latter work, with its extensive treatment of compassion in the path to Buddhahood is probably the single most influential text in the Dalai Lama's own religiosity. From among the many Indian and Tibetan commentaries on these two texts I shall therefore mainly use a Tibetan commentary to the *Bodhicaryāvatāra* written by one of the founders of the dGe lugs pa tradition rGyal tshab rje (pronounced Gyeltsap Jay; fourteenth/fifteenth centuries). One can thus take it that what is said here would be absolutely familiar to, and accepted by, the Dalai Lama, who is himself an important figure in contemporary Christian-Buddhist relations. Having outlined the Buddhist position on God as found in these two texts I shall construct a plausible version of a response true to Thomas Aquinas. Finally, I shall draw some tentative conclusions for an approach to Christian-Buddhist dialogue that could reasonably claim to be based on Thomas ("Thomas-ist").

The Buddhist Refutation of God

I do not intend here formally to define what I mean by "God". And that is just as well, as Aquinas holds that God as He is Himself cannot be defined (see, for example, *Compendium Theologiae* 26). But Aquinas does hold that God can be considered as the source of all things, and as their teleological end (e.g. *Summa Theologiae* (S.Th.) 1a: *principium rerum et finis earum*). God is that from which we come, and to which we seek to return. And to claim God exists is to claim that certain metaphysical questions are genuine questions and worth asking. Specifically, the question is "How come?" asked of *everything*. It is a question "How come there is something, rather than nothing?".[3] It is a peculiar question, of course, but that peculiarity need not bother us here. All I wish to say at this point is that any concept we want to construct of God necessarily includes that of "creator".[4] Whatever else God is—or, indeed, even if we can know anything else about God—"God" is the term we use for the *creator* of everything (e.g. *S.Th.* 1a. 2. 3: *et hoc dicimus Deum*).

Thus it seems clear to me that if the Buddhist refutes the existence of a creator of everything, then the Buddhist refutes the existence of God, at least the existence of God as that would be understood by Thomas. In other words, under such circumstances Buddhism is quite straightforwardly a form of *atheism*. This is regardless of other concepts included in the notion of God here that might not be part of the Christian or Thomist notion. I say this because it is sometimes held that since our Indian Buddhist sources were familiar with only Hindu ideas of God, and not those of Christians, in their refutations of God they should not be taken as attacking the God of Christians.[5] Perhaps on that we have to think of them as being agnostic. But this is simply wrong. If there can be no creator of everything then God as He is understood by Christians does not exist. When the Buddhist says there is no such thing as a creator of everything, he directly contradicts in the strongest way possible Thomas's assertion that *Deus sit,* or *Deum esse sit,* or *Deus est.* On the existence of God, let alone the possibility of demonstrating the existence of God, when Thomas says that "from the effects of God one is able to demonstrate that God exists" (*S.Th.* 1a. 2, 2 ad 3: *ex effectibus Dei potest demonstrari Deum esse*) he and Śāntideva adopt directly contradictory positions. This is regardless of any subsequent metaphysical subtleties relating to what it *means* to speak of the existence of God. Thomas holds that while we cannot know the existence (or being) of God (*esse Dei*) in the sense of His act of existing (*actum essendi*)—that is beyond us—we certainly frame a true proposition about God when we say that God exists.[6] And we can know it to be true.[7] Once more, we can know this from God's effects, i.e. everything as created. Since knowing such a proposition to be true is a possibility for us, we can properly refer to such matters as the existence of God as "preambles to faith" (*S.Th.* 1a. 2, 2 ad 1: *non sunt articuli fidei sed praeambula ad articulos*). They are not matters that are available to us in this life through faith alone.[8] If one person states that a proposition is true, and another person states at the same time and without equivocation that it is false, they contradict each other. If Buddhist texts refute the existence of a creator of everything then they deny the existence of God as understood by Christianity. Other aspects of that refutation are irrelevant.[9]

The Sanskrit term normally used for "God" as creator in Buddhist sources is *Īśvara.* The Pali, from the very earliest sources, is *Issara.* This word is usually translated as "the Lord". In Tibetan it becomes *dbang phyug* (pronounced: "wongchuk")—literally "the Powerful One". The word *Īśvara* is most familiar in the expression *Maheśvara,* the Great Lord, which is a common epithet for the Hindu god Śiva. Notice here that the word used for the creator God in Sanskrit or Pali is not commonly or simply *deva,* a god[ling] (cognate to *deus,* or English "deity"). Hinduism knows any number of devas. Buddhism accepts the existence of devas, but denies the existence of a real *Īśvara.* To be a deva is part of the cycle of unenlightened rebirth. Devas are born, and devas die. We have all been devas in previous rebirths many, many times.[10] Thus when our Buddhist sources want to refer specifically to *the* creator God, the final God who is creator of all, including the devas themselves, they use another term, *Īśvara* or *Maheśvara.* One can thus talk of theistic Hindus as holding that actually (for Vaiṣṇavites) Viṣṇu is *Īśvara,* or alternatively (for Śaivites) Śiva is *Īśvara.* Buddhists contradict them in asserting that truly there is no such thing as *Īśvara.*

Īśvara is unnecessary, and can be refuted. And no one in India would doubt that there is here a contradiction.

The topic of Īśvara is addressed in the *Bodhicaryāvatāra* in connection with the metaphysics of causation. This is crucial. Īśvara is here presented as an example of a particular type of cause. rGyal tshab rje names this section of the text "the refutation of production from a cause that is other [than the effect] and that is permanent".[11] Some people mistakenly hold that there is a creator God, an Īśvara who is causally responsible for things. For their own part our Buddhist texts address the path to final fulfilment of Buddhahood, and the topic of a creator God occurs nowhere else than in discussing the possibility of a particular generic type of causation. In other words, the very lack of interest in God in these works shows *de facto* the fundamental absence of God in Buddhism. The spiritual path as conceived and understood by our Buddhists does not require any reference to God. God, even if He were to exist, would be irrelevant to final spiritual fulfilment. There is no place for God in these central Buddhist texts. Therefore even if there were to be a creator God, He would not be—as He is for Thomas—the teleological goal as well as the origin of creation, in whom lies our final spiritual perfection.

I want at this juncture to make a point relating to methodology in these Buddhist philosophical texts. rGyal tshab rje summarises what is going on here as follows: "The very root of the continued cycle of rebirth [and thence suffering] is apprehending things as truly existing. That is tainted ignorance. Without refuting its object there is no final spiritual freedom."[12] In other words, spiritual freedom is bound up with the complete refutation of anything at all having true existence, and hence letting go in the deepest possible way all craving attachment. "True existence" here is a technical expression. It is not the same as existence *per se*, for example, mere existence as given to us in our everyday practical, socially-conditioned lives, "things as apprehended by cow-herders", as one Buddhist scholar disparagingly remarks. For our purposes in this context we can take "true existence" as meaning "existence in the fullest possible metaphysical sense".[13] It is certainly what Thomas holds God, and God alone, has when he speaks of God as *per se necesse esse* ("necessary existence through itself": see *Summa Contra Gentiles* 1: 22). An equivalent in Sanskrit writing about God is "self-originated" (*svayambhu*). If there were such an existent (the Buddhist suggests) it would be a worthy object for our clinging, our attachment (we might say, our love) as holding forth complete immutable satisfaction. But there is not. Final freedom comes precisely through letting go all vain search for something that will provide complete immutable satisfaction, thus finally bringing to an end the infinite series of rebirths—and thence misery—that it has generated. The method in these texts is to take something put forward by a rival school as having the plenum of existence and, through critical exploration, to show that it collapses under rational probing. The result is that "it is not found under critical investigation". Thus it is said to be "empty of true existence". The very quality of emptiness of true existence—its mere absence (in Sanskrit *abhāvamātra*)—is the actual ultimate truth concerning that thing. This is the famous Buddhist notion of emptiness (*śūnyatā*).[14]

If the subject under investigation is such that if it were to exist it could *only* exist with the fullest possible existence, then clearly not being found under this critical probing means that it is simply incoherent, it does not exist at all even in everyday pragmatic or transactional usage. It does not exist at all for cow-herders in their normal cow-herding lives. It is a complete fiction comparable, our texts tell us, to hallucinatory hairs seen in front of the eyes by people with a rather debilitating eye disease. An example of such a fiction would be God. The Buddhist texts are clear (correctly) that if God existed (as the source of the existence of everything) He would have to exist with the fullest possible existence Himself. Thus in critically investigating the concept of God, and finding (it is argued) that it collapses into incoherence, our texts consider that God is shown not to exist at all. God—the God accepted as existing by Thomas, as the creator of everything—is here held to be a complete fiction. Even those ordinary people with no philosophical or religious sophistication would not hold that such could exist without being taught so by deluded followers of false religions who have simply assimilated, without sufficient critical thought, mistaken ideas.[15]

The God that is refuted in Śāntideva's text (*Bodhicaryāvatāra* 9: 118–125) is introduced as that which is "the cause of the world" (*īśvaro jagato hetuḥ*). That is what He is. Such is the position that is put forward by the opponent, and attacked by Śāntideva. Implicitly in Śāntideva, but explicitly in the commentaries, this God has five characteristics. He is pure, worthy to be worshipped, permanent, one only, and the creator of everything.[16] This is the God that is being refuted here. It is not some special *Hindu* conception of God. It is God for whom this is a suitable description. I do not see that Thomas would have a problem with allegiance to this as a minimal characterisation of God, although of course he would want to give it a particular interpretation and also add (in his own way) further features. In actual fact, Śāntideva's attack is really directed at God as the cause of all things who is also permanent. If there could be no such God, then it would *de facto* include Thomas's God as well.

And how does Śāntideva critically analyse the concept of a creator God? First (verse 118), he asks what exactly the expression "God" truly refers to. And in typical Indian philosophical fashion he methodically examines the options. It is clear both in context and in his subsequent treatment that actually the main characteristic of God that really matters is that of being the creator of everything. Granted this is what God is alleged to be, the first logical possibility is that "God" is an expression used for the primal elements that make up the universe itself. These are referred to (in Ancient Indian cosmology) as earth, water, fire, and air.[17] So when we say "God is the cause of everything", all we really mean is that the cause of everything is the cosmological primal elements. And Śāntideva agrees that these are indeed in a sense the cause of the world.[18] We might draw a parallel here with those who seem to think "God" is the set of trees, mountains, the oceans etc.—in other words, the (Natural) World. Okay, but why call it "God"? Śāntideva states he has no intention of arguing over a mere name (*nāmamātre'pi kiṃ śramaḥ*). In effect, his opponent and he hold the same position. It is just that his opponent wants to call it "God". As rGyal tshab rje points out, the words differ but the meaning is the same (*don khyad par med pa'i ming mi 'dra ba tsam la*). But, Śāntideva goes on to argue, clearly this will not really do. That superficial harmony is only the case because the theist has actually abandoned just about all that is meant by the term "God". For our Buddhist points out (verse 119) that the primal elements fail to match the other features of our working characterisation of God. It simply is not the case that these primal elements are one only. They are actually four, and thus multiple. They are clearly not permanent. And they are inert. A commentary explains this as meaning they are not active in the sense of mental knowing and volition. We might say that they "lack intentionality". They neither know nor could intend creation. There is indeed no element of divinity about them. And we walk on them. They clearly lack purity.[19] It seems so obvious. Those who say Nature is God should recognise that there is nothing God-like about Nature. Thus what Śāntideva wants to say is that in terms of logical options we could call the elements "God", and there would then be only a matter of verbal difference from the Buddhist denial of God. Nevertheless in actual fact the theist in using the term "God" wants to bring with it a whole range of connotations and implications that are simply incompatible with the plain non-theistic sense implied by the cosmological elements. And there Thomas would surely agree.

Well, there are other logical possibilities. Perhaps "God" is just another name for the fifth element, space (or in some Indian traditions whatever it is that fills space, the gap between things). Or perhaps God is really one's own true Self, the *ātman* spoken of in Indian philosophy. But Śāntideva has little time for either of these options (verse 120). Space is still an inert primal element. It does not *do* anything. It cannot be said to be creative. It too lacks intentionality. It is just there. No theist would call space "God". And although there are some who think that their true Self is God, it could not be acceptable to Śāntideva the Buddhist. We are not talking about ourselves. We are talking about God, the creator of everything. The issue of Buddhism and the *ātman* is a complex one, but no Buddhist would claim to accept the existence of the *ātman* understood in this way as a permanent unchanging creator of the universe.[20] Certainly not Śāntideva. He points out that such a Self has already been refuted earlier (see *Bodhicaryāvatāra* 9: 56 ff.). In perfectly appropriate conventional pragmatic life and discourse there may be the person that I am, conceptualised in dependence upon a flow of consciousness, mental contents, and physical processes, and given the name

"Paul Williams". But there is simply no such thing as a permanent and unchanging metaphysical Self behind it all. This is basic Buddhism. The metaphysical Self is another example of a complete fiction, not needed even in everyday transactional usage let alone in reality. In fact, Śāntideva says (verse 77), even thinking that there is such a Self must lead to egotism and thence misery. He would certainly add that the notion that I have (or am) a Self that is truly God, standing behind the universe as the unchanging creator of all things, is patently false.[21] It is also surely a path to megalomanic confusion. And here, again, Thomas would certainly agree. All of these attempts to identify God are utterly mistaken in that they are suggesting as the creator of everything something that (Thomas would insist) is actually a creation.[22] They are examples, therefore, of idolatry. And for Thomas this would not just be a case of wrong selection from a range of options. Idolatry is not simply a misidentification of God. Idolatry is a failure to understand *what God must be and what God cannot be*. As the creator of everything God is not a member of any class. So there can be no options from which to make a misidentification. In other words, the opponent criticised by Śāntideva here is as wrong as one can possibly be, so wrong that he or she is not even on a continuum of wrongness. Idolatry is utterly, utterly wrong, and the wrongness is *metaphysical*.[23] But need it follow from this (as Śāntideva seems to think) that God does not exist?

The opponent has tried to identify God with the primal elements, and with the Self. On one simplified model of Hindu thought (say, the tradition known as *Sāṃkhya*) these two classes exhaust everything. What is left? Śāntideva considers that the theist might resort to one last stratagem. God exists but is simply inconceivable (*acintya*), beyond the mind's ability to fathom. Thomas might be prepared here to see some progress. For, famously, Thomas too holds that while we can know *that* God exists, as the creator of everything, we cannot know *what* God is but only what God is not (*S.Th.* 1a, 3: *sed quia de Deo scire non possumus quid sit sed quid non sit*). That is, we can know that God exists through reference to effects as created by Him, but concerning what God is in Himself, apart from His effects, as far as our natural rational faculties are concerned apart from faith through revelation we have no idea. God as He is in Himself is beyond the range of our natural unaided minds. Yet there must be more to it than this. Śāntideva argues that if God is literally inconceivable, beyond all our understanding, then it makes no sense also to refer to Him as creator. Indeed, we could not even know Him as "God".[24] And that is surely correct. We find it stated sometimes that God (or whatever) is in every sense beyond all language and conceptualisation. If so, what of any interest whatsoever can follow from this? We can do without it.[25] However much God is transcendent, there has to remain some slender thread connecting us with a true awareness of Him. For Thomas, we can certainly make true statements about God, even positive statements (like "God is intelligent") grounded on what, as cause of everything, He is not (in the case of intelligence, He is not subject to material limitation).[26] Of course, such statements are used analogously and we cannot know through our natural minds what these statements mean for God Himself. Moreover Thomas's approach to God is apophatic as regards our natural reasoning, but firmly cataphatic when God is seen by means of the revelation that comes through Christ, who is God Himself. Thus while we know God exists, we know of God's nature (as Trinitarian, for example) through God actually coming to us, not through our natural reasoning. Thomas's theology is through and through Christocentric precisely *because* of his apophatic approach to God. But his apophaticism does not involve saying simply that God is *acintya*, inconceivable. Thomas's apophaticism is subtle, and capable of theological development. That (no doubt) is why he was able to write so much.

There is also a further point that should be made against Śāntideva here. Śāntideva's opponent has, it seems in desperation, declared God to be inconceivable. But Śāntideva ignores the fact that the opponent declares God inconceivable *while at the same time being the creator of everything*. In other words, one could argue that the opponent is not committed to saying that God is literally inconceivable in all respects. Rather, God is inconceivable save being the creator of everything and what follows from that alone. Śāntideva has assumed that in order to be able to say that God is the creator of everything we have to be able to specify *additionally* what God is. But why should that be the case? Why should we have to say anything beyond specifying that God is the creator of everything? Of course, we can infer some things that God cannot be if He is to be the creator of everything. He cannot be something created. And Aquinas devotes a great deal of space to saying what follows from this, what God cannot be (composite, for example) if that is to be the case. Thus Śāntideva is correct to rule out e.g. the primal elements, or the Self, as God. But the theist could plead unreasonableness in an argument that requires he or she to be able to say, *in addition* to being the creator of everything, what God is, in order for a claim that God is the creator of everything to stand. At least, Thomas would certainly have thought it unreasonable. In order for the expression "God" to be meaningful, we have to know what is to count as being God. That is explained as "the creator of everything". We then ask whether that expression has a referent. That is what Thomas is doing when he asks whether the expression *Deus est* frames a true proposition. And, Thomas wants to say, he is entitled to argue that it does. He can also say various things about what could not be true concerning God, if *Deus est* expresses a true proposition where God is indeed the creator of everything. To be able to say more about *what* God actually is would be to have *scientia* of God. Thomas denies that we can have any *scientia* of God. And he is entitled to do that, too.[27] As his argument begins to move closer to something recognisable to Thomas himself Śāntideva precisely fails to take into consideration the potential sophistication of the theist's position.

For Śāntideva, the theist has failed to show what God is supposed to be. It is also not totally clear *why* one needs to appeal to God as a cause of things (verses 121–122). For example, some things the theist opponent himself holds actually to be permanent. An example would be the Self. Why does one need to appeal to God as the creator of something that is permanent?[28] Why too do we need God as the creator of temporal events, like seeing an object or an occurrence of pain, for example. We all know what are the causes of those. Seeing an object is produced by functioning visual awareness, the presence of an appropriate object, and so on. Likewise Śāntideva the Buddhist holds that when I feel a pain, or indeed when pleasure occurs, they result from *inter alia* the force and process of *karman*, my own previous wicked or meritorious intentions and deeds. Even without karman, the genesis of pain-events is perfectly explicable in psycho-physical terms. In other words Śāntideva appeals to a sort-of Ockham's razor. Causal explanations should not require causes beyond those necessary to explain their effects. We do not need to appeal to God as a cause in order to explain all the events with which we are familiar. The same is the case with natural kinds such as trees, or artefacts such as pies. If we want a tree, we plant a seed, add water, and so on. Only as an act of desperation would we also pray. No one thinks that the seed failed to germinate because although everything else was in place God failed to do His bit! If we want to bake a pie we assemble the ingredients and engage in the pie-generating processes. No one would add "Don't forget the secret ingredient—God"! The causes of me were my parents and what they got up to. The causes of our children were me, my wife, bottles of wine, and a power-cut. And so on for all effects. Moreover, Śāntideva points out, in common with Indian tradition, one also does not need to appeal to God to start the whole temporal series off. The temporal series is eternal—there never was a first beginning. Nothing in reason forces us to think there was one. Even Thomas accepts that. And a first cause arguably involves more complex suppositions than no beginning at all. So God is needed neither to start the series of causes and effects, nor to produce each effect during the series. God is a useless extra.

These arguments are enormously important in Buddhist refutations of God. The presupposition of the Buddhist here is that when a theist speaks of God as the creator of everything he or she means that, rather than the causes we thought were generating their effects, really it was God bringing those effects about. God is a *rival* cause in the cosmos, excluding the supposed generating causes. They merely appear to be causes. Actually all effects are generated by God. Or perhaps God is an *additional*, but the principal, cause in a causal collection. But, the Buddhist wants to argue, we know perfectly well that everything can be explained in terms of their generating causes, the sorts of causes we all (including, or perhaps especially, cow-herders) have recourse to in the relevant pragmatic contexts. What additional factor is added by bringing in God? There is simply no causal question to which God is the answer. No asking "How come?" needs to receive the reply "By God".

Notice, however, what Śāntideva is and is not doing here. While he is committed to the claim that our actual experience of causation is such that nowhere is there an explanatory gap that requires the insertion of God, he is not committed to any *particular* naturalistic or scientific *explanation* of causation. He is nevertheless as a matter of fact committed as a Buddhist to further claims about causation that are arguably metaphysical. For Śāntideva, in common with all Buddhists, accepts that the universe always operates in terms of strict, regular and discoverable causal patterns. Indeed this was felt to be one of the great discoveries of the Buddha himself. It is called "dependent origination" (*pratītyasamutpāda*). In its most general form this entails that things and events result quite impersonally from their natural causes, without recourse to occult factors like God or a true Self. The formula is "This being, that occurs. With the nonoccurrence of this, there is the nonoccurrence of that". Many causes are psychological (greed always arises accompanied by the following other mental factors . . .), some are physical (although these too may reduce to psychological events like sense-data), and some important causal processes are moral. Thus Buddhist texts (like those of the Abhidharma) explain at length and in detail how it is part of the very order of things (the *dharmatā*) that—quite independently of whether a Buddha comes to tell us about it—wicked deeds, for example, lead eventually to suffering for their perpetrator. It is not just that this has been observed in the past to be the case. Barring other more elaborate causal factors coming into play it is *always* the case. The regularity of the causal complex itself is objective and absolute. The cosmos is an intricate dynamic network of causal patterning. That explains the occurrence of effects, and God is nowhere in it. For the Buddhist, regular causality *replaces* God. The idea that God is needed to perform any causal function represents nothing more than the remnants of a primitive anthropomorphism ignorant of the objective and universal nature of impersonal causal laws.

How could God be a cause of things and events in the world anyway? Śāntideva (verse 123) points out that it makes no sense to speak of a permanent unchanging cause of an impermanent changing world.[29] If X is a cause, then X produces its effect. That is what being a cause is. So if X is an eternal and unchanging cause, the effect must be eternal too. This is because *qua* cause throughout all eternity X is the same. Thus X, since it is always the cause of effect Y, always produces its effect. So the effect is throughout all eternity. But if the effect is eternal, why do we need X (God) as a cause to produce it? We do not need a cause of an eternal effect because, Śāntideva wants to say, it is eternal and therefore no effect at all. Moreover it is patently obvious that effects are not eternal. They come into existence sequentially, remain for a time, and then cease. Otherwise every feature of the cosmos would be eternal and unchanging. There would be no sequential causation in the universe at all. Since effects are sequential, their causes must be sequential too. A permanent unchanging being like God could not act as a cause of an impermanent effect. Śāntideva takes cognisance of a suggestion that God might create in sequence because of other causal factors coming into play. But this will scarcely work with God. Imagine before creation. God then creates. How can God possibly rely on other causal factors in order to create things in a temporal sequence? Before creation there can be no other causal factors. We cannot argue that He would create one thing, then another thing with the help of the first, and so on. The ability of a permanent and unchanging cause to create one effect, *then* another effect, is precisely the point at issue. Thus as permanent and unchanging God must create everything in one go. And that simply does not happen.

There would be other problems with the suggestion that God needs to rely on co-operative causes in order to produce a temporal sequence of effects (verse 124). Who or what then would really be the cause of things? For example, God might generate the first effect, but after that He cannot produce subsequent effects without relying on that first effect as a co-operative cause. Since a cause is that without which the effect will not come into existence, it follows that God is no longer the cause. The cause would be the co-operative factor(s). And since they would now be the cause, if they came together even God could not stop them producing the effect. And if they did not come together, even God likewise could not bring about the effect. What a mess!

And for the theist (Śāntideva thinks) the mess gets worse (verse 125). Does God want to create or does He not? If He does not want to create something, yet such things are still created, He must have been forced to create by some factor apart from Himself. For example, rGyal tshab rje considers (1973: 265) that perhaps God does not want to create the sufferings of Hell and so on.[30] The wicked actions of sinners create those pains. God is thus forced to go along with it by something—perhaps the moral law, or the "law of karman" —that is actually higher than Himself. Thus God is subject to something other than Himself and we cannot say that He creates everything by His own creative power. And if God is said to want to create all the things He does create, then it is His desire for the effects that actually produces things. He desires a thing to exist, and thus creates it. Then He desires another thing to exist, and thence creates that. And so on. Thus creation becomes dependent upon a sequence of desires in God. Thus either God is not unchanging, or if He is then the real creator is a series of desires, not God at all. And as rGyal tshab rje puts it, "if desire generates the effect, how is that God? Desire is impermanent." (*'dod pas 'bras bu byed na'ang de dbang phyug ga la yin te 'dod pa mi rtag pa yin pas so*).

So not only is God unnecessary as a creator of everything, the very concept of a creator God is quite absurd. This is not to say, however, that the Buddhist is uninterested in the question of where the world comes from as given to us now in our own phenomenal experience. Imagine standing and spreading your arms out around you in every direction. "Where does all this come from?", you ask. Your question is perhaps more psychological, or epistemological, than metaphysical. Śāntideva the Buddhist might gloss it as "How come I am having all these experiences?", or "How come it's like this?". Well, Candrakīrti explains it in *Madhyamakāvatāra* 6:86/89. Rather than from a creator God, or any other thing like the Self, as taught by non-Buddhist thinkers, actually the Buddha has discerned that it all comes from our own minds. From the continuum of our minds it arises in regular causal patterns, determined by karman, our previous acts (of which the most important dimension is mental volition, *cetanā*) in this and former lives.[31] From what Candrakīrti says it is clear that this is not intended as a metaphysical theory of the ultimate origins of the cosmos, perhaps from some sort of Absolute Mind. Rather we have an explanation (perhaps a quasi- or proto-scientific explanation) for the origins from previous mental events of all the world of my experience (where "my" should be applied by each of us). In terms of our experience in the world, which is all we really have, the creative agent is said by the Buddha to be simply the mind (*rgyal bas sems tsam 'jig rten byed por gsungs*). Thus along with my previous claim that Buddhism replaces God with regular causality, we now have an account of what it is for Buddhism about regular causality that substitutes for God as creator. At 6:89 Candrakīrti explains that "as far as the world is, its sentient beings and the various environments they occupy are fabricated by the mind alone [or 'by the nature of mind']. All beings are declared to be born from karman, and without the mind there is also no karman".[32] Thus it is regular causality based on mental events of a karmically determinative sort that power the process of *my* phenomenal construction, the world as lived by me. And this is here explicitly offered in rivalry to e.g. a creator God, to account for the world in the only way it can be accounted for. The Dalai Lama too confirms this in a commentary on the *Bodhicaryāvatāra*:

> According to our view, sentient beings and our environment are produced by our own actions. Tracing the source of actions leads one to the mind. Thus, the source is awareness. This is not to say that the world is of the nature of consciousness. Actions are brought forth by wholesome and unwholesome states of awareness, and on this basis the world of phenomena is established.... According to our view, the production, transformation and destruction of all natural phenomena can be understood without resort to the hypothesis of a Creator God.[33]

In teachings attributed to the Buddha himself, in some of the very earliest of Buddhist texts, there is a mocking attempt—undoubtedly intended as a joke—to explain the origins of the notion of a creator God. The idea of a Creator springs from an elementary and foolish confusion on the part not only of His worshippers, but also on the part of God Himself. Buddhism accepts no first beginning to the process of unenlightened rebirth. But it does

accept the Indian notion of "cosmic cycles", an endless series of cosmic evolution, collapse, and devolution. All this occurs due to impersonal causal
processes. At the beginning of the current cosmic cycle a sentient being, due
entirely to karmic causes relating to previous deluded deeds, was reborn in
a sort-of heaven. This was Brahmā. He was there all by himself. And he felt
jolly lonely. So he thought to himself that it would be lovely if there were
some company. At that very moment other beings, also due to karmic causes,
were born around him. He thus inferred that he must have created them
solely by wishing that they should be there. They, for their part, assumed
that since he was there already, by himself, he must have created them. Thus
Brahmā came to be worshipped as the creator God. But actually, of course,
there is no creator God. All happened due to impersonal causes, based on
previous karman.

In another of these early attempts to mock the creator God, a monk travels
to visit Brahmā's heaven to ask him a question. Brahmā simply keeps repeat-
ing "I, brother, am Brahmā, Great Brahmā, the Supreme Being, the Unsur-
passed, the Chief, the Victor, the Ruler, the Father of all beings who have
been or are to be."[34] The monk, receiving no answer to his specific question,
eventually gets quite fed up. Whereupon Brahmā takes him on one side and
explains that actually he, Great Brahmā, has not the faintest idea what the
answer to the monk's question is. But Brahmā does not want to be seen by
his worshippers to be ignorant, since they think he knows everything. Truly,
if the monk really wants to know the answer to his question he should return
and ask the Buddha. He is the one who truly knows.[35]

So What is Thomas to Make of All This?

It seems to me that in so many ways Thomas would be enormously grateful to Śāntideva and his colleagues. For Śāntideva has disposed of any
notion of God as a chunk of, or all of, Nature. That ought to get rid of quite
a number of so-called "nature mystics". Śāntideva has disposed of God as
just one's own True Self. For there is nothing about me (or you, I suspect)
that is at all Godlike. And he has demolished God as the Unknown, the Non-
conceptual, the Great Unutterable, or the Complete Mystery. We certainly do
find those who express the idea that they believe in God because they
"accept the existence of something behind it all", although they haven't the
faintest what that is or what it might entail. True to their beliefs, *nothing
follows*. For these people, with suchlike expressions, taken at their face value,
simply make of God nothing at all, or at least nothing granted any conceiv-
able meaning. And Śāntideva has also demolished any idea of God as a
substitute for or rival to the supposed causes of things, causes that are the
subjects of the various empirical sciences. When the theist says that God
creates everything he or she cannot mean that God created the Mona Lisa
instead of da Vinci. Moreover Śāntideva does not see the need for God in

order to give punishments and rewards. God is not the Cosmic Policeman. God does not create in the sense of *doing something*, perhaps through operating on some prior principle. And God can be no creator in time, creating one thing after another, maybe through different wishes that occur to His inscrutable mind, perhaps through the help of other willing supporters. That is, Śāntideva dissolves away any idea that the creator of everything could be a godling, a super-powerful (or perhaps fairly powerful) being in the universe, like poor old Brahmā (or the Zeus of Greek myths), perhaps living with a long white beard on a cloud. Off goes the idea of God as requiring our help to get creation right, or perhaps a God like Moltmann's who apparently joins in with us empathetically through being miserable whenever we are suffering. Maybe there is such a god, but Śāntideva would not be impressed. Nor would Thomas.

So Thomas, I suggest, would be enormously grateful to Śāntideva for showing (as far as he is concerned) the incoherence of many people's ideas of what God is. Inasmuch as the attack on the existence of God proceeds through attacking that which simply could not ever have been God—that is, therefore, through undermining idolatry—Thomas would be quite happy:

> [T]he Church considers all goodness and truth found in [other religions] as "a preparation for the Gospel, and given by him who enlightens all men that they may at length have life" . . . [But] very often, deceived by the Evil One, men have become vain in their reasonings, and have exchanged the truth of God for a lie, and served the creature rather than the Creator. Or else, living and dying in this world without God, they are exposed to ultimate despair.[36]

What Śāntideva simply has not shown, however, is that *God* does not exist, the (for Thomas) true God, the actual Creator of everything.[37] Of course, Śāntideva thinks he has shown the falseness of *all* notions of a creator God. But he has not. And the falseness of idolatry does not entail the falseness of God. Let me make the following distinctions with reference to our question "How come?".[38]

(A) How come the bus arrived late?
(B) How come Archibald and Fiona have just had a baby?
(C) How come doing things like *that* leads to results like *this*?
(D) How come there is anything at all, such that the previous "How come?" questions can have (in principle) answers?

When we ask questions (A) and (B) we are asking for an enumeration of the causes sufficient, in context, to explain the result. In the case of (A) the causes may differ depending on occasion. In the case of (B), a natural process, some of the causes will be of the same *type* each time an effect of this type occurs. (C) is a different sort of question. It asks about the way the world is, and it may not always be obvious how to go about answering such a question. Nevertheless there is in principle an answer, and the process of scientific discovery is one in which answers are mooted and verified or otherwise. But note that questions (A)–(C) all necessitate that there *are* things, that there *is* a world. Answers, whatever they are, take place within a framework of an existing world that occurs as it does occur. Such answers, to be adequate, *presuppose* the existing world, and their adequacy is to be gauged with reference to accepted things within the world. The bus was late because the driver woke up late. The existence of the driver, the process of sleeping, and so on, are taken for granted in framing an answer. Of course, we can also ask about them. But again an answer will be given, and judged adequate or otherwise, in terms of further beings and processes within the world. And such explanations cannot proceed to infinity. This is because an infinite regress would cease to be an explanation. Or, put another way, there is no *context* that would require an explanation proceeding to infinity.

When the Buddhist asserts that the existence of things can be explained in terms of natural causes, and does not need reference to God, his position depends on the adequacy of natural causes—further beings and processes within the world—to answer questions of type (A)–(C). In terms of what is to count as an adequate causal explanation in context, surely we can all see (the Buddhist wants to say) that it is not necessary to refer to God. God does not explain why the bus was late, or why Archibald and Fiona have just had a baby. The difficulty for the Buddhist with this perspective that would seek to eliminate God, however, is that Thomas the theist would be in entire agreement. No one *needs* in context to mention God in explaining the lateness of the bus. God provides not that sort of causal explanation.[39] "God" is the name we give to the answer to question (D). Question (D) asks how come there is anything at all? In other words, (D) asks *how come there is a context* for answering (A)–(C)? How come there is context for answering all our normal causal questions?[40] Let us note here the following:

   (i) Question (D) is not a question about how come there exists particular things or bundles of things (where "thing" here just = *X*). It is not a question about how come *X* exists, or how come any totality of *X*s exists. It is emphatically a question about why there is something—anything at all—rather than nothing—nothing at all.

  (ii) (D), while clearly a strange question compared with (A)–(C), is not obviously a pseudo-question, a misphrased question, or a question that in some radical sense contradicts itself. It appears to be a legitimate question capable of being meaningfully asked.[41]

 (iii) Granted this, the question asked by (D) is itself a genuine *causal* question.[42] It is asking for the cause of there being something rather than nothing. Thus if the Buddhist seeks to replace God with an explanation in terms of causes, this question should interest the Buddhist.

(iv) Any plausible answer to (D) could not refer to any *thing* within the world. It could not be part of any *context*. Purported answers that did refer to something within the world would have radically missed the point. For Aquinas, this "missing the point" is idolatrous.

 (v) If there were an answer to (D) it would be an answer to a genuinely causal question, yet not an answer in terms of things within the world, an answer in terms of contexts. Thus it would perhaps be better to use a different expression for the causal activity of the answer to (D). Christian theology from the beginning has spoken of this activity as *creation*. (A)–(C) are questions of causation, but not of creation. (D) is also a question of causation, but any answer also refers us to something known as "creation".

(vi) Since any plausible answer to (D) could not refer to any thing, it could not refer to any thing of which it would make sense to ask of *it* "How come?". The answer to (D) would not be a natural cause within the world. It would be a creator. Thus the Buddhist disposal of the need for God as a natural cause within the world in order to explain the occurrence of individual events simply misses the question of whether a *creator* is still needed. In other words the Buddhist, while supremely interested in causation, has failed to make a crucial distinction between two different types of causation. Only causation as creation is of interest to Aquinas the theist. Moreover there is no reason why causation as creation should operate in exactly the same way as natural causation between things in the world. And this is an issue or distinction the Buddhist simply fails to recognise or discuss.

(vii) Since (D) is a question about the existence of something rather than nothing, any answer to (D) would by definition be an answer that would ground the existence of *anything-as-such* (rather than nothing-as-such). Thus as creation it would necessarily involve creation *ex nihilo*. Indian arguments for the existence of God, and their refutation, based not on creation *ex nihilo* radically miss the point. Creation *ex nihilo* necessarily involves a creator who is outside time and thus unchanging. Creation *ex nihilo* cannot be understood on any model of *doing something* derived from causal activity between things within the world. The answer to the question "Why is there something rather than nothing?" (if there were one) would by definition be a cause adequate to its effect. But there need be no commitment to a particular model of *how* that cause brings about its effects. All Śāntideva's arguments about changes in the creator, whether the creator wants certain things or not, how the creator causes, whether He requires additional subsidiary causes—all these are utterly irrelevant. They all involve conceiving of the causal activity of God on the model of causal activity among *things*. The question is how God does it, who helps Him, and so on. But God as Creator, Thomas would argue, is not like that.

(viii) As Herbert McCabe points out, it is simply false that a change in creation necessarily entails a change in God as its creator. All that happens
in creation can depend on a timeless and unchanging God without this
entailing that events must be timeless and unchanging.[43] There is no
contradiction in talking of God, i.e. the reason why there is something
rather than nothing, as being outside time and willing timelessly the
occurrence of events as they occur sequentially within creation. Of
course, we have no idea what that would be like in terms of the nature
of God Himself. This is because what that is *like*, is quite simply that
it is not like anything. Thomas holds that (short of revelation) we
simply have no idea of what things are like for God Himself. But *if*
there is an answer to the question "Why is there something rather
than nothing?" then the arguments of Śāntideva at *Bodhicaryāvatāra*
9:122–125, resting as they do on probing the creative activity of God
as if it were an example of natural causation, are simply irrelevant.
And it has not yet been shown that there is no answer, or that the purported answer is illegitimate.

(ix) Note therefore that with all this Thomas's inability to be more specific
about the nature of the Creator does not entail as such the illegitimacy
of (D). For Thomas "God" is the name we give to whatever answers
this question. And much of Thomas's *Summa Theologiae* is spent detailing what follows from this. One is reminded here of the response of a
Christian to the "gentile" in Nicholas of Cusa's *Dialogus de deo abscondito*, a response very much within the Thomist frame of reference. The
gentile sees a Christian worshipping God with great emotion and
involvement. On asking who or what this "God" is that he worships,
however, the Christian replies that he hasn't the faintest idea. But
surely (the gentile urges) it is stupid to worship something of which
one has no idea? Not at all, replies the Christian. It would be much
more stupid to worship as God that of which one *did* have an idea.[44]
Any answer to (D) would be of such a nature that one could know virtually nothing of it. That necessarily follows from (D). If there is an
answer to (D), necessarily one could know next to nothing of it. But it
would not follow *from that alone* that it is not an answer to (D). The
only answer that could not be would be one that involved a contradiction. And, Thomas wants to argue, once we make (as Śāntideva
does not) the distinction between creation and natural causation, there
can be an answer to (D) that allows for a creator without involving
contradiction. Anything of which one did have greater knowledge
(short of faith in its own self-revelation, Thomas would add) could not
be an answer to (D), and thus should not be worshipped as God. To
do so would be idolatry.

(x) The fact that the Buddhist fails to recognise the issue of creation and
thus does not refute specifically a "Creator" in Thomas's sense, does

not mean, however, that there is no radical disagreement between Thomas and Śāntideva, or that the Buddhist cannot be genuinely referred to as an "atheist". This is because while the Buddhist does not recognise the issue of creation, and thus does not refute it specifically as such, the Buddhist does set out to refute *all* explanations that entail a God as *cause*. In other words, since the category of causation is conceptually a wider one than creation (creation is a subclass within causation), in setting out to refute causation the Buddhist also sets out implicitly to refute Thomas's God. There is no need for causes over and above natural causes. Thus (the Buddhist contends) there is no need for God as cause. Thomas replies that while we may have no need to bring in God (explicitly) in order to explain the natural processes of causation, as given to us in the world, in a worldly context, there remains the issue of creation. That too is a causal issue, and should very much interest the Buddhist. But unfortunately the Buddhist has not even appreciated that there is such an issue.

Thus Thomas is making a claim about things that is indeed being denied by Śāntideva. Things have an additional characteristic that the Buddhist fails to realise. For things are *created*. This is not a statement about God. It is a statement about things. "God" is what we call whatever it is that explains how come things are created. In other words, we come to God here as an inference from the created nature of things. Thomas considers that there is a particular causal question about things—a question of createdness—that is omitted by asking simply what *in the nature of things* caused something newly arisen to come into existence. And Thomas holds that the question of createdness—"Why is there something rather than nothing?"—is a perfectly legitimate question, a question that comes within the remit of an interest in issues of causation. The Buddhist is supremely interested in such issues. So the Buddhist should be interested in this question, the question of createdness. The answer to it (whatever that is) we all give the name "God". But the Buddhist is not interested in this question. The Buddhist never even asks the question. And that, Thomas would hold, is a defect—an incompleteness —in the *Buddhist's own project* of seeking for causes. It is a project that started well, for it dethroned the idolatrous claims that would elevate something less that God, little godlings, as final explanations. But (as Catherine of Siena will urge below) it ends in confusion.

The Difference it Makes is One of Everything

The Buddhist's failure is a failure in his own project.[45] But it is not just an ontological failure. We are here in a world where (as Alasdair Macintyre has pointed out) the Humean separation of "is" from "ought" does not form a framework for our discussion. For Thomas the fact that things are created is not only a matter of their ultimate *origin*. It is also an issue, teleologically, of their final *goal*. In not comprehending the ontological origin of things in God, the Buddhist also cannot be oriented towards the true spiritual end of things. In anthropological terms, that end is the return to that which we always were, creatures of God. Thus (Thomas would urge) the Buddhist's failure is not just a failure of ontology. It is in spiritual terms a *complete* failure. It is a failure in goal, and a failure in striving—the path—for striving is a striving for the goal. And I want to illustrate this with specific reference to the thought of Thomas's fellow Dominican Saint Catherine of Siena.

Catherine was writing at a time in Europe so much more fraught politically and socially compared with the relatively tranquil times of Thomas. While Thomas contemplated and explained, Catherine contemplated and acted.[46] But in her book, the book that came subsequently to be called simply the *Dialogue*, Catherine brings out particularly well how not understanding the fact that things are created, that all things depend on God for their very existence, affects *everything*. Without that central thread, the entire tapestry of our lives instantly (quicker than instantly) unravels. Catherine begins in a way that might appeal in an Indian context, with reference to "self-understanding" (*cognoscimento di sé*). But self-understanding here lies precisely not in "finding the true nature of oneself"—self-knowledge—as such.[47] Rather it lies in a displacement of concern from self to God *through realising that one's own true nature is one of createdness*. For, Catherine says, the purpose of this self-understanding is "better to understand the goodness of God towards oneself (in sé), for love follows understanding" (*per meglio cognoscere la bontà di Dio in sé, perché al cognoscimento seguita l'amore*). Ontological understanding here leads to God, leads to gratitude, and thus leads to love.[48] The Buddhist, in patently not loving God, in not knowing God, also shows *de facto* a failure in ontological understanding of himself.[49] This is because the Buddhist does not realise that he is *created*. And ontological understanding of oneself (in order to engender detachment and thus cessation of the forces that lead to rebirth) is what Buddhism is *on its own terms* all about. There cannot be humility, Catherine wants to say, without acknowledging createdness. The supremely radical ontological re-evaluation needed is one of self-displacement that comes only through realising this createdness. And that re-evaluation is simply impossible without such realisation. But createdness requires God, for "God" simply is the name we give to whatever grounds the truth of createdness. And without humility there can be no charity. Without charity there is no true virtue.[50] Thus, Catherine would say, in not knowing God the Buddhist yet again fails in his own (this time, moral) terms. And charity on our part requires that we tell him so.

Catherine's explicit linking of knowledge of Truth, hence createdness, with the growth of virtue highlights an important affective implication that is absolutely central to Christian life and must be completely lacking in any relevant sense in Buddhism. It is that of *gratitude*.[51] Without acknowledgement of createdness, hence God, there can be no such radical gratitude, a gratitude that shakes and reorients one's entire being, a gratitude to God out of which flows a concern for His creation that is the prerequisite for the development of virtue. I want to underline this point, for it is sometimes thought that Christian emphasis on dependence on God, and the Buddhist stress on dependent origination, amount to the same thing. Both simply state that we are not complete in ourselves. But it should be clear by now that they do not amount to the same thing at all. Buddhist dependent origination concerns natural causation, and is thus radically different, as different as is possible, from Christian createdness. Not surprisingly, given his stress on natural causation—causation within the world—the Buddhist has no interest in God and hence in createdness. Thence the Buddhist has no use for the gratitude spoken of here. For createdness is not just dependent origination but creation through, as Dante puts it, "the love that moves the sun and other stars" (*Paradiso* XXXIII: *l'amor che move il sole e l'altre stelle*). Gratitude is actually what follows from createdness, and is thus for Catherine and for Thomas what life (and, of course, Christianity) is all about. It is gratitude that springs from recognition of createdness, gratitude that leads to love of the God who loves us into existence first, and gratitude that thence engenders concern for His creatures. Thus gratitude too is, for Catherine, a prerequisite for the development of virtue. It is because the Buddhist, without God, cannot develop this radical gratitude that, Catherine would hold, the Buddhist could not develop true virtue.

The importance of gratitude for Catherine can be illustrated from some of her other writings, such as her extensive correspondence. Important here is a letter to a prior in Montepulciano in which Catherine points out that piety felt in the heart should be nourished through gratitude, but not gratitude simply in words. One needs to act to help the poor and hungry. One does works of charity out of direct gratitude to God, seeing as nothing we can do will be of benefit to God Himself. For He, of course, has no need of us, or our acts towards Himself. Thus we demonstrate our gratitude to God by working for our neighbours.[52] That is, after all, what He has asked us to do. And, Catherine urges, all virtues are practised through such gratitude. Similarly, ingratitude gives honour to oneself. It is the very nourishment of death.[53] And for Catherine the Christian—as indeed for Thomas—there is another dimension of gratitude to this wonderful God. For a Christian, gratitude is not just for createdness, but also for the activity of God, particularly the Incarnation itself, in which God became man in order to return man to God.[54] God comes to man, for man cannot come to God. This, of course, would be another thing quite (radically) beyond Śāntideva's frame of reference.

But then, as Thomas says, it is not something we know from natural reason at all but only from Christian revelation. Revelation itself is only possible, however, because the statement "God exists" is a true one.

Conclusion—and some implications for Christian-Buddhist dialogue

The real difference between Thomas and Śāntideva is not over the existence of an additional something called "God". Rather, it is a dispute concerning not God as such but concerning *things*. For Thomas, the Buddhist does not know something supremely important about things—whatever things, for this refers to *every* thing. What the Buddhist does not know is that every thing is *created*. Knowing this changes everything. For it has supreme soteriological import.

Thomas as a Christian theologian wants to argue that without friendship with God—the actual God, not something other than God mistakenly portrayed as God, which would be idolatry—a person cannot attain his or her own final goal, that for which one was made. With Augustine he holds that without recourse to God there can be no true peace.[55] Thus, corresponding to the falling short of Buddhist ontology in not turning to God, is a parallel soteriological failure. For Thomas (and Augustine), without God there can be no freedom. And we have seen what Thomas means by God—the creator of everything with Himself as its teleological goal. As we have also seen, this is denied by Śāntideva. Thus it is not possible to argue in Thomist terms that Buddhists too (*qua* Buddhists) attain true peace.

However, in terms of the minimum characterisation of the final soteriological goal as being true peace, both Buddhists and Christians agree. This is something held in common. There are varying Buddhist concepts of the final goal, but all agree it incorporates true peace (*śānti*).[56] Therefore, Thomas would argue that Buddhists could not, *qua* Buddhists, attain even what is actually the goal of Buddhism. Buddhism requires God in order to attain its *own* true goal. Thus God not only completes Buddhism ontologically. He also fulfills Buddhism soteriologically. As a Christian theologian Thomas is therefore entitled to argue that in not facing up to the real differences between Buddhism and Christianity as the *starting point* of any Christian-Buddhist dialogue, one who would enter into dialogue with Buddhists cannot in charity help Buddhists to their own true Buddhist goal.

But we should note that Śāntideva would be happy to reverse all this. We have seen that rGyal tshab rje (in common with Buddhist tradition) holds that any conception of something enjoying the plenum of existence would inevitably entail selfish grasping and thus the suffering that is the very antithesis of any Buddhist soteriological goal. Therefore Śāntideva would urge that since the Christian holds God as having that plenum of existence, any concept of God (such as Thomas must have in holding "God exists" to be a true proposition) inevitably entails grasping and thus suffering in this and in future lives. Since Thomas (and Augustine) both have a soteriological goal of true peace, neither can actually attain *their* goal so long as they think there is a God. Finally one has to do away with any notion of God in order to attain true peace. Fortunately one can show that the concept of God is incoherent. The soteriological goal of cutting all selfish attachment is facilitated by ontological analysis that shows God not to exist.

Thus focussing on ontological differences between Buddhism and Thomas's vision of Christianity highlights also radical differences between Śāntideva and Thomas in the way to attain their respective, or indeed their common, goals. Here, I want to suggest, we have a real basis for dialogue because we have a real and honest appreciation of difference based on a common search for true freedom and peace.

But it might be suggested that with focussing on differences here the dialogue is sterile, and not really going anywhere. Is that right, however? Where should we expect inter-religious dialogue to go? Surely all dialogue requires as a starting point an accurate understanding (all too often lacking) of each tradition involved. And (much as some may regret it) traditions are different. There is nothing to say that realising such difference entails a failure of dialogue. We can also gain a real practical basis for a different type of "going somewhere", a going somewhere that might otherwise be obscured. I mean here the possibility of religious *choice*. Choice between two options (whatever they may be) entails recognition that they *are* two options, that is, that they are *different*, and that as well as saying "yes", saying "no" to either entails consequences.[57]

And let me note one other point about this dialogue that starts from and appreciates seemingly irreconcilable differences. The Christian has to recognise that it may turn out to be the case that the question "Why is there something rather than nothing?" simply does have no answer. It may be that the existence of something just is a brute fact, with no justification beyond itself. And the Buddhist has to recognise that it may turn out to be the case that this most primordial of questions does have an answer, and that answer is (as Thomas says) what we call "God". In such an answer all questions of "How come?" find their resolution and fall silent. Thus each—the Buddhist and the Christian—has to recognise that they may be *wrong*, really, genuinely, wrong. Each makes a choice and takes a risk. That choice, and the risk, can only be real in recognising their authentic differences, and the nature of those differences. It can only be recognised as real by one who accepts (as do both Śāntideva and Thomas) the objectivity of truth. We have each taken a risk. We may be wrong. And it is here, I want to suggest, that we find in dialogue the openness to the other that we seek, and tolerance. It is the nature of our human situation, our "Being-there", if you like, that we take risks. To be human is to make choices, and is thus one way or another to take these deep metaphysical risks. Realising that we have each done just that in our own way is perhaps itself the starting and the final point of our dialogue.

NOTES

I am grateful to my colleague Gavin D'Costa for comments on an earlier draft of this paper.

1   Although, compared with Christianity, for Buddhists the urgency of mission is ameliorated by an infinite series of lives available through reincarnation. For those unfamiliar with Buddhist doctrine wanting background reading here, see Paul Williams, with Anthony Tribe, *Buddhist Thought: A Complete Introduction to the Indian Tradition* (London: Routledge, 2000).

2   For additional information on Mahāyāna, see Paul Williams, *Mahāyāna Buddhism: The Doctrinal Foundations* (London: Routledge, 1989), and Paul Williams, with Anthony Tribe, *Buddhist Thought* (Routledge, 2000). Candrakīrti and Śāntideva are both classed by Tibetans as following the *Madhyamaka* school of Buddhist philosophy, and as such both are usually said to teach the real, final truth. They are held to portray things exactly as they are.

3   Herbert, McCabe, O. P., *God Matters* (London: Mowbray, 1987/2000), chapter 1.

4   I do not mean by this that God necessarily had to create. I simply mean, with Thomas, that when we talk of creation we mean the creation by God.

5   See, for example, The Padmakara Translation Group (trans.), *Khenchen Kunzang Palden/ Minyak Kunzang Sönam: Wisdom—Two Buddhist Commentaries* (Peyzac-le-Moustier, Editions Padmakara, 1993), p. 106 n. 1, which claims that Śāntideva's arguments are aimed at the theistic notions of Hinduism and not at those of Judaism, Christianity and Islam "to which only some of Shāntideva's [sic.] arguments are relevant". Just which arguments those are is left unexplained. But it is clear that Śāntideva's arguments are aimed at God as creator of everything *per se*, and not specific versions of God as creator.

6   *S.Th.* 1a. 3, 4 ad 2: *scimus enim quod haec propositio quam formamus de Deo cum dicimus Deus est vera est*. St. Thomas Aquinas, *Summa Theologiae* (London: Eyre and Spottiswood; New York, NY: McGraw Hill Book Company, 1964–1980). Hereafter *S.Th.*

7   Thus strictly speaking, as Brian Davies has pointed out, Aquinas does not really want to say that we know the existence of God. See Brian Davies, O. P. *Aquinas*, (New York, NY: Continuum, 2002), p. 39. This is (at least, in part) because actually God is the *source* of all existence (*esse*), and as such the existence of God—what God is like from His own side, as it were—is quite beyond us as created beings. And all we can say on that score is that unlike things that exist, God *is* existence itself, not *an* existent (something that exists). Thus Thomas says in his *Commentary on Aristotle's Peri Hermeneias* 1:14 that "God's will is to be thought of as existing outside the realm of existents, as a cause from which pours forth everything that exists in all its variant forms" See Timothy McDermott, (trans.), *Aquinas: Selected Philosophical Writings* (Oxford: Oxford University Press, 1993), pp. 282–283. One could thus imagine someone saying (perhaps a Meister Eckhart, or a Nicholas of Cusa), for rhetorical or pedagogical effect, that we cannot talk of the existence of God. Providing the sense of this could be explained—and it can be done so quite easily in Thomist terms—there would be nothing unorthodox about it. But one could also imagine a hasty modern enthusiast suggesting that this shows that when we really get down to it (perhaps through "mystical" insight) we find that the Christian and the Buddhist do not contradict each other at all on the existence of God. That is nonsense. What Aquinas wants to say, strictly speaking, is that the utterance "God exists" expresses a true proposition. And actually this is about as far as one can get from the position of our Buddhist, for whom it very definitely expresses a false proposition.

8   One implication of this, notice, is that for Thomas if one holds that God does not exist one cannot have faith and be saved. But if one holds that God *does* exist it does not follow that one does have faith and might be saved. For example, if one holds through one's own natural reasoning that God (as the creator of everything) exists, but denies all the matters known only through revelation but still to be believed, one still will not have faith. The existence of God is a preamble to faith, not the content of faith, even for those who as a matter of fact *do* hold to the existence of God through faith and not through rational demonstration.

9   Let us try the following thought-experiment. Let us suppose that Thomas's apophatic approach to God is held to be no different from the approach to God in Buddhism. Buddhism, perhaps it is thought, is just an extreme form of *via negativa* Absolutism. Let us also suppose that in the modern world past confusions over too anthropomorphic approaches to God suggest that what is wanted (in the interests, maybe, of tolerance and broadmindedness) is a good dose of *via negativa* apophaticism. Then (it might be urged) perhaps the Christian would be better off adopting the Buddhist's view of God. But what is going on

here? This *cannot* be the same as Thomas's apophatic approach to God. The Buddhist simply does not hold that Thomas's God exists. Thus if this approach were correct, what then should Thomas do with Christ? For Thomas Christ, and revelation through Christ, is the main means by which we know about the actual nature of God. See e.g. St. Thomas Aquinas, *Summa Contra Gentiles*, five volumes, trans. Anton Pegis, James F. Anderson, Vernon J. Bourke and Charles J. O'Neill (Notre Dame, IN: University of Notre Dame Press, 1975), 1:5. But on the suggested scenario revelation must be wrong. Perhaps it is, as a Buddhist might urge, simply an adaptation to suit the mentality of people in first-century Palestine. Moreover Christ cannot actually be God, since there is no God. Christ must therefore be simply a very good, perhaps supremely good, man. Thus with adopting a "Buddhist explanation" of God, we lose God and we end up with Christ as just a good human being adapting His teaching to the level of His listeners. Again, since in the modern world we are now more aware of the plurality of religions, perhaps Christ is not truly unique. Perhaps He is just one among many good men, each adapting his teaching (the perennial teaching) to the level of his hearers. But clearly these conclusions do *not* provide us with a basis for Christian dialogue with Buddhists. They *are* (modern) Buddhism. This is exactly the view held by Buddhists (at least, commonly in Mahāyāna Buddhism). But for its part Christianity starts from God and is all about God. Buddhism simply does not. In not beginning discussion from what Christianity is all about, but side stepping it in the interests of closeness as a basis for dialogue, it is not surprising that the Christian is left with nothing to dialogue about at all.

10   For more details see Paul Williams, with Anthony Tribe, *Buddhist Thought*, pp. 4–5.
11   rGyal tshab rje, *Spyod 'jug rnam bshad rGyal sras 'jug ngogs* (Sarnath, Pleasure of Elegant Sayings Printing Press, 1973), p. 262: *rtag pa'i rgyu gzhan las skye ba dgag pa.*
12   *Ibid.*, p. 239. Tibetan commentary to Śāntideva *Bodhicaryāvatāra*: *bden 'dzin 'khor ba'i rtsa bar gyur pa'i nyon mongs can gyi ma rig pa yin la de'i zhen yul sun ma phyung bar thar pa thob pa mi srid pa'i phyir ro* / The philosophical school of Buddhism here is again *Madhyamaka*. See Śāntideva, *Bodhicaryāvatāra*. Sanskrit text in P. L. Vaidya, ed., *Bodhicaryāvatāra of Śāntideva, with the commentary Pañjikā of Prajñākaramati* (Darbhanga: The Mithila Instititute of Post-Graduate Studies and Research in Sanskrit Learning, 1960).
13   For those interested in this sort of thing the Sanskrit in this Buddhist context is *sasvabhāva*—possessing intrinsic existence. It can be taken as an equivalent for (among others) *dravyasat*—primary existence—and *paramārthasat*—ultimate existence.
14   On the meanings of *śūnyatā* in Buddhism see Paul Williams, *Mahāyāna Buddhism: The Doctrinal Foundations*; Paul Williams, "Emptiness: Buddhist ideas of" in *Routledge Encyclopedia of Philosophy*, 10 volumes, general editor, Edward Craig, (London: Routledge, 1998); and Paul Williams, with Anthony Tribe, *Buddhist Thought*. In this sort of Madhyamaka it is commonly given as an equivalent for *niḥsvabhāvatā*—lacking intrinsic existence.
15   Perhaps this is why the Dalai Lama commonly refers to "the God hypothesis": "According to our view, the production, transformation and destruction of all natural phenomena can be understood without resource to the hypothesis of a Creator God." Dalai Lama, *Transcendent Wisdom: A commentary on the ninth chapter of Shantideva's Guide to the Bodhisattva Way of Life*, trans. ed. and annotated by B. Alan Wallace (Ithaca, NY: Snow Lion Publications, 1988), p. 97. And:

> There are many different religions in this world. Each of them has its own special qualities, its own unique way of presenting the spiritual path. We Tibetans chose Buddhism as our national religion. Buddhism is an especial tasty and profound religion because it is not a path of faith but a path of reason and knowledge. Buddha himself stated that his doctrine should be accepted not on faith but only in the light of reason and logical inquiry. . . . Had Buddha not relied upon truth in his teachings, were his teachings mere superstition, he would not have advised us to critically judge his words in this way. Instead, he would have given us a dogma like, "Believe what I say or else you will come to experience misery." . . . Many religions begin with the idea of a God . . . Although this is an easy answer, it is not logically proveable [sic]. Therefore Buddha avoided it and tried to present a doctrine that in every way could be established through reason. . . . By avoiding the use of the God-theory, Buddha also avoided the many problematic side-effects that come with it. . . . [R]eligions based on

the "God-theory" usually do not permit rejection of the "Words of God", even should they contradict all reason. This can very easily stunt the growth of philosophical enquiry.... Buddha tried to present a path based purely on reason, and a path expressed solely in terms of human problems and human goals. Tenzin Gyatso, Dalai Lama XIV, *Universal Responsibility and the Good Heart* (Dharamsala: Library of Tibetan Works and Archives, 1980), pp. 8–11.

This is taken from a relatively early work given originally in Tibetan to Tibetan refugees in Delhi, and published in India. It is described as representing "the direct and personal nature with which His Holiness communicates with his people" (*ibid.*, p. 2). I also used and discussed it in *The Unexpected Way: On Converting from Buddhism to Catholicism* (T. & T. Clark, 2002), pp. 69–70.

16 Taken for convenience from the Tibetan commentary by dNgul chu thogs med (fourteenth century): *dbang phyug ces pa lhar gtogs pa | gtsang zhing mchod par 'os pa | rtag pa | gcig pu | kun gyi byed pa po yin pa ste | chos lnga ldan zhig 'gro ba kun gyi rgyu yin par 'dod na.*

17 The fifth element, that of "space" (or sometimes "ether", what fills space: *ākāśa*) is treated separately in the next verse (verse 120). Indian commentaries make it clear that the reference to the elements in verse 119 is only to the first four of the elements. One is reminded here of suggestions in e.g. presocratic works that "air", or perhaps "fire" or "water" is the primeval element from which all things spring, the source of all. For a Biblical criticism see, e.g. the *Wisdom of Solomon* 13.

18 But see later on the primary role of the mind in phenomenal causation.

19 There is a cultural association at play here. Purity in India is an important concept bound up with caste and class status. God by definition is therefore the most pure. The feet are the lowest part of the body, regularly in contact with impure pollutants. Feet are thus thought to be highly impure. The fact that one walks on the ground, composed of the primal elements, indicates that there can be no sense in speaking of them as pure (as God should be).

20 Actually there have been some Buddhist traditions associated with the "Buddha–nature" (*tathāgatagarbha*) particularly in Tibet and East Asia that might suggest some similarity with this. But they vehemently deny any real similarity with the *ātman* teachings, and were anyway accused by their opponents with having precisely abandoned Buddhism in adopting a position so clearly akin to that of the Hindus. Śāntideva would agree. For more, see Paul Williams, *Mahāyāna Buddhism: The Doctrinal Foundations*, (London: Routledge, 1989), chapter 5.

21 Some people seem to think this is actually a Buddhist view. It is not.

22 But see below for the sense in which our Buddhists would accept the mind as the actual creator of the everyday world given to us in experience. The mind is, we might say, the *phenomenal* creator.

23 We might want to say that the idolater simply does not know what "God" *means*. But would that absolve him or her of responsibility?

24 *acintyasya ca kartṛtvam apy acintyaṃ kim ucyate.* See also rGyal tshab rje (1973), p. 264: *de yang bsam bya min pa byed pa por byed pas ci zhig bya khyod kyis kyang dbang phyug su yin mi shes pa bsam du med pa yin pa'i phyir ro ||*

25 For more in a Buddhist context see Paul Williams, "Non-conceptuality, critical reasoning and religious experience: Some Tibetan Buddhist discussions", in Michael McGhee, ed., *Philosophy, Religion and the Spiritual Life* (Cambridge, Cambridge University Press/Royal Institute of Philosophy Supplement Vol. 32, 1992).

26 On God as intelligent, and its dependence in Thomas's thought on God as not subject to material limitation, see Herbert McCabe, O. P., *God Still Matters*, ed. and introduced by Brian Davies, O. P. (New York, NY: Continuum, 2002), pp. 24–26.

27 See Herbert McCabe, O. P., *God Still Matters*, chapter 2.

28 Thomas too could recognise this argument. He held as a matter of faith that God (who is outside time) has not brought into existence a world that is literally eternal, existing through all time. But he also held in defence of Aristotle's view of the eternality of the world that there is no *contradiction* in God being the creator of something eternal. Thus God could have done so if He had wished. Thomas wrote a short work to prove just this point. It can be found translated in Ralph McInerny, (trans.), *Thomas Aquinas: Selected Writings*

(Harmondsworth: Penguin Books, 1998), chapter 27. As a general point there is no contradiction in arguing that were X not to exist, Y would not exist (but not also vice-versa), even where as a matter of fact (or, in the case of X, necessarily) X and Y are eternal. Cf. here the relationships between the three "persons" of the Trinity.

29   There are some very technical reasons in Buddhist thought why something truly permanent must also be unchanging. Please take my word for it.

30   rGyal tshab rje, *Spyod 'jug rnam bshad rGyal sras 'jug ngogs*, p. 265.

31   *Madhyamakāvatāra* 6: 86: *ji bzhin rang gi bstan bcos de de las | mu stegs rnams kyis gang zag sogs de dag | smras pa de dag byed por ma gzigs nas | rgyal bas sems tsam 'jig rten byed por gsungs ||*

32   *sems nyid kyis ni sems can 'jig rten dang | snod kyi 'jig rten shin tu sna tshogs 'god | 'gro ba ma lus las las skyes par gsungs | sems spangs nas ni las kyang yod ma yin ||*

33   Dalai Lama, *Transcendent Wisdom: A commentary on the ninth chapter of Shantideva's Guide to the Bodhisattva Way of Life*, trans. ed. and annotated by B. Alan Wallace (Ithaca, NY: Snow Lion Publications, 1988), pp. 96–97. And remember there is not thought to be any ultimate *first* origin. The series of causes and effects powered by mental events is for Buddhism literally beginningless. Such, again, is basic Buddhism. It is expressed in the formula of the "twelve links of dependent origination" (*pratītyasamutpāda*). This is attributed to the Buddha himself, where although one causal link leads to another in a circle, so that the cycle of unenlightened rebirth (*saṃsāra*) continues, primacy in Buddhism is always given to ignorance (*avidyā*) that generates selfish craving (*tṛṣṇā*). Ignorance and selfish craving are, of course, mental in nature and incorporate a series of mental events. It seems to me, incidentally, that in stressing the creative power of the mind in these and other ways all Buddhist thought has great difficulty avoiding one form or another of idealism and eventually solipsism. At least this would apply (I would argue) to all formalised Buddhist philosophical schools thought. And I would also suggest that even where Buddhist thought concerns other issues such as meditation practice rather than explicit philosophical issues, its orientation is always towards the mind and thus personal experiences. It is, in that sense, always *subjectivist*.

34   Narada Maha Thera, *The Buddha and His Teachings* (Singapore: Stamford Press, 1980), p. 230.

35   The first of these two texts is the *Brahmajāla Sutta*. The other is the *Kevaddha Sutta*. For the benefit of readers unfamiliar with Buddhism, I should perhaps point out here that Buddhists consider the Buddha to be someone who has through his insight developed over many incarnations *become* a Buddha. He is basically a human, the same as the rest of us, who has come to "see it as it is" and thus put a stop to the process of rebirth. Out of his compassion he has taught this way to his disciples so that they too can come to see things the way they really are and put a stop to the process of rebirth and thence suffering and unfulfilment. Throughout infinite time there are infinite Buddhas. Buddhas are not, repeat not, considered to be God (or gods). The distinguished Sri Lankan monk Walpola Rahula, writing within a more modern tradition of explaining away belief in God, comments that "[f]or self-protection man has created God, on whom he depends for his own protection, safety and security, just as a child depends on its parent". See Walpola Rahula, *What the Buddha Taught* (Bedford, Gordon Fraser, 1959), p. 52. In the light of this it might seem surprising that when Pope John Paul II visited Sri Lanka there was such a terrible fuss concerning his statement that "Buddhism is in large measure an *'atheistic' system*". John Paul II, *Crossing the Threshold of Hope*, ed. Vittorio Messori, trans. Jenny McPhee and Martha McPhee (London: Jonathan Cape, 1994), p. 86; italics original. I am not quite sure why "atheistic" is put in quotation marks. It is quite clear that Buddhism *is* atheistic, and Buddhists are very proud of the fact. Buddhists consider the notion of a creator God to be incoherent and immature. I suspect that the fuss in Sri Lanka may have owed something to cultural and linguistic misunderstanding. Throughout the Third World, particularly bearing in mind that usually the first language is not English, "atheism" has come to be associated with a materialist anti-religious stance most familiar from Marxism. Thus if a Buddhist hears that his religion has been termed "atheist" it may be that a natural response will be to think that Buddhism is being disparaged, linked with anti-religious movements, and with crass materialism or political revolution. It should have been explained that "atheism" (to most Westerners at least, in terms of the development of Western intellectual history) simply means denying a true, real creator God. Many Westerners consider the

atheism of Buddhism to be to its advantage as a religion. Then it seems to me there should not have been any great problems with Buddhist objections. As so often with such issues, it is important to remember sensitive understanding and presentation.

36   *Catechism of the Catholic Church* (London: Geoffrey Chapman, 1994), p. 196.

37   To quote a wonderfully written and very relevant essay, "in the sense in which atheists of this sort say God 'does not exist', the atheist has merely arrived at the theological start-ing point. Theologians of the classical traditions, an Augustine, a Thomas Aquinas or a Meister Eckhart, simply agree about the disposing of idolatries, and then proceed with the proper business of doing theology". Denys Turner, *Faith Seeking* (London, SCM Press, 2002), p. 8.

38   In my explanation of what is going on in Aquinas's so-called "proofs of the existence of God" here I am indebted to the work of Herbert, McCabe, O. P., *God Matters* (2000), and McCabe, *God Still Matters* (2002), and to Denys Turner, *Faith Seeking* (2002). Similar expla-nations, also relying on McCabe, can be found in Brian Davies, O. P. *The Thought of Thomas Aquinas* (Oxford, Clarendon Press, 1992), and Davies, *Aquinas* (2002). As will be clear, I think Aquinas here provides a brilliant theistic reply to Buddhist atheism, one that uses the very presuppositions and interests of the Buddhist himself. I do not know if Aquinas's approach to the existence of God (in terms of the answer to the question "Why is there something rather than nothing?") originated with him. But I strongly suspect it did, for it requires a mature understanding of Aristotle and the potential of his application to Chris-tian theology. It rests on an Aristotelian interest in science as an explanation of causes, the search for first causes as a search for final intelligibility, and metaphysics as the science of being-as-such (see *Metaphysics* 1003a21 ff.). When this is combined with a Christian concern that theology should be the First Science, and God the first cause, we reach Aquinas's God. God is the reason why there is anything at all, understood as the reason why there is being-as-such, rather than specific individual beings. Although, of course, for Aquinas the fact that God is the reason why there is anything at all also makes God the final reason why there are individual things as well. See here the "Prologue" to Thomas's commentary on Aristotle's *Metaphysics*—available in, for example, Mary T. Clarke (ed.), *An Aquinas Reader* (London: Hodder and Stoughton, 1974). If Thomas did originate this perspective and argu-ment for God, it was arguably a supreme point of Western philosophical theology.

39   See here Nicholas Lash, *Believing Three Ways in One God: A reading of the Apostles' Creed* (London: SCM Press, 1992/2002), pp. 39, 53.

40   Another variant on this question, that Thomas might also offer to the Buddhist, is to ask how come regular causal processes take place at all? Buddhists base their view of the world on regular causal processes, including causal processes of a moral kind, referred to as *karman*. But how come it is like that? It is not enough to say that "this being, that occurs". How come? That this is the case (known in Buddhism as the *dharmatā*) is not self-explanatory. It too is a question that occurs within the context of "Why is there something rather than nothing?". Why, given the Buddhist understanding of how things truly are, is it like that?

41   Thus, Denys Turner, *Faith Seeking* (2002), chapter 1 says, if one truly wants to be an atheist one has to work very hard at it, restricting one's imagination in order to limit the range of questions asked. One must keep to (A)–(C) type questions, avoiding questions like (D). The Buddhist would agree. Indeed, the Buddha himself is supposed to have urged his follow-ers to do just this, not to ask "big" metaphysical questions but to concentrate on the process of spiritual liberation. Of course, the problem here is that the process of spiritual liberation may precisely itself depend upon asking (and answering) certain "big" metaphysical ques-tions. For Thomas, the existence of God is essential to spiritual liberation.

42   Here I find myself in disagreement with Nicholas Lash, *Believing Three Ways in One God*, p. 39, a book and thinker I otherwise much admire. Lash goes too far, it seems to me, in dis-solving away the *causal* nature of God's creativity. As such, I am not sure he is left with any meaning for "creation", and is in danger of loosing the causal thread between God and the world. For me, as should be clear, God's creation is a *sui generis* type of causation. The fact that we cannot know what it is like for God to create is irrelevant. Creation is still caused by God in whatever way God causes, and reference to God is in terms of a type of causal explanation—a causal explanation that (as Lash notes) brings to a stop further talk of explanations.

43 See McCabe, *God Still Matters*, (2002), chapter 4. A change in a relative of mine—say, she becomes a mother, and hence I become an uncle—need not entail *as such* an actual change in me. The Buddhist arguments rely very often on unstated principles that can be questioned. For example, a very common principle in Buddhist metaphysics is that if there is a change in the set of propositions true of a thing, it follows that there must be a change in the thing itself. Thus if it becomes true of me that I am now a grandfather, when previously it was not true of me, that involves a change in *me* such that strictly speaking I am no longer ontologically identical with me before this became true. But various *prima facie* absurdities result from this principle (it would follow—and Buddhists frequently argue this—that I lose ontological identity constantly), and the absurdities themselves suggest (to me) its unacceptability. For much more on the philosophy of this, see Paul Williams, *Altruism and Reality: Studies in the Philosophy of the Bodhicaryāvatāra* (Richmond: Curzon, 1998), chapter 5.

44 See Nicholas of Cusa, *Dialogus de deo abscondito*. Latin text (with Italian translation by Franco Buzzi) in Niccolò Cusano, *Il Dio Nascosto* (Milan: Biblioteca Universale Rizzoli, 2002), p. 46.

45 We can see in all of this the sense in which Thomas would agree that Buddhism represents a searching, a reaching out, for *its own fulfilment* that can be found in Christ. See here also the *Catechism of the Catholic Church* (London: Geoffrey Chapman, 1994), pp. 195–199).

46 It is striking how portrayals of Thomas in, for example, the famous frescoes by fellow Dominican Fra Angelico at St. Marco in Florence, often show Thomas standing in the background observing, and half facing the viewer, explaining to us what the action is about, what it all *means*. This is the case even where (as in the great fresco in the Chapter House of St Marco) the portrayal of the crucifixion has other Dominicans like Peter Martyr and Dominic himself on their knees in active wonder and adoration.

47 Which is why I have preferred "self-understanding" as a translation of Catherine's Italian to Suzanne Noffke's translation "self-knowledge". St. Catherine of Siena, *Il Diologo della Divina Provvidenza ovvero Libro della Divina Dottrina*, ed. Giuliana Cavallini, (Siena: Edizioni Cantagalli, 1995). First edition 1968, p. 1. Cf. English translation by Suzanne Noffke, O. P. (1980), *Catherine of Siena: The Dialogue* (New York/Mahwah, NJ: Paulist Press, 1980). In terms of how the latter expression is used in contemporary spirituality it seems there remains the possibility of assimilation into the contemporary obsessive "self spirituality". But Catherine's whole point is that we come to understand ourselves when we displace self-concern with a realisation of our complete dependence on God. Self-understanding is *understanding* that we are created by God. It is not at all knowing the self. Self-understanding is, if you like, *knowing* God. This is through knowing correctly our relationship to Him. It is precisely *not* knowing the self as such.

48 Cf. St. Catherine of Siena, *Il Diologo della Divina Provvidenza ovvero Libro della Divina Dottrina*, ed. Giuliana Cavallini, (Siena: Edizioni Cantagalli, 1995), p. 10. First edition 1968. Truth (Christ) speaks: "Never depart from understanding what you are (*cognoscimento di te*—i.e. understanding yourself).You are sunk down as you are into the valley of humility; and you understand Me in yourself . . . No virtue is able to have life in itself except from charity, and humility is the wetnurse (*baglia=balia*)—the very nurse who feeds from herself (*nutrice*)—for charity. In understanding yourself you will attain humility, seeing as you will that you do not exist through yourself. You will come to understand that your existence is from Me, and that I loved you even before you ever were". (*tu non esca mai del cognoscimento di te, e abbassata che tu se' nella valle dell'umilità, e tu cognosce me in te . . . Niuna virtù può avere in sé vita se non dalla carità; e l'umilità è baglia e nutrice della carità. Nel cognoscimento di te ti umiliarai, vedendo te per te non essere, e l'essere tuo cognoscerai da me, che v'ò amati prima che voi fuste*). Cf. English translation by Suzanne Noffke, O. P., *Catherine of Siena: The Dialogue*, (New York/Mahwah, NJ: Paulist Press, 1980), p. 29. For Thomas, God is in all things not in any literal sense of location but inasmuch as God is always acting directly on any thing whatsoever, without intermediaries (*Su. Th.* 1a, 8, art. 1). In particular, God always acts directly on each thing as its creator and sustainer. Thus God is always immediately present to each and any thing. Hence God can be said to be present in oneself *inasmuch as—and only in the sense that—one is created by God*. For Catherine humility comes from an understanding of oneself—what one really is. One understands, specifically, one's own createdness by God. This humility gives rise to charity, and thence to virtue. Without an awareness of createdness, there can thus be no true virtue.

49   If self-understanding is not rooted in God, rooted in an awareness of createdness, Catherine has Christ say, "if this understanding were not united in Me it would end in confusion" (*finirebbe nella confusione se questo cognoscimento non fosse unito in me*), *Il Diologo della Divina Provvidenza ovvero Libro della Divina Dottrina*, ed. Giuliana Cavallini, (Siena: Edizioni Cantagalli, 1995), p. 30. In her notes here Cavallini comments that this theme is central to Catherine's thought. She cites Christ's words to Catherine in the standard and important *Vita* of the saint (the *Legenda Maior*) by her confessor Raimundo da Capua: "You are that which you are not; I am He Whom I am" (*tu sei quella che non sei, Io sono colui che sono*). It should be obvious by now how radically different this is from any Buddhist position of "not-Self" (*anātman*), to which it could so hastily and superficially be assimilated. The Buddhist, Catherine wants to say—and how could Thomas disagree—is *radically confused.*
50   Catherine agrees with the Buddhist that virtue is to be grounded in ontological realisation. But Christianity—for Catherine, Truth—is all about God. *For us, from our side*, God is all about createdness. Thus where understanding God is lacking, ontological realisation is lacking. Hence there can be no virtue. You cannot love your neighbours, Catherine says, without loving God. See *Dialogo* (1995), p. 17: *E così ogni male si fa per mezzo del prossimo, ciò è che non amando me, non è nella carità sua.* Once again we see that the dispute between the Buddhist and the Christian is not simply one of words. It is radical to the core, because it is about createdness and inasmuch as the Buddhist does not accept createdness and the Christian (at least in any orthodox sense recognisable to Thomas and Catherine) must do so there is simply no room for compromise. There is no love of neighbours without love of God. There is no true virtue without love of God. See *Dialogo* (1995), pp. 20 ff.
51   Certainly Buddhists speak of gratitude to "all sentient beings", and specific gratitude to one's teachers, for what one has received from them. In the case of the former there follows an implication of duty, duty to strive for their welfare out of gratitude for benefits received. The theme of gratitude to the Buddha Amitābha (Japanese: Amida) for his salvific acts is also important in Shinran's Jōdo Shinshū Buddhism in Japan. But this "temporal gratitude" (that corresponds morally to the ontology of "temporal causation") is radically different from the gratitude owed to God for existence as such. The latter is a "transcendental gratitude" that is lacking in Buddhism just as God through the question "Why is there something rather than nothing?" and its answer, is lacking in Buddhism. And the goal of Buddhism, as indeed for much of Indian spirituality, lies in a state beyond essential dependence. The goal lies precisely in no longer needing others. An enlightened being, or a Buddha, *as such* does not need anyone or anything else at all. That is what "attaining the goal" means. Thus the goal here cannot involve the sort of radical dependence necessitated by gratitude to God on whom, as Creator, one is *always* in a relationship of grateful dependence. Contrast this with Dante, who in his *La Divina Commedia* reserves for the lowest reaches of Hell traitors, those who show different sorts of ingratitude. See Dante Alighieri, *La Divina Commedia*, ed. with a commentary by Fredi Chiapelli (Milan: Mursia, 1965). The very lowest place in Hell is for ingratitude to benefactors. But what greater ingratitude to a benefactor could there be than ingratitude to God? This is why, perhaps, Satan himself is at the very bottom of Hell (gnawing away at Judas Iscariot, who betrayed Christ, God Incarnate). Satan was an angel, in the presence of God, an angel who showed complete ingratitude. Those who would reach the heights, yet fail to understand God and their dependence on Him, fall to the lowest depths. The one who would be literally, truly, perfect—that is, wants to be God—in fact wants to bring about an absurdity, for by definition only God can be God. Thus the one who would be God essentially never knew God or what God is. That, I suppose, is Hell. Gratitude is a much-neglected virtue, and I plan to return in the future to this topic, its contrasting nature in Buddhism and Medieval Christian thought, and its philosophical and theological presuppositions.
52   Cf. here the centrality of gratitude in Catherine's impassioned *Orazioni*: "One does not even love his neighbour for himself, but rather for You in order that one might render You glory": *E neppure ama il prossimo per sé, ma per te, acciò che ti renda gloria.* St. Catherine of Siena, *Le Orazioni di S. Caterina da Siena*, ed. Giuliana Cavallini (Siena: Edizioni Cantagalli, 1993), p. 42. Interestingly enough, we find the importance of gratitude particularly stressed for female Dominicans in a sermon given by Humbert of Romans (elected Master of the Dominicans 1254). See here Simon, Tugwell O. P., *Early Dominicans: Selected Writings* (Mahwah, NJ: Paulist Press, 1982), p. 329. But for Catherine (as it would certainly be

for Thomas) gratitude becomes the right response, a right ordering, of *all* creation to God. Gratitude is what we have to become by nature.

53 See St. Catherine of Siena, *Lettere alle Religiose: Brani scelti raccolti da una claustrale domenicana*, (Milan: Editrice Massimo, 1982), pp. 88–91. Cf. here Pope John Paul II's frequent observations on the modern world as purveying a "culture of death". We see in this letter, incidentally, Catherine's frequent use of food-imagery that, combined with her fasting, has led some modern commentators to see in her life signs of an unhealthy obsession with food, perhaps even anorexia.

54 See e.g. Catherine's *Orazioni*, pp. 112–113.

55 *Confessions* 1:1: "For You made us for Yourself, and our hearts are not at peace until they rest in You" (*quia fecisti nos ad te et inquietum est cor nostrum, donec requiescat in te*). St. Augustine, *Confessions*. Latin text (with Italian translation by Carlo Vitali) in *Sant'Agostino: Le Confessioni*, (Milan: Biblioteca Universale Rizzoli, 1998). Original edition 1974; twenty-fifth edition: 2000.

56 "*Nirvāṇa* is peace" is often said in Tibet to be one of the four points common to all Buddhists.

57 An example of how createdness makes all the difference is in the way it displaces the primacy of relationships within the world to the total and complete primacy of relationships between things-within-the-world and God. One implication of this is that it is no longer an obvious premise that one has complete rights over, for example, one's own body. One's "own" body is created by God. Thus one does not even *own* one's own body, let alone have absolute rights over it. Hence the claim, for example, that one has absolute rights over one's own body and *therefore* one can commit suicide or undertake abortion does not follow. It is as if one's body is not one's own, but on loan. One does not have absolute rights in the use of something on loan. If one's body is on loan from God then, if God so wills, He can also lend your body, or parts of your body, to a fetus without you having any right to curtail that loan.

6

AQUINAS AND ANALYTIC PHILOSOPHY: NATURAL ALLIES?

FERGUS KERR, O.P.

I

For over forty years now, developments in mainstream Anglo-American philosophy have been significantly affected by a handful of students of the work of Thomas Aquinas, while attention to his work by some of the same people has helped to establish one more version of Thomism.[1] This interaction is little recognised by philosophers at large or indeed by the majority of Thomists. For one thing, as we shall see, Aristotle is often at the forefront, with the presence of Aquinas somewhat concealed. On the other side, the vast majority of Thomists throughout the world remain gloriously ignorant of any other tradition than their own. The recent papal encyclical *Fides et Ratio*, for example, addressed to philosophers among others, recommends Aquinas's philosophy of being as a way of combating scepticism, subjectivism, relativism, scientism, nihilism etc. While not unfriendly allusions are made to phenomenological, hermeneutic and post-modern tradition(s), there is no informed reference to analytic philosophy, let alone recognition of the decades of intense and fruitful argument on precisely these matters.[2]

Analytic philosophy—unbelievably—is regularly dismissed as nothing but "talk about talk", or deplored as reluctant or even impotent to discuss the Big Questions (evil, death, the meaning of life, etc.). Worse still, in the judgement of many Christian theologians, and Catholics especially, it is, in John Haldane's words, "something to be avoided as a serious threat to one's grasp of God, goodness and truth".[3]

It is hard to understand how anyone who has ever even dipped into the writings of philosophers from G. E. Moore and Bertrand Russell to Willard Van Orman Quine, Donald Davidson, Hilary Putnam and such like, could think their work is mere "talk about talk", or that they never advert to the Big Questions. Essays such as Russell's "Mysticism and Logic" and "The Place of Science in a Liberal Education" would not make Christian theologians happy; but their beauty and passion are surely undeniable.[4] Putnam's work, for a quarter of a century now, has dealt with some of what must by any standards be regarded as some of the most fundamental and persistent problems in philosophy: the nature of truth, knowledge and rationality.[5] It would not take long, in a good bookstore or library, to see that, compared with recent products of Continental philosophy and Thomistic philosophy, Anglo-American philosophers have no reason to be embarrassed.

Amazingly, to philosophers in the analytic tradition, Catholic theologians at the present time, if they regard philosophy as a congenial or anyway unavoidable interlocutor, mostly prefer to engage with Continental philosophy: phenomenology, *Seinsdenken*, the hermeneutic tradition, deconstruction, etc. As regards modern philosophy, that is to say, they find Nietzsche, Heidegger, Levinas, Derrida and their kin much more accessible, more challenging, or anyway less threatening, than Frege, Russell, Wittgenstein, Quine, Davidson, and their followers. They are unlikely to be studying the works of Thomas Aquinas.

II

"While it is fairly clear what Thomism is", so Dagfinn Føllesdal says, "it is far from clear what is meant by 'analytic philosophy'".[6] However diverse the forms that Thomism takes, presumably he means, they may all be traced back to a single corpus of writings. Mainstream Anglo-American philosophy is plainly not a monolithic homogeneous tradition either—on the contrary, there has always been much internal conflict. While librarians and booksellers have little difficulty in deciding which authors belong on which shelves, there is now considerable dispute among philosophers of a broadly analytic persuasion as to what counts as analytic philosophy and how it originated. It is sometimes contended that there is nothing special about analytic philosophy—that all philosophy is in some sense "analytic".[7]

Then, even while recognizing the difference in the respective canons, post-Nietzschean and post-Fregean, analytically trained philosophers have sought recently to bring out how much the two traditions have in common. Richard Rorty, for example, contends that "post-phenomenological" philosophy and "post-analytical" philosophy are converging, even merging. Since he is inclined to blur the distinction between philosophy of any kind and literary studies in general, his view is perhaps not very helpful. His point is that analytic philosophers lean towards science for their examples while in the Continental tradition philosophers prefer to look to poetry—just a matter of emphasis. There is obviously something in this claim: from Frege to Quine and Davidson philosophers turn to mathematics and physics for examples, whereas Heidegger and Derrida happily invoke poetry and fiction. In the end, however, for Rorty, philosophy is "culture criticism".[8]

Others acknowledge the difference but highlight what the traditions have in common. Samuel C. Wheeler III, himself an analytic philosopher, argues in detail that, beneath the obvious surface differences, there are common-alities in strategy and concern between Donald Davidson and Jacques Derrida.[9] Henry Staten, comparing Derrida and Wittgenstein, argues that Derrida is a lot more sensible than some think (the dust wrapper carries enthusiastic endorsement by Derrida himself).[10] Simon Glendinning reads Wittgenstein in the light of Heidegger and Derrida, again undermining the supposed gap between analytic and Continental philosophers.[11] J. E. Malpas argues that Heidegger's notion of truth as *aletheia* complements Davidson's insistence on the presuppositional character of truth, with both emerging as opponents of relativism about truth.[12]

Such efforts are welcome. For theologians, particularly, these compari-sons offer the opportunity to approach major figures in the analytic tra-dition in the light of the Continental philosophers with whom they are more likely to be *au fait*. Independently of such explorations of common problems and strategies in current practice in the two schools, a number of recent historiographical studies trace the origins of analytic philosophy back to the time before the trajectories divided. Michael Dummett, for example, himself a major figure in analytic philosophy contends that the two schools have common roots, chiefly in the work of Bolzano and Brentano.[13]

Dummett attacks the very idea of "Anglo-American philosophy": a mis-nomer, which has the "vicious effect" of encouraging philosophers to think that they need not read, let alone write in, any language but English. More-over, far from being created in Cambridge by G. E. Moore and Bertrand Russell, in the opening decade of the twentieth century, as many would have supposed until recent genealogical investigations,[14] the sources of analytic philosophy, Dummett argues, lie in the writings of philosophers writing in German—which "would have remained obvious to everyone had it not been for the plague of Nazism which drove so many German-speaking philoso-phers across the Atlantic".[15]

Dummett first realized this by examining the career of Gilbert Ryle, the most prominent philosopher at Oxford in the 1950s, editor of *Mind* for many years, creator of the Oxford B.Phil.,[16] author of *The Concept of Mind* (1949). Before 1939, he used to lecture on Bolzano, Brentano, Frege, Meinong and Husserl—"It is a great pity that little of his knowledge of those authors was preserved in print, and, equally, that, as far as I can see, little that he learned from them survived into his later work".[17]

Bernard Bolzano (1781–1848) belongs as much to the history of mathe-matics as to that of philosophy. He developed a form of logico-ontological atomism directed against radical scepticism and subjectivism. Essentially, he sought to secure the objectivity of knowledge by positing non-linguistic enti-ties (ideas, propositions, and truths) independent of human cognition. In effect, Bolzano anticipated Frege's sharp distinction between logic and psy-chology, breaking radically with the tendency in the empiricist tradition to found logic on psychology and in the Cartesian tradition to confuse logic and epistemology.[18]

For Dummett, Gottlob Frege (1848–1925) is the key figure in the development of analytic philosophy. Yet, if Frege is "the only grandfather" of analytic philosophy, then Bolzano was "a great-grandfather": "In Bolzano there is the same rejection of the psychological approach that one finds in Frege, but not the richness of the semantic analysis".[19] That is to say, putting it simply, there are truths which are there whether or not they are discovered by human beings: the laws of logic are not identical with, or derived from, the ways in which the human mind works. From the outset, Bolzano and Frege rejected psychologism: the result of failing to understand that logic is a normative discipline, giving laws of truth to which thought ought to conform, thus in no way a construction based on patterns to which our thoughts do in fact conform.

Of course all this is much disputed: that analytic philosophy originated principally in Frege's rejection of psychologism—in effect, of Cartesianism and empiricism. In various forms, psychologism remains a tempting option: Quine's interest in naturalised epistemology and the later Wittgenstein's attempts (as some would say) to base logic and mathematics on our natural reactions, for example. Frege's concern to secure objectivity for logic and mathematics leads to accusations of Platonism: the view that abstract objects, such as those of mathematics, are real, independent, and timeless entities, which are there, whether or not human beings discover them.

The point here is, however, that the question is at the centre of debate in analytic philosophy. Since the appearance in 1959 of the translation (by J. L. Austin) of Frege's *Grundlagen der Arithmetik*, and particularly with Michael Dummett's seminal paper on "Truth",[20] there has been deep and wide-ranging conflict between those who affirm, and those who deny, the real existence of mathematical objects, but also of other minds, moral and aesthetic properties, the past and the future, universals, possibilities, and the external world. The debate spreads all the way through metaphysics, philosophy of mind and perception, epistemology and ethics.

While Thomists are (or should be!) realists, the realist/anti-realist debate in analytic philosophy owes nothing to them, even indirectly.

Franz Brentano (1838–1917), ordained priest in 1864, was a zealous Thomist from student days (he was to leave the Church because of the infallibility dogma). Brentano's thesis, as it is called, first proposed in 1874, is to the effect that it is the *intentio*, the directedness of the mind to an object, which marks off the mental/psychological from the physical.[21] He believed he was retrieving the medieval notion of the intentionality of mental states: that is to say, one cannot believe, wish or hope without believing, wishing or hoping *something*. This seemingly platitudinous claim opened the way to reconnecting beliefs, thoughts, wishes, etc. with things—thus overturning the solipsistic assumptions in much post-Cartesian philosophy.

This too has given rise to much debate. Under the heading of externalism philosophers contend that what is thought, or experienced, or said, is essentially dependent on items or aspects of the world external to the mind. It is not just that mental states are typically caused by factors in the environment. The claim is that thoughts, experiences, *et cetera*, could not exist as they now do without the subject's being embedded in an external world of a certain kind—which it is now up to the philosopher to describe. Over against this, obviously, is the "Cartesian" separation of the mental from the physical, in many different versions, including the very plausible assumption that we have "privileged access" to the contents of our own minds, such that solipsism may become quite tempting.[22]

The turn against subjectivism, in the analytic school, thus owes a great deal to Brentano's retrieval of the medieval Scholastic idea, that mental states are what they are by reference to something other than themselves.[23] That our mental states depend on objects in the environment remains the minority view in current debates: the mind, or more commonly now the brain, is supposed to construct items in the external world from representations of these items, impressions, sense data, raw feels, neurophysiological occurrences, *et cetera*.

Second only to the realism/anti-realism debate in analytic philosophy there is this dispute within the philosophy of mind, dividing those who defend some form of externalism (the mind as situated in the world) and those who advocate some kind of representationalism (minds have no immediate knowledge of the world). Clearly these disputes are interconnected, with the first occupying the traditional ground of metaphysics and the second the field of epistemology.

Far from there being an unbridgeable gap between the philosophical assumptions of Thomism and analytic philosophy, then, the truth is that, under the heading of intentionality—that what our understanding grasps primarily and most readily is the specific nature of material things—one of Thomas's most distinctive assumptions has been central all along. A thesis in nineteenth-century Aristotelian Thomism, one may say, had a crucial effect in twentieth-century Anglo-American philosophy.

III

Where the analytic tradition departed radically from the Continental, according to Dummett, was that the analytic school took the "linguistic turn", whereas followers of Husserl did not do so. Frege's idea that the analysis of thought is what philosophy is about, and that this analysis proceeds through the analysis of language, was, according to Dummett, the decisive factor.[24]

This debt to Frege, on the other hand, is not what led to "linguistic analysis", "ordinary language philosophy" or "Oxford philosophy", so Dummett insists. From his days as a young philosopher in Oxford, he was out of sym-

124 Fergus Kerr, O.P.

pathy with that "amazingly complacent" movement. He regarded, and regards, Gilbert Ryle and J. L. Austin, the leading Oxford philosophers in the 1950s, as quite unimportant. They were much overrated by visiting American philosophers; "Oxford philosophy" acquired a reputation in the United States from which he dissociates himself. He stood apart, along with others such as Elizabeth Anscombe ("needless to say") and Philippa Foot.[25]

No doubt both Dummett and the other two were regarded, and regarded themselves, as mavericks on the Oxford scene at the time. From this distance, however, neither Anscombe nor Foot seems so eccentric. Ryle's book, *The Concept of Mind* (1949), a landmark attack on the Cartesian myth of the self as "the ghost in the machine", is very much an essay in philosophical anthropology in the spirit of Aristotle. The new generation of philosophers in Oxford were all more or less openly students, not so much of Frege as of Aristotle.

J. L. Austin is also clearly in the Aristotelian tradition.[26] In the classic paper "A Plea for Excuses" (1956), for example, his scrupulous examination of the kind of thing that we say when trying to excuse ourselves is, as he says, a contribution to an examination of freedom and responsibility. He observes that this is only one way of proceeding ("talk about talk" we may say), which he justifies on the grounds that "our common stock of words embodies all the distinctions men have found worth drawing, and the connections they have found worth marking, in the lifetime of many generations". This, in turn, means that we can learn important things about freedom and responsibility by attending to what we find appropriate and inappropriate to say. As he insists, this is "not merely looking at words . . . but also at the realities we use words to talk about". Once again, this sounds very like Aristotle's method of "setting down the appearances (*phainomena*)" and attending to "the things that we say (*ta legomena*)".[27]

Elizabeth Anscombe (no admirer of Ryle's philosophy) and Philippa Foot, distinctive as each is, and different from Ryle and Austin, nevertheless also shape their projects around the relationships between philosophical psychology and moral philosophy. Moreover, in doing so, they too appeal to Aristotle. For many years now, a small number of philosophers in the analytic tradition have been reading Aristotle, but also Thomas Aquinas, more or less obviously, in ways which enable them to resist, criticise and reshape the agenda in ethics. Few as these philosophers are, they have exercised an influence far beyond their tiny number. Through them, Thomas has long been an important resource, with some of his key ideas incorporated, anonymously or obliquely, into mainstream philosophy.

As Hayden Ramsey notes, analytic philosophers owe gratitude to Thomists—and other Aristotelians—for initiating and extending the retrieval of "virtue ethics".[28] By the same token, Thomists, and others concerned with Christian ethics, owe gratitude to analytic philosophers. Indeed, as John Greco notes, analytic philosophy and Thomism have long been natural allies, in regard to ethics, though on neither side is this much understood or appreciated.[29]

Here again, the existence of lively debates within analytic philosophy seem unknown to Thomists. It is, of course, excusable to disregard analytic philosophy as offering little or nothing to Thomists or Christian theologians in general. For example, many philosophers in the analytic tradition defend, and have defended for over fifty years, positions and projects, which belong to the family of utilitarian theories. These might simply be regarded as wrong. That does not mean that the entire tradition can be ignored. On the contrary, there is a debate. Versions of emotivist and utilitarian ethics have been extremely controversial for half a century. It is hard to understand why philosophers interested in inquiry and argument should avoid engaging in this debate.

Nor is this a merely academic matter. Utilitarianism, after all, is not just a cluster of theories. On the contrary, in societies like ours in which success, achievement, happiness, *et cetera* are measured in economic terms, utilitarianism as a philosophical theory expresses the view of life (love, family, death, and so on) that determines political and social planning, as well as the individual's desires and aspirations.

The antecedents are well known. In John Stuart Mill's statement of the position (first in *Fraser's Magazine* in 1861), "actions are right in proportion as they tend to promote happiness, wrong as they tend to produce the reverse of happiness". As every first-year philosophy student knows, Mill's conception of happiness recognised qualitative differences between different kinds of pleasure ("better a Socrates satisfied than a pig satisfied"), over against the position expounded in 1789 by his great predecessor Jeremy Bentham ("other things being equal, pushpin is as good as poetry").

To many people now, Mill sounds aristocratic and elitist; Bentham, on the other hand, seems to voice in advance the values of our pluralistic egalitarian mass culture. Such views frequently go with emotivism ("it's right if it feels right to me"): the function of ethical utterances in conversation is to express emotional or affective states of one's soul, rather than to state truth or falsehoods about what is the case in the realm of actions or events. The emotive theory first appears in the inaugural years of analytic philosophy, at Cambridge. The classical text is *The Meaning of Meaning* (1923) by C. K. Ogden and I. A. Richards. Little read nowadays by philosophers, or anyone else, the book amounts to a manifesto for the "technologico-Benthamite age".[30]

Ogden, at Bertrand Russell's suggestion, had translated Wittgenstein's *Tractatus Logico-Philosophicus* (thus inviting the wholly misguided logical-positivist reading). He went on to invent Basic ("British American Scientific International Commercial") English: surviving in a diluted form in programmes for teaching English to foreigners but originally much more ambitiously intended to replace "ordinary language" by the kind of logically perfect ideal language recommended by Russell. Richards had already introduced "analytical" methods into literary criticism. He distinguishes between the referential use of language and the emotive use, poetry being concerned exclusively with the latter, and as having a "therapeutic" function. Almost single-handedly, Richards created the New Criticism which dominated literary studies in American universities for decades.

Much more might be said. This perhaps suffices to indicate the roots of the utilitarian and emotivist components of Anglo-American culture in the early years of what would become analytic philosophy. Under such labels as expressivism, non-cognitivism, quasi-realism, projectivism, *et cetera*, the theories continue to proliferate. Prevalent as these ideas are in standard moral and political discourse in the English-speaking world (not only there!), as well as in the theorising of many analytic philosophers, their authority has never gone unchallenged.

Without tracing the genealogy back to the beginning, we must content ourselves here by highlighting a few of the classics in the canon of the long resistance to the hegemony of non-cognitivist utilitarian ethics. The point to be established is that the opposition within analytic philosophy to these ideas owes a good deal to philosophers who have studied the work of Thomas Aquinas.

IV

To begin with, as a glance into any history of analytic philosophy would show, the revolt against the versions of moral philosophy we have just sketched is usually dated from Elizabeth Anscombe's paper "Modern Moral Philosophy", published in 1958.[31]

Anscombe did not think of herself as practising analytic philosophy, as distinct from some other kind, even less as doing "linguistic analysis". She never shows any knowledge of, let alone interest in, Nietzsche, Husserl, Heidegger and the like. This does not mean that she was indifferent to the history of philosophy, as English-speaking philosophers have often been accused of being. She published a dozen notable essays on earlier philosophers including Parmenides, Plato, Aristotle, Hume and Brentano, as well as Aquinas and Wittgenstein, nearly all deserving and indeed demanding close attention. The seminal paper itself includes a reading of the history of philosophy.

The main theme is as follows. We should jettison the concepts of moral obligation and moral duty, of what is morally right and wrong, and of the moral sense of "ought"—"if this is psychologically possible"—on the grounds that these are "survivals, or derivatives from survivals, from an earlier conception of ethics which no longer generally survives"—these concepts "are only harmful without it". These concepts, in Anscombe's view, depend for their sense on belief in God as lawgiver and judge—a belief which, she thinks, few in our society now retain. That is why, she thinks, the concepts now only do harm: it is a form of false consciousness to go on using moral language which is now uprooted and detached from its original home in biblical revelation. We need to take the "moral" out of ethics and return to something like the philosophy of psychology to be found in pre-Christian thinkers such as Aristotle. This means that we need to rehabilitate the concept of virtues as "excellences"—intellectual as well as social skills.

Anscombe never mentions Thomas Aquinas. It is solely to Aristotle that she directs philosophers who seek to break out of the Kantian ethics which is now so injurious, as she thinks, in a post-Christian culture. Anscombe's book *Intention*, a classic in twentieth-century English-speaking philosophy— ninety-four pages in length—appeared in 1957. Here again, while she refers a few times to Aristotle and to Wittgenstein, she does not make anything of Aquinas.

It seems to have been her work on translating Wittgenstein's *Investigations*, and no doubt many conversations with Wittgenstein himself, that allowed her to see that, in his relatively few and always somewhat enigmatic remarks about intentions and reasons for action, she had the basis of powerful arguments against behaviourist attempts to explain action in mechanistic-causal terms; or, more positively, she could have the clues to retrieve something like Aristotle's concept of practical reasoning.[32]

Readers of *Intention* are usually left dissatisfiedly wondering what an intention is; it takes many re-readings to understand that what Anscombe means us to see is that we do not need to ask. There is no such thing as we think an intention is—or so she contends. Of course, not everyone agrees with her. Intentions, we are strongly inclined to think, are antecedent events inside our heads which explain our intentional actions.[33] For many philosophers, this supposition is translated into the theory that intentional actions are movements caused by certain mental states or events, the occurrence of which explain the occurrence of these movements. Of course there are many variations on this causalist thesis; but Anscombe's objection, to put it simply, is that, whereas causalist theories are all supposedly very "scientific", they only substitute neurophysiological occurrences for the hypostatised introspectable mental items we are more likely to postulate. While there may in fact often be mental events which immediately precede intentional actions— hesitations, qualms, calculations, and so on—most of what we do intentionally (Anscombe wants us to remember) is neither preceded nor accompanied by such occurrences.

In short, prompted by her reading of Wittgenstein, Anscombe treats as a myth the parade of mental events that supposedly determine one's intentional acts. She reminds us of the obvious fact that our psychological concepts are grounded in the natural reactions and attitudes that we have to the world. In other words, most of what we do, intentionally, purposely, voluntarily, is provoked or guided by events in the world, and happens without our having to stop and think—which does not mean that it is unintelligent and unintentional. On the contrary, Anscombe wants us to see that our actions and reactions can be intended, reasonable, and explicable, though not preceded or accompanied by our first entertaining thoughts and intentions. Indeed, she might say, this is how things usually are. As Wittgenstein famously remarked: "voluntary movement is marked by the absence of surprise".[34]

V

The project of getting the word "moral" out of ethical discourse and returning to something like Aristotle's account of what we call "virtue" as one kind of "excellence" among others was not advanced very far by Anscombe; it has been brilliantly achieved by Philippa Foot. They were colleagues. Foot's first published papers appeared in 1957. When she collected her papers in 1978 she dedicated the book to Iris Murdoch, expressed gratitude to Donald MacKinnon as her first teacher in moral philosophy, and referred to many lunchtime discussions with Elizabeth Anscombe.[35] In her second collection, published in 2002, Foot repeats her gratitude to Anscombe, this time thanking her specifically for helping her to see the wrong-headedness of the distinction between "evaluative" and "descriptive" language. Finally, as she writes in the preface to her recent book, *Natural Goodness*, "It will be obvious that I owe most to the work of Elizabeth Anscombe, and to early discussion with her".[36]

The essay "Virtues and Vices" which opens the first collection mentions Thomas Aquinas in the second paragraph—"it is best when considering the virtues and vices to go back to Aristotle and Aquinas". Foot has already referred to herself, in the very first sentence of the essay, as a moralist "working within the school of analytic philosophy". Foot contends that we can learn a great deal from Aquinas that is not in Aristotle: "It is my opinion that the *Summa Theologica* is one of the best sources we have for moral philosophy, and moreover that St Thomas's ethical writings are as useful to the atheist as to the Catholic or other Christian believer". Again: "it was reading Aquinas on the individual virtues that first made me suspicious of contemporary theories about the relation between 'fact' and 'value' ".[37]

We may surely assume that Foot and Anscombe discussed Aquinas together during some of their lunchtime conversations. Foot's moral philosophy remains a minority enterprise—the majority of Anglo-American moralists (Catholics included) defend some version of utilitarianism, often accompanied by some non-cognitivist theory. Nevertheless, as a quick glance through the current journals would show, moral realism, or ethical naturalism, flourishes; and Foot's name appears.

Natural Goodness—at just under one hundred and twenty pages—is longer but will clearly also, like Anscombe's *Intention*, become a classic of modern moral philosophy.[38] Here, in wonderfully lucid prose and with many examples from current politics and ethics, Foot sets herself against the whole sub-jectivist movement in ethics, deriving (as she assumes) from David Hume. She ranges over such topics as practical rationality, erring conscience, and the relation between virtue and happiness, ending with a critique of Nietzsche's immoralism.

The main theme, to simplify, is that evaluations of human will and action have the same conceptual structure as evaluations of characteristics and operations of other living things: "Life will be at the centre of my discussion, and the fact that a human action or disposition is good of its kind will be taken to be simply a fact about a given feature of a certain kind of living thing".[39]

Foot takes up Anscombe's discussion of promising: "getting one another to do things without the application of physical force is a necessity for human life". This is what Anscombe, a little arcanely, called an "Aristotelian necessity"—"that which is necessary because and in so far as good hangs on it".[40] In the sense that it is necessary for plants to have water, for birds to build nests, for wolves to hunt in packs, and so on, and of course allowing for the vast differences embodied in culture and language, so Foot maintains, human necessities, and that means skills at coping, are similarly related to what human beings are and what they do. For example, human parents are simply failures to the extent that they do not teach their young the basic skills they need to survive. Quite seriously, Foot likens the basis of moral evalua-tion to the basis of the evaluation of behaviour in animals. For human beings, she argues, the following and teaching of morality is something necessary, vital, for our survival, just as flying is for birds, *et cetera*.

What Foot likes is the thought that the evaluation of moral action is set in the wider context of the evaluation of other features of human life but also of evaluative judgements of the characteristics and operations of other living things. There is nothing unique or *sui generis* about moral behaviour—what is morally good or bad is what is positive or negative for the kind of living beings that we humans are. The "moral" is an aspect of what is "natural" for our kind.

Foot never evinces the least interest in religion. For Aquinas, as she of course knows, all living things are creatures—there are certain necessities about how they are to behave if they are to flourish, certainly, but Aquinas's account of flourishing is ultimately theocentric. Yet, Foot urges, philosophers should not be embarrassed to recognise teleological language. It is not merely a leftover from theology. On the contrary, natural-teleological judge-ments, as she calls them, organise and articulate the necessities and capaci-ties of our form of life.

Foot cites Peter Geach: "Men need virtues as bees need stings".[41] The nat-uralistic theory of ethics which Foot keeps on the analytic-philosophical agenda is mainly Aristotelian—but there is no doubt that it is deeply indebted also to her years of studying Thomas Aquinas.

VI

In the work of philosophers such as Anscombe and Geach it is difficult, and ultimately fruitless, to separate ethics from philosophical psychology, logic from epistemology, metaphysics from natural theology. As just noted, we could have taken Geach instead of Foot as an example of the interaction of moral philosophy and the study of Aquinas. Another of the ways in which Geach has affected developments in the last half-century of English-speaking philosophy is, however, his contribution to the dislodging of "abstractionism".[42]

Mental Acts is a wholesale attack on *The Concept of Mind*. Basically, "the entire programme seems to me misconceived".[43] According to Geach, reports of mental acts are logically different from reports of physical events, and here he cites Wittgenstein and Aquinas in support; but Ryle's view is that psychological statements, while not reports of mental acts understood as private events, are hypothetical statements about overt behaviour—and that's all.

In other words, Ryle may have learnt from Wittgenstein to reject the picture of mental acts as radically private events inaccessible to anyone else—but he has succumbed to a crassly behaviourist alternative. Admittedly, Geach concedes, Ryle is inconsistent: he allows some reports of mental acts without translating them into hypothetical statements about overt behaviour, though his deflationary practice of referring to them as "itches", "tingles", "tweaks" and suchlike, as Geach says, is "highly depreciatory". Mainly, however, Ryle runs "counter to a very deep-rooted way of thinking", by explicitly and repeatedly comparing psychological accounts of behaviour to physical events. The ways we picture "the mind" are potentially misleading, Ryle sees, and indeed the philosophers he calls "the Cartesians" have, he thinks, been misled into picturing the mind as "the ghost in the machine", the agent or site of mysterious non-physical states, happenings, and acts. Yet, he keeps suggesting the radically different account, according to which all talk seemingly about what is going on in one's mind is really only a way of talking about one's body. Contrary to what ordinary ways of speaking suggest, there really are only physical objects and physical happenings.

Ryle's view is perhaps more ambivalent than Geach's polemic allows. Ryle's adoption of Wittgenstein's attack on the Cartesian self was threatened with misunderstanding, given the way that he opted for a semi-behaviourist reduction of the mind as the alternative.[44] Overtly, *Mental Acts* is an attack on Ryle's behaviourist tendencies but, less obviously, Geach is even more dismissive of Aquinas's "soi-disant followers".[45] They are inclined to abstractionism, a complete misreading of Aquinas.

By abstractionism Geach means the assumption that psychological words are given a sense "privately", by the private and uncheckable performance of consulting one's own psychological experiences (another version of psychologism in effect). Those who hold this view need to notice Frege's distinction between sense (*Sinn*) and reference (*Bedeutung*). What Wittgenstein denied was not the private reference of psychological expressions—that "pain" stands for an experience that may be totally "private" (I grit my teeth, you have no idea that I am in pain at all; I am much more sensitive than you, it is no surprise that you don't understand how acute the pain I have is; etc.). Wittgenstein's point was that psychological expressions could not receive a sense, by our just attending to our experiences.

The classical statement of abstractionism, Geach says, is to be found in Locke: psychological concepts are abstractively derived from inner experience; we are supposed to possess a quasi-sense that is related to mental occurrences in much the same way as our senses are to physical occurrences.[46]

According to Geach—though he names no names—many would-be Thomists are abstractionists, in the sense he has defined. This is despite the fact that Aquinas himself holds anti-abstractionist views. In comparing the mind's concept-forming power with a light that enables the mind's eye to see the intelligible features of things, on analogy with how the bodily eye sees colours, Aquinas is careful to note that the analogy works only if we take it that colours are generated by kindling the light. In other words, the light does not just reveal colours that already existed in the dark, so to speak (cf. *ST* 1a 79, 3 ad 2). Moreover, when he says that we frame a judgement in words, our use of concepts is to be compared, not with seeing something, but rather with forming a visual image of something we are not now actually seeing, or even never have seen (*ST* 1a, 85, 2 ad 3).

In other words, both as regards the formation and as regards the exercise of concepts Aquinas rejects abstractionism—forming or having a concept never means being able to recognise some feature we have found in direct experience; rather, the mind makes concepts. "We must resist the perennial philosophical temptation to think that if a thought is to be true to reality, then it must copy it feature by feature, like a map".[47]

VII

Much more might be said about the interaction of analytic philosophers with the study of Aquinas. Most Thomists have little interest in analytic philosophy, as we noted (§I). This is less excusable than it perhaps used to be, now that the origins of analytic philosophy are being explored: Brentano's Aristotelian-Thomist thesis helped to constitute the analytic-philosophical school (§II). Admittedly, the moral philosophy that has dominated for decades is incompatible with Catholic Christian ethics (§III). On the other hand, in the work of Anscombe (§IV) and Foot (§V), we have very fine philosophers who challenge the dominant utilitarian/emotivist ethics, appealing to Aristotle but clearly with Aquinas in the background. That analytic philosophy has never been a monolithic homogeneous tradition is plain: there has always been debate. To a philosopher trained on Frege's distinction between reference and sense, many would-be Thomists have been inclined to misread Aquinas in Cartesian/empiricist terms (§VI).[48]

This does not mean, however, that competent readers of Aquinas are always happy with the use made of Aquinas by analytic philosophers. M. W. F. Stone, for example, argues that talk of Aquinas's naturalistic theory of ethics is highly contentious.[49] At its weakest the theory holds that moral predicates can be identified somehow or other with facts about the natural world. More strongly, naturalism in ethics is the idea that goodness and rightness can be related to a set of natural properties. In whatever form, naturalism rejects any theory according to which moral properties are unique and *sui generis*.

According to Stone, however, Aquinas cannot be "hijacked" to produce a naturalist ethics or for that matter an anti-naturalist theory. There are important texts, which simply contradict each other. In one passage, much cited by proponents of naturalistic ethics, Aquinas writes as follows: "all things to which men have a natural inclination are naturally apprehended by reason as being good, and consequently as objects of pursuit" (*ST* 1–2.94.2). In other words, our moral ends are natural ends, much as Philippa Foot contends.

On the other hand, in an equally important passage Aquinas writes this: "moral ends are only accidentally related to a natural thing, the notion of a natural end is accidental to the moral end" (*ST* 1–2. 1, 3 ad 3). This seems an explicit denial that the object of a moral end is supplied by anything natural. Here, the moral and the natural seem quite clearly distinct, and quite specifically the idea that the moral can be founded on the natural seems to be excluded.

Stone's argument, positively expressed, is that we have to attend to Aquinas's account of the roles of reason and will in his explanation of human action. By the standards of modern ethical naturalism, he contends, what Thomas says is bound to appear ambiguous. His anxiety about much recent appeal to Aquinas in virtue ethics stems from his suspicions of the desire to connect goodness and rightness with facts in the natural world. This would simply have been incomprehensible to Aquinas. Like all the medievals, Thomas was concerned, in ethics, to develop a theory of practical conduct in which the agent's actions would be judged from the perspective of the ultimate end. In short, curtailment or suspension of the theocentric intention of Aquinas's ethical considerations is bound to distort his account.

Even here, however, one might contend that analytical-philosophical misreadings, if that is what they are, sharpen understanding of what Thomas actually means—thus bringing him and philosophers of the analytical school into the kind of debate, in metaphysics and in ethics, which both he and they would regard as essential.[50]

NOTES

1 For Wittgensteinian Thomism see Roger Pouivet, *Après Wittgenstein, saint Thomas* (Paris: PUF 1997), discussing G. E. M. Anscombe, P. T. Geach and Anthony Kenny; and for Analytical Thomism see *The Monist* Vol. 80 (1997), pp. 485–618; *New Blackfriars* Vol. 80 (1999), pp. 158–216, edited by John Haldane, with Select Bibliography, pp. 214–216, including work by Anscombe, Geach, Kenny, and Haldane himself, as well as David Burrell, Brian Davies, John Finnis, Norman Kretzmann, Alasdair MacIntyre, Christopher Martin, Herbert McCabe, Hugo Meynell, Hayden Ramsay, James Ross, Eleanore Stump, Linda Zagzebski, among others.

2 *Faith and Reason* Encyclical Letter of Pope John Paul II (London: Catholic Truth Society 1998).

3 *New Blackfriars* Vol. 80 (1999), p. 168.

4 First published in 1914 and 1913 respectively, these essays appear in Bertrand Russell, *Mysticism and Logic and Other Essays* (London: George Allen & Unwin, 1963).

5 See for example Hilary Putnam, *Reason, Truth and History* (Cambridge: Cambridge University Press 1981).

6 *New Blackfriars* Vol. 80 (1999), p. 175.

7 Some say "analytic", others say "analytical": it seems purely a matter of euphony.

8 Richard Rorty, *Consequences of Pragmatism* (Minneapolis, MN: University of Minnesota Press, 1982), passim.

9 Samuel C. Wheeler III, *Deconstruction as Analytic Philosophy* (Stanford, CA: Stanford University Press, 2000).

10 Henry Staten, *Wittgenstein and Derrida* (Oxford: Basil Blackwell, 1985).

11 Simon Glendinning, *On being with others—Heidegger-Derrida-Wittgenstein* (London: Routledge, 1998).

12 J. E. Malpas, *Donald Davidson and the Mirror of Meaning : Holism, Truth, Interpretation* (Cambridge: Cambridge University Press, 1992).

13 Michael Dummett, *Origins of Analytical Philosophy* (London: Duckworth, 1993).

14 In the now quite extensive literature see *Midwest Studies in Philosophy Volume VI: The Foundations of Analytic Philosophy* edited by Peter A. French and others, (Minneapolis, MN: University of Minnesota Press, 1981) and more recently P. M. S. Hacker, *Wittgenstein's Place in Twentieth-century Analytic Philosophy* (Oxford: Blackwell, 1996); *The Story of Analytic Philosophy: Plot and Heroes* edited by Anat Biletzki and Anat Matar (London: Routledge, 1998); *The Rise of Analytic Philosophy* edited by Hans-Johann Glock (Oxford: Blackwell, 1997); *Early Analytic Philosophy: Frege, Russell, Wittgenstein* edited by William W. Tait (Chicago, IL: Open Court, 1997); and *Future Pasts: The Analytic Tradition in Twentieth-Century Philosophy* edited by Juliet Floyd and Sanford Shieh (Oxford: Oxford University Press, 2001).

15 Dummett, p. ix.

16 Bored by reading doctorate dissertations running to 100,000 words by recent graduates, Ryle took the lead at the University of Oxford in creating the B.Phil., three stiff papers and a compact, rigorously argued dissertation of 30,000 words, for the elite; still regarded (not only at Oxford) as the most testing qualification for teaching analytic philosophy.

17 Dummett, pp. ix–x; Ryle's review of Heidegger's *Sein und Zeit* might have been mentioned, in *Mind* (1929), reprinted in Gilbert Ryle, *Collected Papers* volume 1 (London: Hutcheson, 1971); it might even be that *The Concept of Mind*, that classic of "Oxford philosophy", owes a good deal to the philosophical anthropology which Ryle found in *Sein und Zeit*.

18 Bolzano, ordained as a Catholic priest in 1805, much too early for him to be any kind of Thomist, belonged to the "Bohemian Enlightenment"; he was forced out of the ministry in 1819 by imperial decree on account of supposed heterodoxy and political unreliability.

19 Dummett, p. 171.

20 Originally in *Proceedings of the Aristotelian Society* NS Vol. 59 (1959), pp. 141–162; reprinted in Michael Dummett, *Truth and Other Enigmas* (London: Duckworth, 1978).

21 For Brentano see *The Philosophy of Brentano* edited by Linda L. McAlister (London: Duckworth, 1976).

22 Gilbert Ryle, *The Concept of Mind* (London: Hutchinson, 1949).

23 It was probably through the Cambridge philosopher/psychologist G. F. Stout (1860–1944) that Brentano's thesis reached Bertrand Russell and G. E. Moore.

24 Dummett, p. 4: "What distinguishes analytical philosophy, in its diverse manifestations, from other schools is the belief, first, that a philosophical account of thought can be attained

through a philosophical account of language, and, secondly, that a comprehensive account can only be so attained".

25   Dummett, p. 170.
26   Dummett, p. 168: "I thought he was a very clever man, but I felt his influence on philosophy to be noxious"—through the formalization of Austin's *How To Do Things With Words* (Oxford 1961), the posthumously published text of lectures at Harvard in 1955, particularly by John Searle, *Speech Acts* (Cambridge, 1919) "speech-act theory" has spread quite widely into literary criticism and theory and into feminist theory (as in Judith Butler). "A Plea for Excuses", Austin's Presidential Address to the Aristotelian Society in 1956, appears in his *Philosophical Papers* edited by J. O. Urmson and G. J. Warnock (Oxford: Clarendon Press, 1961).
27   Aristotle, *Nicomachean Ethics* 1145b1ff; see the seminal essay by G. E. L. Owen, "Tithenai ta phainomena", in Suzanne Mansion, ed., *Aristote et les problèmes de méthodes* (Louvain, Publications Universitaires, 1961), pp. 83–103.
28   *New Blackfriars* Vol. 80 (1999), p. 198.
29   "Whereas almost all of Continental philosophy has gone 'post modern', Anglo-American philosophy continues to defend truth and objectivity. Ironically, analytic philosophy has become the natural ally of Thomism and Catholic philosophy. But old images die hard. The developments in analytic philosophy that have turned it from natural enemy to natural ally have gone largely unnoticed by Thomist philosophers, largely because of the historical, institutional and cultural barriers that are now firmly in place." *New Blackfriars* Vol. 80 (1999), pp. 182–183.
30   F. R. Leavis, *English Literature in Our Time and the University* (London; Chatto & Windus, 1969), passim.
31   Originally in *Philosophy* Vol. 33 (1958), reprinted in her *Collected Philosophical Papers Volume III* (Oxford: Basil Blackwell, 1981).
32   The thesis is worked out in much greater detail by Charles Taylor, *The Explanation of Behaviour* (London: Routledge, 1964).
33   See Rosalind Hursthouse, "Intention", in *Logic, Cause and Action: Essays in honour of Elizabeth Anscombe* edited by Roger Teichmann (Cambridge: Cambridge University Press 2000), pp. 83–105—a collection which is the best introduction to the seminal contributions Anscombe has made to metaphysics, ethics, and the philosophy of mind and action.
34   Ludwig Wittgenstein, *Philosophical Investigations*, translated by G. E. M. Anscombe (Oxford: Blackwell, 1953), §628.
35   Philippa Foot, *Virtues and Vices and other essays in moral philosophy* (Oxford: Blackwell, 1981). Iris Murdoch, hostile to Aristotle, preferred to retrieve Plato to combat the antimetaphysical ethics of the day; see *The Sovereignty of Good* (London: Routledge, 1970); Donald M. MacKinnon was one of the most influential teachers of ethics and philosophical theology at Oxford, Aberdeen and finally Cambridge.
36   Elizabeth Anscombe died on 5 January 2001, a few weeks short of her eighty-second birthday.
37   Philippa Foot, *Virtues and Vices*, pp. 1–2.
38   Philippa Foot, *Natural Goodness* (Oxford: Clarendon Press, 2001).
39   Philippa Foot, *Natural Goodness*, p. 5.
40   Philippa Foot, *Natural Goodness*, p. 15; citing Anscombe, *Collected Philosophical Papers Volume III*, p. 18.
41   Peter Geach, *The Virtues* (Cambridge: Cambridge University Press, 1977), p. 17; one of the first contributions to "virtue ethics", largely a reading of Thomas Aquinas, *Summa Theologiae*, 1-2 and 2-2.
42   Peter Geach, *Mental Acts: Their content and their objects* (London: Routledge, n.d. but actually 1957).
43   Geach, 4.
44   Ryle and Wittgenstein were friends in the 1930s; in 1942, after considering the question, Wittgenstein said that Ryle was one of the only two philosophers who understood his work, see Ray Monk, *Ludwig Wittgenstein: The Duty of Genius* (London: Jonathan Cape, 1990), p. 436 (the other was no doubt Rush Rhees).
45   Peter Geach, *Mental Acts*, p. 131.
46   Peter Geach, *Mental Acts*, p. 21.

47   Peter Geach, *Mental Acts*, p. 41.
48   P. J. FitzPatrick, an analytically trained philosopher with a sound knowledge also of
      Aquinas, deals with neoThomism very succinctly: "Neoscholasticism", in *The Cambridge
      History of Later Medieval Philosophy* edited by Norman Kretzmann and others (Cambridge:
      Cambridge University Press, 1982), pp. 838–852.
49   "Practical Reason and the Orders of Morals and Nature in Aquinas's Theory of the *Lex
      Naturae*", in *Mind, Metaphysics, and Value in the Thomistic and Analytical Traditions* edited by
      John Haldane (Notre Dame, IN: Notre Dame University Press, 2002), pp. 195–212.
50   In metaphysics the seminal essay is by Peter Geach, in *Three Philosophers* by G. E. M.
      Anscombe and P. T. Geach (Oxford: Basil Blackwell, 1961), pp. 65–125; the other two
      philosophers are Aristotle and Frege; for a brief but impressive argument that Geach's
      Fregean reading converts Thomist realism into Scotist conceptualism see Stephen Theron,
      "The resistance of Thomism to analytical and other patronage", *The Monist* Vol. 80 (1997),
      pp. 611–618; for a sympathetic reading see *The Philosophy of Thomas Aquinas Introductory
      Readings* edited by Christopher Martin (London: Routledge, 1988).

7

ON DENYING THE RIGHT GOD: AQUINAS ON ATHEISM AND IDOLATRY

DENYS TURNER

Eadem est scientia oppositorum, says Aristotle in the Latin translation of the *Peri Hermeneias*[1] with which Thomas Aquinas was familiar: "one and the same is the knowledge of opposites", or, "to know an affirmative proposition is to know what would count as its negation". You would think, on that account, that a theologian as much preoccupied with the logic of "God exists" as is Thomas would accordingly have something to say about the logic of atheism, about the logic of the proposition "There is no God". For, just as (in the spirit of Aristotle's remark) the analytic philosophers used to ask concerning some proposed assertion or other, "that *as opposed to* what?", so Thomas in that connection seemed often to share the analytic disposition.[2] Alas for the author commissioned to write on my subject, it is hard to find material in Thomas which relates in any very direct way to those issues of explicit theoretical atheism which arise for us today. We all know that professed atheism was not a theological issue in Thomas' time, nor was it for several centuries thereafter, largely because there were no intellectuals professing it. Thomas evidently did not feel intellectually challenged by what we today know of as atheism and, for all that I will argue for a view which differs from them in many another respect, I do share the opinion of the theologians of the "nouvelle théologie" persuasion that even the famous "five ways" are not intended at least primarily as a response to an atheist challenge, but have rather different purposes.

I used to maintain that if not Aquinas, then Anselm thought that at least in principle a theologian needs to sort out what an atheist position looked like, for though he does not explicitly acknowledge Aristotle's *mot* in that

Denys Turner
The Divinity School, University of Cambridge, West Road, Cambridge CB3 9BS, UK

place, Anselm does note in *Proslogion* 2 that the fool who says in his heart "there is no God" must know what he is denying—that is to say, must deny what the true believer affirms—if his denials are to have any properly atheistic effect. At any rate I took it to be Anselm's view that there is not any real argument to be had with an atheist unless theist and atheist alike agree on what it *means* to say "God exists"—for they would have to agree on that much if the one is to be affirming what the other denies; and that if the atheist can be got to see what exactly it is that he is denying, his position can be shown to be logically self-defeating. But I have been persuaded by my colleagues in Cambridge, Anna Williams and Catherine Pickstock, that what is bothering Anselm in the *Proslogion* is not some atheistical position of *intellectual* denial, but rather the spiritual condition of the fool whose lips acknowledge God but whose *heart* is not in it: for it is "in his heart" that this fool says there is no God.[3] On this account, therefore, what we get in the *Proslogion* is less a formal argument against professed atheism than a persuasion offered to the nominally professing theist that his life of indifference to God is a bundle of practical contradictions.

Knowing what Atheistically to Deny

Which considerations lead one back to Thomas and to the possibility that there is a parallel strategy in his theology, of promise for today's author in pursuit of Thomas' views on atheism. If Thomas has little—perhaps nothing—to say about atheism in any modern sense, does he not have a great deal to say about what might seem to be its equivalent in his time, namely idolatry? And there is indeed promise here, in so far as much of Thomas' preoccupation with the logic of "God exists" seems to be motivated by a desire to insure against the innumerable ways in which one can "get God wrong": worship the wrong God, pray to the wrong God, love the wrong God and even perhaps *deny* the wrong God—the latter, of course, being what the theist and a certain kind of atheist both do, the one in the conduct of good theology, the other concluding (mistakenly) that in seeing off an idolatry he has succeeded in seeing God off *tout court*. Hence, we might say that the value in Thomas' account of the logic of "God exists" for us today, preoccupied as we are with all sorts of theoretical atheisms, lies in his setting some pretty high standards for truly atheistical denial: unless, dear atheist, you are denying what the true believer affirms, all you are doing is rejecting an idolatry that the true believer anyway rejects (I suppose Richard Dawkins springs to mind as being among the softer targets) and are engaging in the sort of conceptual ground-clearing which is the proper preliminary to any positive theology. Doing this is what we sometimes call today (as Thomas did in his) "negative theology". To put it as briefly as I may, a true atheist has to work hard and fast at his denials if he is to keep up with Thomas' "we do not know what God is",[4] never mind to get ahead of him with a convincing "there is no God". Most atheists of my acquaintance today know all too well what they are denying.

Of course to a simple-minded atheist of the Dawkins sort (a sort which elsewhere I have described as a "parasitical" or "mirror-image" atheist[5]) negative theology will seem like a mere intellectual evasion: he will naturally insist on some hard and limited proposition of the kind his sort of limited denials are good for, and negative theology can sometimes be mistakenly represented as if to disallow any affirmation of God, leaving the atheist with apparently nothing to do. But even those atheists who do take negative theology seriously, such as Jacques Derrida, and concede that a non-idolatrous God is going to have to be "on the other side of language"—or, as they acknowledge the pseudo-Denys to say, as speaking with an authentic theological voice, God is "beyond both similarity and difference", which is the same thing—will balk at what appears to be surreptitious re-insertion of a spurious "hyper-essentiality" hidden in the "to be": "to be on the other side of language" is, it would seem, an oxymoron. For on which side of language is this "to be" itself supposed to lie? If on the "inside of language", then this may give us a notion of the divine existence which is intelligible, but just because it is intelligible must affirm an idolatrously onto-theological God, an instance of "being". And if on the "other side of language" how can there be anything asserted by this "to be"? A God so different as to be "on the other side of language" is, therefore, reducible to the ultimacy not of God, but of "difference" itself: not, that is, that "there is" *an* ultimate difference, ontological or otherwise—for that would still seem to imply that there is a something or other which is "ultimately different"—but that it is difference itself which is ultimate, and so not God. It seems that the "to be" will have to go altogether, conceding its place at best to some God "without being", as Marion would have us say.[6]

Of course Thomas does not know of such issues in those terms, but in his own terms he is perfectly alive to them. Today we might ask: Does negative theology, as a means of avoiding an idolatrous onto-theology, entail a merely vacuous God, a God of pure undifferentiation or—which might seem to be the opposite of that, but is not—a God who is nothing but difference itself, alterity as such, the *tout autre*, which, as Derrida says, could not be the "bringer of good gifts",[7] and so could not be God? But Thomas himself acknowledges that there is an equivalent problem with his doctrine of the divine simplicity—the root, as he says so clearly and emphatically, of his negative theology.[8] And this is because, in turn, he locates the root meaning of God's simplicity in the identity of God's *essentia* and *esse*,[9] to which doctrine the quasi-derridean objection rather obviously re-surfaces, one which Thomas takes seriously enough to feel constrained to offer a complex and difficult response. If God's *esse* and God's *essentia* were identical, he objects,[10] if God is to be described as *ipsum esse subsistens*, it would seem to follow that God's existence (*esse*) is an existence of no particular kind—"unspecific existence". From that it would seem further to follow that the name "God" would simply name "existence in general", that is, unspecifically any kind of existence, whether created or uncreated—and this would appear fatally to break a firm rule of Thomas' own devising concerning the logic of *esse*: *esse per se convenit formae* . . .[11]—it makes no sense to speak of *esse* but of no particular kind.

Now this would seem to be a telling objection, particularly as posed for so enthusiastic a follower of the pseudo-Denys as Thomas, for the pseudo-Denys's famous saying "there is no kind of thing that God is"[12] could easily be interpreted as entailing the consequence: "God exists, but his existence is of no kind; hence, God is, unspecifically, 'existence as such' ". In turn, that could be interpreted in one of two ways: either as meaning that "God" names the overarching category of "being" of which all beings other than God are instances, from which the pantheistic consequence would follow that all created beings are "instances" of God; or else as meaning that both God and creatures are instances falling under the general category of "being". Both would be forms, one supposes, of onto-theological error, since either way the difference between God and creatures would be reduced to that which could obtain between "beings" belonging to the same, albeit most general possible, category.

God as "Pure Act"

The objection can be put in another way, equally problematic for Thomas' negative theology and in turn for the doctrine of the divine simplicity, insofar as both are rooted in the related doctrine that God is "pure act". This is a closely related doctrine because, of course, for Thomas, the fundamental meaning of *esse* is as "act", "actualization", just as also the fundamental mean of "act" or "actualization" is that in which it is *esse* that actualizes. You refer to a thing's *esse* not when you consider it as this rather than that, nor when you consider it as this kind of thing rather than that kind of thing; nor even (in its most fundamental sense) when you consider its existence by contrast with *its* non-existence, but when you consider its existence by contrast with there being nothing at all: in short, for anything created, when you consider it precisely in its character *as* created. A thing's *esse* is what God has brought about so that it should be at all, and the divine action of creating is always set against the "background" of that *ex nihilo*—which is not, of course, a "background" at all, for "nothingness" is not some context within which God creates. As Thomas says, it is not the case that when God creates "out of nothing" the "nothing" is some sort of soupy negative "something" which God makes things out of. The negation, he says, negates the "out of" itself, as if to say: there is a sort of making here, but no "out of", just as when we say that a person is "speaking of nothing" we do not mean that "nothing" is the subject of his speech (as it might be with Heidegger) but that he is not speaking at all.[13] For which reason, when speaking of God "as the source of *esse*" as McCabe rightly says, we are speaking of "the being of the thing not just over against a world-without-it, but over against nothing, not even 'logical space'".[14]

Of course, for Thomas, "act" has many other meanings—or at least uses— than that of "act of existence", for Thomas happily speaks, by extension from this primitive meaning, of how a person's running is an act, in the sense that it is the "actualization" of a person's potentiality to run when that person might have been sitting;[15] or of the way in which a material object's being red is the actualization of one of the colours it could be, and not others; or of the way in which my thinking about the square of minus one is the actualization of the intellect's capacity to think indifferently about anything at all. But all these uses of the word "act" are parasitical upon a basic use and meaning, which is that according to which *esse* is the most fundamental actualization of anything at all. Why?

Because in every other, parasitical, use of "act", what is actualized is some already existing potentiality. If Frieda runs, then Frieda existed in such and such a nature which can run; if the lintel is red, then the lintel existed in bare pine to be painted one colour or another; if I think of the square of minus one then I have a mind which could think of that, or of something else. But if what actualizes is a thing's *esse*, and if the existence which *esse* denotes is that it exists rather than that nothing at all exists, then it cannot be the case that in the same sense there exists some potentiality which *esse* actualizes. God can do anything *possible*. But nothing is *potentially* creatable. For the potentiality which *esse* actualizes is brought about by its actualization: the potentiality only exists *as actualized*, and cannot exist prior to it, as it were "awaiting" actualization.

It does not of course follow from this that what exists cannot not have existed, nor that it cannot cease to exist. It is crucial to Thomas' understanding of *esse* and *essentia* that they are "really distinct", for anything at all which exists as an actualized potentiality has been caused to exist and can be caused to cease to exist, even were it the case, as he thinks it coherent counterfactually to say, that it has endlessly existed and will endlessly exist.[16] The contingency of a created thing lies in its createdness, not in any finite parameter of endurance. That said—the real distinction notwithstanding— a thing's *esse* is that by which the potentiality exists which it actualizes. It makes no sense to say of what *esse* makes to be that it in any way "exists" in potency "to be".[17]

But if that is so, if *esse* is therefore to be understood in relation to the potentiality it actualizes, how can we in any way speak of God as "*ipsum esse subsistens*", and so as "pure act"—as Thomas does? It is clear to Thomas why we must say that God is "*pure* act". There cannot be anything in God which his existence "actualizes", no potentiality of any sort, for God cannot be brought into existence or be caused to cease to exist, else God would be, simply, a creature. On the other hand it seems hard to know what sense it makes to say that God is "pure *act*" but that there is nothing of which that act is the *actualization*, as if we were to say that Frieda is running, but that her running is not the exercise of any capacity to do so. For, as we have seen, *esse* is intelligible only as the function of some form. But God is not some kind of thing, possesses no "form" which his *esse* actualizes. So what sort of sense can we make of saying that God is *just* his actualization, *esse*, but nothing actualized?

It might seem that once again Thomas' own argument has, by his own devising, maneuvered him into the jaws of the derridean trap. If we are to be permitted to say that God exists at all, the predicate ". . . exists" will have to retain some connections of meaning with our ordinary senses for the term as we know how to use it of creatures, even if falling infinitely short of God. And it will be enough to meet this condition that we know all alternatives to be worse, because falsifying of God, since to "fall short" of God is not the same as to speak falsely of God. But that "ordinary sense" in which we use it of creatures is, it would seem, intrinsically tied in with their creatureliness—*esse creaturae est creari*—as the actualization of a potency. But if it cannot be in that sense that God may be said to exist, what sense can there be left to the term "act" when, as Thomas says we must, we describe God as "pure act"? Is this an *aporia*, an impossible dilemma?

It would seem not. It is clear from Thomas' latest writings—from the *Summa Theologiae* in particular—that far from seeing this problem as an intractable dilemma or theological blind-alley, the "pincer movement" which leads to it has been a carefully designed theological strategy, designed to manoeuvre the theologian into exactly that position where she ought to find herself—just in that place where, constrained by our ordinary discourse of "to be" we discover that that ordinary discourse is incapable of capturing the meaning it must nonetheless point to. Of course we could not know what it means to say that God is "pure act", *ipsum esse subsistens*—Thomas is quite emphatic about this: "we cannot know the *esse* of God any more than we can know his essence".[18] In fact the statement's incomprehensibility, "God is 'pure act' or *ipsum esse subsistens*", is not an *aporia* that reduces Thomas' theological metaphysics to absurdity. It is, on the contrary, a precise theological statement, intended to mark out with maximum clarity and precision the *locus* of the divine incomprehensibility, the *ratio Dei*, the most fundamental of the "formal features" of God, to use Burrell's terminology.[19] Since it is far from being the case that describing God as "pure act" gives us some firm purchase on the divine nature, one may go so far as to say that talking about God thus is a kind of "babble": for to pretend that we remain in full command of the meaning of such words through any self-evidently meaningful extension of their ordinary senses is idolatrously reductive of theological language. It is only just *in*appropriate to call such theological speech "babble" in so far as, unlike mere babble, calling God by the name "pure act", or *ipsum esse subsistens*, retains that degree of connection with the logic of our ordinary discourse which licenses us to derive, with consistency and coherence, what follows from saying it, and what does not. And once again, Thomas is emphatic: the proper response to this objection is not to abandon all talk about God as *esse*, confining the predication of *esse* to creatures, as some do, believing that to say that *esse* is predicable "in common" of God and creatures is bound to lead you through some form of "Scotist" univocity into an onto-theological outcome. At any rate, you cannot reasonably read Thomas as having allowed some such retreat from what is for him a central doctrine, given that he explicitly blocks that way out of the dilemma: "to be caused is not of the definition of being *simpliciter*, for which reason we can come to know of an uncaused being".[20]

On the other hand, this strategy is not absurdly to attempt to eat one's cake and have it. We know that, insofar as a creature is "in act" it is, Thomas says, to that degree "perfect" and so "good" in some respect, *secundum quid*. From this we know that if God is "pure act" then God is wholly perfect and good in every respect, *simpliciter*. We know this because we know what *esse* as "act" means of a creature: it means the actualization of a potentiality. Hence, whatever "pure act" means, we know better than to attribute to God, in his character as pure act, anything which follows from a thing's having potentiality: so we cannot avoid saying both that God is "pure act" but that there is no potency in God of which *esse* is the actualization. But if for that reason we cannot know what "pure act" means, in the sense that we would if we possessed some concept of it, then it follows that we know no better what "wholly perfect" or "good *simpliciter*" mean than we know what "pure act" means, except that they must be true of God, which is enough to know that their contradictories are false.[21] We can, in short, know enough about what God is to know what God is not; and so we know in saying anything we are entitled to say affirmatively about God—"God exists"—what we are denying in so saying. To that extent, theological talk has a grammar. It is a language. But that said, it is the grammar of a mystery, of language which breaks down according to determinable rules of breakdown. Theological speech is subject to a sort of *programmed* obsolescence. To be "theological" you have to get language to self-destruct.

An "Empty" God?

But does not so heavily negative a theology still leave us with a vacuous God of pure "undifferentiation", a *mere* "otherness"? The objection provides Thomas with an opportunity to clarify what could possibly be meant by the pseudo-Denys' famous *dictum*, God is not "any kind of thing",[22] or that, as he himself puts it, God is *ipsum esse subsistens*. In agreeing to this statement of negative theology Thomas is not consenting to some notion—as one might be tempted to suppose—that the name "God" names an utterly empty category. That we cannot form any "concept" of God is due not to the divine vacuousness, but, on the contrary, to the excessiveness of the divine plenitude. That excessiveness eludes our language because we could not comprehend it except in a surplus of description which utterly defeats our powers of unification under *any* conception, an excessiveness which is exactly captured in the full text of the dionysian formula: "There is no kind of thing which God is, *and there is no kind of thing which God is not*". If ever there were a compendious statement of the relationship between the apophatic and the cataphatic in the pseudo-Denys's writing, this is it: for it says that God is beyond our comprehension not because we cannot say anything about God, but because we are compelled to say too much. For the pseudo-Denys, and for Thomas following him, the "apophatic" consists in the *excessus* of the "cataphatic".[23] It is not that, for Thomas, we are short of things to say about God: just that anything we do say of God falls short of him.

And so Thomas makes a distinction between two logically different kinds of "unspecificness", or, as we might put it, two kinds of "undifferentiation", or, as we might put it in a third set of terms, between two ways of being "beyond both similarity and difference".[24] In the first kind of case, he explains, further specification is *excluded*, as "reason is excluded by definition from irrational animals". In that case, he adds, the exclusion of the specification "rational" adds content to the concept "animal" since by virtue of the exclusion of the *differentia* "rational", we know that what is referred to is, specifically, non-human animals—brutes. By contrast, in the second kind of case, "unspecificness" is achieved by *indifference to either inclusion or exclusion*, as when we speak of the *genus* "animal in general" indifferently as between "rational" and "non-rational", between humans and brutes.

When we say, therefore, that God is *ipsum esse subsistens*—hence, that there is no kind of thing that God is—we could mean that God's existence is "unspecific" in either sense. To mean it in the second sense would turn out to mean that God's existence is such as to be indifferent to any kind of specification—and that, for sure, would be "onto-theological" error, since it would certainly entail that the name "God" named the entirely empty category of *"ens commune"*, as if God were some most general "concept" of which beings are "instances"—or, on the contrary, that God is just another "instance" of "beings" falling under that general concept.

And, of course, Thomas denies that the identity of *essentia* and *esse* in God entails that second kind of "unspecificness". For God's simplicity consists, on the contrary, in this alone, that in God all specification of this and that *is excluded*—"there is no kind of being that God is", or, as we might put it, if "specificness" is excluded from God, then "exclusion" is excluded from God. The paradox is, therefore, that this kind of "unspecificness" of the divine *esse*, this "otherness", this being "beyond similarity and difference", is such as to be totally *inclusive*, which is the opposite of what one might have supposed.

For note that the specific difference "rational" divides the *genus* "animal" into exclusive species ("rational" and "non-rational"), such that, if the one then not the other: if any animal exists, then it is either a rational animal or a non-rational animal. Both belong to the same *genus*, but, of course, there cannot exist an animal which is, just, generically-an-animal, being neither rational nor non-rational. But if, *per impossibile*, a generic animal could exist, it could not exclude *either* "rational" *or* "non-rational", for then it would have none of the character of either; it would have to be *both rational and non-rational* in some way which excluded the exclusion of each by the other, and thus allow for both in some non-disjunctive way.

No doubt, such a supposition of an actually existent *genus* is absurd, for a *genus* as such cannot exist. But the hypothesised absurdity brings out a central paradox of language about God of which, at this point in his argument, Thomas is acutely observant. For it is by virtue of the divine nature's excluding every possible specification—that is to say, by virtue of excluding every *differentia* whatever—that God's nature is such as to exclude all exclusion; hence, God stands in no relation of any kind of *exclusion* with anything whatever. God, as Eckhart says, is distinct in this exactly, that God alone is "indistinct"[25]—not, as Thomas observes, by virtue of an "indistinctness" which is an excess of indeterminacy taken to the point of absolute generalised vacuousness, but by an excess of determinacy, taken to the point of absolutely total plenitude: "there is no kind of thing", the pseudo-Denys says, "which God is not", or, as Thomas himself put it, God is "virtually" everything that there is, containing, as it were, every *differentia* as the cause of them all, but such that "what are diverse and exclusive in themselves pre-exist in God as one, without detriment to his simplicity".[26] That is why we cannot comprehend God: the "darkness" of God is the simple excess of light. God is not too indeterminate to be known; God is unknowable because too comprehensively determinate, too *actual*. It is in that excess of actuality that the divine unknowability consists.

If there are therefore no grounds in logic, and certainly none having the sort of idolatrous consequences which Marion fears, for disallowing Thomas to say, as he does with some essential clarifications and precisions of terms, that *esse* is predicable "in common" of God and creatures, what can justify our predicating *esse* of God? The full answer to this cannot be obtained until later in this essay, but what we can say in the meantime is that, whatever the grounds are on which we are enabled to understand created *esse* as that which stands against there being nothing at all, just the same are the grounds on which we are able to say that the *esse* of a creature is to be created. But in knowing that for anything to exist is for it to be created is thus far to understand the name "God" as the pure, undifferentiated, wholly inclusive "act" from which all exclusion is excluded, for he brings all things into existence and sustains them in it. We know God, in short, insofar as we know the *esse* of creatures, as creator of all things, "visible and invisible", and as the exemplar and cause of all that is, so that whatever is true of a creature is in some way true of God.

And this is to know how to name the difference between God and everything which exists, which is the "difference" between the Creator and the creature. And just as we are compelled thus to name it, we do not, and could not, understand the difference that it names.

The "Five Ways"

This much, therefore, can be said about what on Thomas' doctrine of God the atheist is going to have to deny if s/he is not to be engaged merely in the preliminary, and essentially theological, exercise of idolatry-busting: that the world, all that is, is created "out of nothing". That, of course, is a statement about the world, a statement which it is possible to contest on common terms of disagreement with those who, like Aquinas, affirm it. But for all that it is a statement "about the world" it does not on that account fail to be a statement about God. On the contrary, it is just that sort of statement about the world which *is* the key to how we are to speak non-idolatrously about God. For which reason, on Thomas' account of the logic of "God exists", there is a genuine argument to be had with those who deny it, with atheists, which is, presumably, why he himself offers arguments in support of it, the famous "five ways". It may be true—I am sure it is—that Thomas does not in fact offer the "five ways" by way of conducting a disputation with atheists; I am just as ready to concede that Thomas does not in fact set out the "five ways" as part of some programme of what we today would call a "philosophy of religion", still less in pursuit of some "foundationalist" programme of philosophical, rational, theologically neutral underpinning for his larger Christian theological enterprise. I am happy to concede that, on the contrary, the sense and purpose of those "arguments" is to be sought entirely *within* those essentially Christian theological purposes of the *Summa Theologiae*. In such respects at least I have no dispute with the anti-foundationalist readings of the "five ways" which are to be found in the recent (though very differently argued) case made by writers in the "Radical orthodox" tendency,[27] by Anna Williams,[28] and earlier by de Lubac[29] and those of the school of "nouvelle théologie" (who undoubtedly source both). And according to all of these, to read the structural place of the "arguments for the existence of God" within the articulation of Thomas' theology as if they were intended to be "free-standing", theologically neutral, exercises in philosophical argument, is very fundamentally distorting of the carefully managed theological strategies of the *Summa Theologiae*. I agree: Thomas, nowhere perhaps, but certainly not in that later *Summa*, offers us a philosophy of religion.

But in thus far agreeing with what such theologians affirm about Thomas' theological purposes, I do contest what they all take to follow from it by way of consequent denial: namely that in setting out those "five ways" Thomas did not set out, and did not intend to set out, formally valid, rational proofs of the existence of God. It is one thing to say (as I do) that Thomas sees there to be reasons of faith, and purposes of theology, in showing that the existence of God can be proved by arguments which stand up on their own grounds of reason; it is quite another thing to say (as Milbank and others do) that the "five ways" stand up as proofs only as assuming faith by way of premise for their inferences. For one thing, that last proposition is simply incoherent. That cannot be regarded in *any* sense as "proof" which presupposes as premise that which it is supposed to entail as conclusion: such is simply the fallacy of *petitio principii*. Hence it is hard to know even what Milbank means when he says that in the *Summa Theologiae* Thomas is not to be construed as offering full-blown formal proofs, "but [only] weakly probabilistic arguments".[30] If Milbank were right, then Thomas could not have been offering anything at all even by way of "arguments", "strong" or "weak", let alone "proofs", and, given the obvious and vicious circularity involved, would have been a poor and foolish logician had he supposed that he was doing so. But Thomas is not a poor or foolish logician, and he says that the "five ways" represent five argument-strategies by which *"Deum esse probari potest".*[31] I know of no stronger mediaeval Latin technical term in point of apodeiticity than *probari*. One would therefore like to know what exegesis of this word is proposed by those who deny that Thomas' "five ways" were meant as proofs in a formal sense, as of his equally emphatic statement that while the divine *esse* is unknown to us, "that God is can be known to be true . . . and we know this from his effects, *as we showed in [ST 1a] q2 a.2".*[32]

It follows from this—and if I am right it will also be true, though much more needs to be said than I have space to say here—that while undoubtedly Thomas *does not* argue with them, his account of the logic of "God exists" is such that for him *there is an argument to be had* with atheists, so long as they know what to deny. There are those who will be ill-informed as to what to deny, of course, but they can get it wrong along two distinct, though ultimately converging, lines: that of the naïve and plodding Dawkinsian atheists, who, misled perhaps by some theists into idolatrously supposing God to be "just another very big thing in the universe", rightly propose to expel an interfering monster from it; and that of the sophisticated postmodern atheists who, in the intensity of their desire to escape from the grasping clutches of a merely idolatrous denial, take the desperate measure of making an absolute of denial itself, of "difference", instead. On the score of the latter sort of atheist, Thomas at least does not feel the pressure to decide between permitting a strategy of proof, as if thereby risking an "ontotheological" God, and a theological apophaticism, as if thereby putting at risk the possibility of proof. Proof is not in itself "onto-theological". Apophaticism is no excuse for abandoning a claim to proof. As I believe a careful examination of the relationship between *Summa Theologiae* q2 a3 and *Summa Theologiae* q3 will show, what the proofs prove is that in showing God to exist we have finally lost control over the meaning of "exists". For Thomas the proofs prove an *unknowable* God, known to exist and known to be unknowable from the unutterable mystery that there is anything at all.

Analogy and Proof: Scotus and Milbank

But it is not only atheists who do not get the hang of this. Scotus did not, believing that the existence of God is demonstrable only if being is predicable univocally of both God and creatures, which, as Richard Cross says, undoubtedly reduces the apophatic pressure on Scotus by comparison with Thomas[33] and is undoubtedly onto-theological, as everyone since Heidegger has learned to say. But it is no better in itself to say, as Milbank does, that the existence of God could not be rationally demonstrable from creatures, since being is *not* predicable univocally of God and creatures, or that, as an interpretation of Thomas, since he thought that only analogy held between God and creatures, he could not have believed rational demonstration of God to be possible: no better than Scotus, because to say this *is* "Scotism". And it is not Thomas. In fact I cannot think of a more openly "Scotist" proposition than that on the grounds of which Milbank purports to demonstrate that Thomas could not have intended his five ways as formal rational proofs, namely, that since terms predicated of God and creatures are for Thomas predicable only analogically, and since (Milbank thinks) for Thomas there can be no strict demonstration of a proposition except from premises which are univocally related to that proposition, then formal demonstration of the existence of God from "creaturely" premises must be ruled out. As Milbank puts it:

> . . . scientific demonstration proper depends, for Aquinas after Aristotle, on a univocity of terms answering to a univocity between causes and effects. For Aquinas, this contention disallowed a transgeneric "science" in the strictest sense . . . Aquinas . . . by identifying God with non-generic *esse*, and by specifically excluding God from *genus* and from substance in the sense either of distinct essence or self-standing individual . . . also ensures that there can be only an analogical or not strictly scientific approach to the divine. Hence . . . his "demonstrations" of God's existence can only be meant to offer weakly probable modes of argument and very attenuated "showings".[34]

Thus Milbank. And so Scotus:

> The active intellect and the sense image cannot give rise to a concept that, with respect to the object revealed in the sense image, is not univocal but rather, in accordance with an analogical relationship, is altogether other and higher than the object. It follows that such an "other",

analogous, concept will never arise in the intellect in our present state. Also it would thus follow that one could not naturally have any concept of God—which is false.[35]

Thomas nowhere says any such thing—in fact, as we will see, he explicitly anticipates Scotus' objection, and rejects it, moreover in what can be construed as a "debate", of course *avant la lettre*, with Scotus about the logic of idolatry.

Scotus and Thomas on Idolatry

If Anselm's "fool", the atheist, is wrong to deny that there is a God, he must at least know what he denies, that is to say, "God exists" must mean the same to him as it does to the theist. And if God does exist, then the atheist is "wrong" in the plainest possible sense, in that what he says is straightforwardly false. That, as we have seen, is an unambiguous application of the Aristotelian principle, *eadem est scientia oppositorum*. But what are we to say about the idolater, the person who worships as God some finite, created object, "fire", "water", or a tree? In what way, precisely, does the idolater get God wrong? Are we to say that the idolater is no better in practice than an atheist, since he worships as if it were God something which is not and could not be God, and so, though nominally a theist, that he fails to acknowledge the existence of the one true God, infinite, Creator of all things visible and invisible, omnipotent, omniscient—which no water, or fire or tree could be? Or, are we to say that he cannot mean by the word "God" what the true believer means? That the idolater says "God exists" is neither here nor there on this account, if the idolater does not mean what the true believer means. If that were the case, then it would follow that the true believer and the idolater use the word "God" equivocally, that is to say, they do not truly disagree, for what the idolater affirms does not have the same meaning as what the true believer denies. In that case there could be no true *oppositio* because there is no *eadem scientia*.

Scotus' answer to these questions is simple, but crucial. The true believer and the idolater straightforwardly contradict one another. Therefore, he concludes, the true believer and the idolater must mean the same thing by "God", and the ". . . exists" in the utterance of either must be predicated univocally in both cases, for they could not be contradicting one another unless the existence predicated of a finite being claimed to be God, "fire" or "water" or whatever, were predicated in the same sense of the infinite being who is the one true God. For univocity of terms is defined thus: "I call a concept 'univocal' if it has that sameness of meaning which is required so that to affirm and deny it of the same subject amounts to a contradiction."[36]

In truth there is some measure of agreement between Scotus and Thomas on how to respond to these questions. Thomas agrees in rejecting the posi-

tion that there is an equivocation between the true believer's and the idolater's use of the word "God", though Thomas is inclined to take the case for
saying that they are equivocating more seriously than Scotus does. As
Thomas puts it, it could very well seem that the idolater simply does not
understand the word "God" at all, if he thinks that a bit of bronze could be
the one true God:[37] and after all, we might ask how *could* you think that a
finite being is the Creator of all things out of nothing? It might seem that the
idolater must be thinking of some other meaning of the word "God" if his
position is to be made intelligible.

But Scotus and Thomas are united in rejecting the understanding of idolatry according to which the idolater simply means something else than
"God" when saying that an idol is God. Moreover, they partially agree on
the grounds for rejecting the position. First Thomas points out, as Scotus also
does, that equivocation does not derive from different subject-terms of predications, otherwise the predicate ". . . is a man" would be equivocal as predicated of Socrates and Plato: so, just because the Christian and the idolater
predicate the name "God" of diverse individuals, it does not follow that the
name is being used equivocally.[38] Equivocity derives from differences of
meaning, not from differences of predication.[39] But secondly, Thomas agrees
thus far with Scotus that there must be some relation of meaning between
what the true believer and the idolater assert, because they contradict one
another, which they could not do if they were using the word "God" equivocally. As Thomas says: "it is clear that the Christian who says that an idol
is not God contradicts the pagan who says it is, because both use the name
'God' to signify the true God".[40] Beyond these points of agreement between
them, however, Thomas and Scotus differ: for Scotus derives from them the
conclusion that existence must be predicable not just non-equivocally—
which is all Thomas believes the argument shows—but univocally of God
and creatures, a conclusion which Thomas explicitly rejects. Let us therefore
recall Scotus' argument.

Scotus says that both the true believer and the idolater are certain that God
exists, but the idolater says that God is fire, while the true believer denies
this, thus contradicting what the idolater says. But on the principle that the
meaning of a predicate is univocal if and only if its affirmation and its negation of the same subject amounts to a contradiction, it follows that it must
be in the same sense of ". . . exists" that the idolater and the true believer say
that God exists. But since the true believer maintains that God is an infinite
being and the idolater that God is a finite being, it follows that there must
be a univocal meaning to the predicate ". . . exists" predicable in common of
finite and infinite being.

Thomas' rejection of this argument anticipates Scotus' defence of it by
some thirty years. Indeed if one did not know that Scotus was writing after
Thomas, one might very well have supposed that Thomas' discussion of
idolatry in the *Summa Theologiae* was written in explicit response to Scotus'

argument in the *Ordinatio*, so precisely in "Scotist" terms does Thomas identify the position he is rejecting. Thomas asks: *Is the name "God" used in the same sense of God, of what shares in divinity and of what is merely supposed to be God?* The question seems odd, but simply means: when "we"—that is, believing Christians, who possess the truth about God—speak about God, we do so in a certain sense. But Christians also have reason to speak of things other than God as having a divine character, for example, a soul in the state of grace may legitimately be described as in some sense sharing in the divine, and pagans call their idols "gods", wrongly supposing them to be so. The question for Thomas, therefore, concerns what the relationship is between the meanings of the word "God" in these two cases of "sharing in the divinity" and "idolatrous supposition" on the one hand, and the meaning the word bears as naming the one true God on the other. So Thomas first sets out the case for the "Scotist" position that the word "God" must be used univocally:

> It seems that the name "God" is univocally predicated of God in all cases, whether as of his [true] nature, whether as shared in, or whether in the suppositions [of the pagans]. For
> 1. Where there is diversity of meanings there can be no contradiction between an affirmation and its denial; for where there is equivocation there can be no contradiction. But when the Christian says, "an idol is not God", he contradicts the pagan who says "an idol is God". Therefore, "God" is predicated in either case in the same sense [*univoce*].

Now while Thomas concedes to this position (as I say, it is "Scotist" *avant la lettre*) that the idolater and the true believer cannot be using the name "God" equivocally, he will allow the argument no power to demonstrate that they are using the name univocally: the argument simply does not prove that conclusion. Thomas explains that if the idolater did not mean to affirm of fire or stone or a tree that it is "the one true God, almighty and worthy to be venerated above all else",[41] then what the idolater says would in fact be true. For in the case that the idolater meant by "God" something other and less than the one true God—for example, that the meaning of "God" is "finite being"—then it would be perfectly legitimate to say that fire is God: after all, the Bible, as Thomas points out, speaks of the "gods" of the gentiles, saying of them that they are in fact "demons" [Ps 95:51]. Hence, if the idolater is to be said to be "wrong about God" it must be because the idolater wrongly claims to be true of fire, or water, or a tree what the true believer claims to be true of the Creator of the universe, one God who is Father, Son and Holy Spirit. This, then, is why Thomas agrees thus far with Scotus: it cannot be the case that the true believer and the idolater have an entirely different meaning for the word "God", or else there would be no contradiction between them. The disagreement between the idolater and the true believer concerns what the name "God" could possibly be true of, the true believer maintaining that it could not be true of fire or water or a of tree that it is "the one, true God".

On the other hand, the difference between Thomas and Scotus emerges from consideration of the answers Scotus and Thomas give to the question: if the idolater is in some way "wrong" about God, in what way is he wrong? For Scotus, the idolater is "wrong" because, knowing what the word God means, he misattributes it to something which could not in *any* way be God in that sense: for there is no sense at all in which something other than God can be said to be "divine".[42] For Scotus, then, the idolater is wrong in the way the atheist is wrong, in that what he says is simply false. For Thomas, however, there is a genuine, if only derived and secondary, sense in which what the idolater calls "God" is truly divine. Therefore, Thomas says, as between what the idolater and the true believer affirm there is neither equivocity, nor univocity, but some analogy.

It is not possible here to say as much as is manifestly needed about what Thomas means by an "analogical" predication, and in this article Thomas gives but a broad and general account: a word is used analogically, he says, when "its meaning in one sense is explained by reference to its meaning in another sense", explaining that, for example, we understand a healthy diet by reference to health in the body, of which health a healthy diet is the cause.[43] Now since the idolater would not be making a mistake in supposing a bronze statue to be God if he did not do so in *some* sense related to that in which the true believer uses the word "God", it follows that the idolater is, as it were, playing the same game as the true believer, for he abides by the same rules for the meaning of the word "God". Hence, if the idolater makes a theological mistake, he is still, we might say, "doing theology" even if he is playing on the losing team—unlike the atheist, for whom there is no theology to do, and will not play the game at all. If the idolater "gets God wrong" he does so not in the way in which the plain atheist does, who, understanding exactly what the theist understands by "God", denies God's existence. Rather, Thomas says, the idolater's mistake is to suppose that that which does, genuinely, share in the divine nature—the bronze statue—is the divine being itself, and this mistake is like supposing that a diet is healthy in the same way in which a body is healthy—which, of course, it is not, for you cannot take a diet's blood-pressure. Thus, the true believer knows *how* to say that the bronze statue is divine—by analogical extension from the true God—whereas the idolater does not.[44]

One further difference between Thomas and Scotus emerges from this, a difference which turns out to be crucial from the point of view of the issue concerning the logical standing of the "five ways" considered as formal demonstrations of the existence of God. If Thomas maintains that the true believer and the idolater contradict one another (as Scotus does), but, unlike Scotus, maintains that the senses in which they use the name "God" are related analogically, not univocally, this is because Thomas does not accept

Scotus' definition of univocity in the first place. For Scotus maintained that a term is predicated univocally if its affirmation and negation of the same subject amounts to a contradiction. But Thomas argues that the affirmation and denial that a bronze statue is God amounts to a contradiction between predicates which are predicated in an analogical relation with one another. Therefore it cannot be entailed that, in principle, propositions may contradict one another if and only if they contain such terms as bear univocally the same meanings: there can be an *eadem scientia* between terms analogically related, and in this case there are. Scotus' argument fails.

Thomas and the Logic of Proof

But so then does Milbank's. If, for Thomas, there can be formal *contradiction* between two analogically related propositions, then it follows, and contrary to what Milbank claims, that there can be formally valid *inference* between premises and a conclusion analogically related to them across the "gap" between creatures and God. Why? For the reason which Scotus gives: if, on Scotus' account, an inference is valid only on condition that the terms related to one another by it are such that "to affirm and to deny [them] of the same subject amounts to a contradiction", then, on Thomas' account, that condition is met by terms which are related to one another analogically. Hence an inference will not, for Thomas, be invalidated by the fact that it connects terms logically related to one another by analogy if, as in the case in question of "God", to affirm and deny of a bronze statue that it is God amounts to a contradiction. As far as Thomas is concerned, all that is required for the validity of such inferences is that there should be no equivocation between premises and conclusion. That premises and conclusion are related analogically can therefore be no obstacle to the inference between them being logically valid.

If this argument may seem to relate with comparative indirectness to the issue of inference to an analogical conclusion, a second text, found in the *Summa Contra Gentiles* could not meet the point more squarely. There Thomas considers "the opinion of those who say that God's existence cannot be demonstrated but can be held by faith alone", and in the course of doing so entertains Milbank's Aristotelian objection to his own view that God's existence is demonstrable: ". . . if the principles of demonstration have their origin in knowledge of sense, as is shown in the *Posterior Analytics*, what wholly exceeds every sense and sensible thing seems to be indemonstrable. But the existence of God is such. Therefore it is indemonstrable".[45]

But Thomas rejects this counterargument. If it were valid, he comments, it would prove too much. For on that account—"if there were no substance knowable beyond sensible substance"—then nothing beyond natural science would be knowable, which even Aristotle denies. He adds—in an oblique reference to the "derridean" objection—that it can be no further objection to the validity of such proof that we cannot know the "essence" of God, and so cannot construct any non-equivocal sequence of premises entailing God's existence, since in proofs of the kind in question it is the divine effects[46] which function as premises, not the divine nature.[47] For we cannot construct an argument for God's existence out of premises definitive of the divine nature, as Anselm (on Thomas' reading of *Proslogion*) supposed, that nature being unknown to us—we are in possession of no definition of God in the first place.[48] But if the arguments for the existence of God are constructed from premises descriptive of the effects of God in creation, and not from any definition of God, then of course the conclusion of such an argument will have to contain terms not univocally related to those of the premises: it could not be an argument for the existence of *God* if that were not so, but only for "just another, creaturely, being". Hence, the only tests of such an argument's validity could be those of ordinary logic: you could not rule out the argument's validity on the grounds alone that the conclusion contained terms not univocally related to the terms of the premises. For that is pure Scotism. Milbank is of course quite right that Thomas is no "Scotist". It is, however, less clear that on this point at least Milbank is not one himself.

The "Five Ways" and Idolatry

If, as I have conceded, Thomas does not offer the arguments of *Summa Theologiae* 1a q2 a3 by way of formal, philosophical response to an "atheist" in any modern sense, this is not to say that they do not stand up as formally valid proofs. Of course, in defending them against a particular case for denying their formal validity I have done nothing to show that they are valid and there is no space in an article such as this for any positive defence of their argument scheme. That is another story which belongs elsewhere. But if their purpose is not to conduct a polemic with the formal atheist, what are they doing at this early point in the *Summa*, what are their purposes in the wider theological scheme of that work? One purpose seems very clear, and would appear to belong within Thomas' explicit intentions, at any rate to such as are evidenced by the close relation between question 2 of the *Prima pars*, which contains the "five ways" of showing that God exists, and question 3, which contains Thomas' most emphatic statement of the divine unknowability, showing that we do not know what God is. A "rational" proof of the existence of God does not yield a God "within the bounds of reason", an all-too knowable and idolatrous "something or other" contained within reason's finite parameters, but, on the contrary, it yields a conception of reason which, in driving our knowledge of the world to the end of its tether, finally cracks that finite world open into a territory of a boundless unknowability which utterly transcends it: *et hoc omnes dicunt Deum*.[49] As I have said, in showing God to exist reason shows that we no longer know what "exists" means. I do not think that Thomas meant the "five ways" to show anything much about God. But they are meant to show a lot about reason. And there is a strictly theological purpose in showing that much about reason, because it is only a conception of reason so "apophatically" construed that can serve the purposes for which it is needed in the theological articulation of Christian faith itself. The reason of the "rationalist" could not do the job at all.

But there is another, related, purpose for Thomas' early inclusion of the "five ways" within the theological construction of the *Summa Theologiae*, which we may identify if we ask why it is, curiously, that in an age such as Thomas', when theologians were not confronted by a serious intellectual challenge from atheists, rational arguments for the existence of God are standard and commonplace theological fare, whereas in our age, when atheism, often in explicitly philosophical and often militant forms, is widespread, theologians have by and large abandoned a rational and philosophical response. It might be said that the reason for this is that we no longer feel that rational proofs can do any good anyway: but I doubt it. I rather suspect that a combination of an intellectual habit of scepticism about reason (inherited uncritically by theologians from "kantian" epistemological assumptions) and complacency about faith, has led theologians to retreat into a position of fideistic invulnerability to philosophical counterargument in principle. Thomas blocks that line of retreat: and as to the false choices between rationalism and fideism, or between an idolatrous onto-theology and a postmodern nihilism, I guess he would have wished a plague to be visited on all their houses.

NOTES

1 *Peri Hermeneias*, 6, 17a 33–35.
2 For example, see *Summa Theologiae* 1a q58 a4 ad2.
3 I do think it worth noting that the distinction between "intellectual" atheism and atheism "of the heart" is more *ours* than any which Anselm would have accepted as a distinction in principle. There is no concept of "intellect" in Anselm which sets it in such contrast with affairs of the "heart" as that in which we tend to set it today.
4 And on the score of this emphatic denial that we know what God is, it makes no difference whether we are on the ground of some purely rational conception of God, or of a revealed conception, known by faith: "we do not know what God is", he says, "*even by the revelation of grace. And so [by grace] we are made one with him as to something unknown to us—quasi ei ignoto*", *Summa Theologiae* 1a q12 a13 ad1.
5 See my published lecture "How to be an Atheist", Cambridge: Cambridge University Press, 2002. In short, atheisms of this kind simply mirror the idolatries they reject: if your theism is of a kind that requires a place for God to be found in the world, then inevitably God's presence in the world is going to have to expel something else from it. And if the place you find for God in the world is such that, say, evolution has to be expelled from it to leave God some elbow room, as "creationists" appear to think, then, conversely, finding a place for evolution in the world will require expelling God from just that place. As Thomas would no doubt say, the common problem with both positions (for *eadem est scientia oppositorum*) is that of idolatrously supposing that if God exists then some place will have to be found for him in the world.
6 Jean-Luc Marion, *God without Being*, trans. Thomas a Carlson, (Chicago, IL: The University of Chicago Press, 1991).

7   Jacques Derrida, "How to avoid Speaking: Denials" in *On the Name*, ed. T. Dutoit, trans., David Wood, John P. Leavy and Ian McLeod, (Stanford, CA: Stanford University Press, 1995), pp. 106–108.

8   *ST* 1a q3 *Prologue*.

9   *ST* 1a q3 a4 *corp*.

10 *ST* 1a q3 a4 obj. 2.

11 *ST* 1a q75 a6 *corp*.

12 *Divine Names*, 817D.

13 *ST* 1a q45 a1 ad3.

14 *God Matters*, (London: Geoffrey Chapman, 1987), p. 69.

15 See *Expositio libri Boetii de Hebdomadibus*, lect. 2, introd., Latin text and trans, Janice S. Schultz and Edward Synan, (Washington, DC: Catholic University of America Press, 2001), pp. 16–17.

16 *De Aeternitate Mundi contra Murmurantes*, in *Aquinas on Creation*, trans., Steven E. Baldner and William E. Carroll, (Toronto: Pontifical Institute of Medieval Studies, 1997), pp. 114–122.

17 This does not mean that created causes cannot cause something to be which did not previously exist. Of course parents can cause children to be. What Thomas means in saying that *esse* is the act of existence by contrast with nothing is that that there is anything at all rather than nothing is, and can be, brought about only by God. No more than any created cause, can parents bring anything about *ex nihilo*. But that created causality which truly causes something to be is itself caused to exist, as everything at all is caused to exist, and so is caused *ex nihilo*, by God alone.

18 *ST* 1a q3 a4 ad2.

19 David Burrell, "On distinguishing God from the world" in *Language, Meaning and God, Essays in Honour of Herbert McCabe OP*, ed. Brian Davies OP, (London: Geoffrey Chapman, 1987), p. 77.

20 ". . . quia esse causatum non est de ratione entis simpliciter, propter hoc invenitur aliquod ens non causatum". *ST* 1a q44 a1 ad1.

21 Of course it does not follow from this that all language about God is logically negative—this conclusion is what Thomas denies in what he understands (correctly or otherwise) to be the position of Moses Maimonides. To confuse "apophaticism" with the view that all statements about God are logically negations is to reduce "apophaticism" to the standing of literal falsehood. If to say "God is good" means "God is not evil", then in any sense in which it is said "apophatically" that God is not good would thereby be reduced to the statement that God is evil.

22 *Divine Names*, 817D.

23 For a fuller discussion of this point, see my *Eros and Allegory*, (Kalamazoo, MI: Cistercian Publications, 1995), chapter two.

24 *ST* 1a q3 a4 ad1.

25 Sermon 83, *Renovamini Spiritu*, in *Meister Eckhart, The Essential sermons, commentaries, treatises and defense*, trans., Edmund Colledge and Bernard McGinn, (London: SPCK, 1981), p. 208.

26 ". . . quae sunt diversa et opposita in seipsis, in Deo praeexistunt ut unum, absque detrimento simplicitatis ipsius". *ST* 1a q4 a2 ad1.

27 *Radical Orthodoxy*, eds. John Milbank, Catherine Pickstock, and Graham Ward, (London: Routledge, 1998).

28 A. N. Williams, *The Ground of Union: Deification in Aquinas and Palamas*, (New York, NY: Oxford University Press, 1999).

29 Henri de Lubac, *Surnaturel: Etudes historiques*, (Paris: Aubier, 1946; second edn, Paris: Desclée de Brouwer, 1991).

30 John Milbank, "Intensities", *Modern Theology* Vol. 15 no. 4 (October, 1999), p. 455.

31 *ST* 1a q2 a3 *corp*.

32 *ST* 1a q3 a4 ad2. There are complex and difficult issues here about the logic of *esse* in Thomas which I have much more to say about in a monograph *Faith, Reason, and the Existence of God* forthcoming from Cambridge University Press in 2004.

33 Richard Cross, *Duns Scotus*, (Oxford: Oxford University Press, 1999), p. 39.

34 *Intensities*, pp. 454–455.

35 "Sed conceptus qui non esset univocus obiecto relucenti in phantasmate, sed omnino alius, prior, ad quem ille habeat analogiam, non potest fieri virtute intellectus agentis et phantasmatis; ergo talis conceptus alius, analogus qui ponitur, naturaliter in intellectus viatoris numquam erit,—et ita non poterit haberi naturaliter aliquis conceptus de Deo, quod est falsum", *Ordinatio* I d3 n. 36. Translation, William A. Frank and Allan B. Wolter, *Duns Scotus, Metaphysician*, (West Lafayette, IN: Purdue University Press, 1995). Otherwise known as the *Opus Oxoniense*, this work is Scotus" first commentary on the "Sentences" of Peter Lombard, begun at Oxford in the last years of the thirteenth century and completed, perhaps by 1304, in Paris. The edition of the text used for translations is found in *Doctoris Subtilis et Mariani, Joannis Duns Scoti Ordinis Fratrum Minorum Opera Omnia*, Civitas Vaticana: Typis Polyglottis Vaticanis, 1950.

36 *Ordinatio* I d3 25. My translation.

37 *ST* 1a q13 a10, *sed contra, praeterea*.

38 ". . . nominum multiplicitas non attenditur secundum nominis praedicationem, sed significationem: hoc enim nomen *homo*, de quocumque praedicetur, sive vere, sive false, dicitur uno modo"; ". . . a multiplicity of names [equivocation] results not from the multiplicity of its predications, but from a multiplicity of meanings. For the word "man", whatever it is predicated of, whether truly or falsely, means just one thing." *ST* 1a q13 a10 ad1.

39 *Ibid*.

40 *Ibid*.

41 *ST* 1a q13 a10.

42 There is an important point implicit here. For Thomas, all creation is in some sense "divine", for all creation in one way or another participates in the divine nature. It is for this reason that the idolater is not unequivocally wrong. By contrast, the Scotist doctrine that the idolater is wholly wrong about God, involving as it does the rejection of all analogy between creatures and God, is bound to cause great difficulty in maintaining consistently any doctrine that creation participates in the divine nature.

43 *ST* 1a q13 a10 *corp*.

44 ". . . when the pagan says the idol is God he does not use the name as signifying a mere [false] supposition about God, for then what he says would be true; and even Christians use the word in this [secondary] sense, as when it is said in Psalm 95:51, 'all their Gods are devils' "—"Cum enim paganus dicit idolum esse Deum, non utitur hoc nominee secundum quod significant Deum opinabilem: sic enim verum dicaret, cum etiam catholici interdum in tali significatione hoc nominee utitur, ut cum dicitur (Ps 95:51), *omnes dii gentium daemonia*", *ST* 1a q13 a10, *corp*.

45 *Summa Contra Gentiles*, 1.12.

46 This is an ellipsis. Kerr is, of course, right (see *After Aquinas: Versions of Thomism*, [Oxford: Blackwell, 2002], p. 59) that you cannot *prove* the existence of God from what you *know* are the divine effects, because that is simply to beg the question. But that is not Thomas' procedure. For Thomas, to prove the existence of God *is* to prove that creatures are "effects" of a divine creating causality.

47 *ST* 1a q2 a2 ad2.

48 *ST*, 1a q2 a1 *corp*.

49 It is sometimes objected that the God of Thomas' proofs could not be the "same" God as the God of faith, because no one of faith speaks of God as "first cause" or "prime mover" or "necessary being", and that Thomas is therefore unwarranted in saying of the God of his proof, *et hoc omnes dicunt Deum*. I think this is mistaken. The Latin should not be translated as "this is how all people speak of God", or even as "this is what all people *mean* when they speak of God", for manifestly they do not, and Thomas knows this. It should rather be translated as "this is the God all people speak of". The square of 1 is 1, and the square root of 1 is 1, but of course "square of . . ." and "square root of . . ." do not *mean* the same. In just the same way, Thomas maintains, the God of Trinitarian faith is the same God as the God of the proofs, though obviously to say "God is the prime mover" does not mean the same as "God is Father, Son and Holy Spirit".

8

SHOUTING IN THE LAND OF THE HARD OF HEARING: ON BEING A HILLBILLY THOMIST

FREDERICK CHRISTIAN BAUERSCHMIDT

The Picture of a Perfect Thomist Gentleman

There are certain things one expects of a good Thomist. He or she will highly prize reason, believing that human nature, though somewhat damaged by sin, on the whole functions quite well, and that assiduous application of human reason forms the basis on which it is possible to enter into dialogue with those who do not accept the Catholic faith. In contrast to Augustinian/Protestant pessimism about human nature, the Thomist affirms the fundamental goodness of human nature and reason. Therefore, when confronted by some variety of unbelief—whether it be atheist, Buddhist, Muslim or Protestant—the good Thomist will wield the weapon of logical rigor deftly, but also serenely, knowing that the doubter's greatest enemy is his or her own natural reason. As the early twentieth-century Thomist Walter Farrell (1902–1951) said concerning Thomas' Five Ways, "The philosopher who, for reasons best known to himself, decides to challenge these proofs has entered a war of cosmic proportions; fortunately for himself, he cannot win".[1]

The commitment of good Thomists to reasoned argument means that they will be rhetorically austere and not prone to passionate exhortation. With human nature and reason on their side, they have no need to inflame the emotions in order to bend the will. Indeed, the more dispassionate the discussion the more the truth will be made manifest. Good Thomists can afford to be gentlemen. The climate of their discussions will be, as John Courtney Murray put it in a different context, "cool and dry, with the coolness and dryness that characterize good argument among informed and responsible men".[2]

Frederick Christian Bauerschmidt
Department of Theology, Loyola College, 4501 N. Charles Street, Baltimore, MD, 21210, USA

Murray's phrase is so vivid that it can be too easily forgotten that Murray himself expressed doubts about the effectiveness of such arguments in what he, in the 1950s, already called the "post-modern" context.[3] Perhaps we live in a world in which informed and responsible men are in short supply, but cool and dry argumentation does not seem to be leading us to any sort of consensus about the "Ultimate Questions", and Murray frankly acknowledges that "the tradition of reason, which is known as the ethic of natural law, is dead".[4] Integral to modern pluralism "is the skeptic or agnostic view that it is useless or illegitimate even to ask Ultimate Questions".[5] And yet Murray, himself a good Thomist gentleman, in the end echoes Farrell's optimism that the "tradition of reason" will ultimately triumph, perhaps by a kind of resurrection from the dead, albeit one foreordained by nature. This is particularly the case with regard to knowing the truth, but it is also the case in the realm of practical reason; people are "by nature . . . natural law jurists" because "they reach the essential imperatives of their own nature and know them to be unthwartably imperative—however much they may subsequently deform them, and destroy their proper bases, by uninformed or prejudiced reflective thought".[6]

Such serene, unpolemical, gentlemanly convictions seem to accord with the tone of Thomas' own writings. The disputational form taken by the *Summa Theologiae*, as well as other of Thomas' works, seems to be a bit of dialectical window dressing; though the form is that of an argument, the tone is "cool and dry". Thomas rarely evinces anger or resorts to sarcasm or employs any rhetorical technique to defeat his enemies. Indeed, it is sometimes hard to conceive of Thomas as *having* any enemies. Standing on the common ground of reason, intellectual opponents are in fact partners in the common search for truth. As Thomas O'Meara has put it, "His writings reveal a sense of tranquility: an appreciative contemplation of the structure of the cosmos is joined to a calm openness to all that exists".[7] Even if one is unwilling fully to endorse A. G. Sertillanges' statement that Thomas "is hardly an 'author,' or even a 'man' but rather a channel connecting us directly with intelligible truth"[8], it does seem that Thomas, too, is a perfect Thomist gentleman.

But without denying the serenity of Thomas' writing, I want to ask whether a cool, dry tone and a direct channel to intelligible truth are really the substance of those writings. Or, to put it perhaps more accurately, does Thomas' theological conviction that "grace perfects nature" necessarily manifests itself in the pragmatic conviction that even non-believers are always at root open to reasoned argument? Is gentlemanliness the "substantial form" of Thomism? Or is it rather an accident of the particular context in which he wrote? And if the latter is the case, might "Thomism" look and sound quite different in our quite different context?

In attempting to address these question I will invoke the aid of the American novelist and short story writer Flannery O'Connor (1925–1964),[9] who once wrote to a friend that everyone who had read her novel *Wise Blood* "thinks I'm a hillbilly nihilist, whereas I would like to create the impression . . . that I am a hillbilly Thomist".[10] Anyone familiar with O'Connor's work knows that it is quite ungentlemanly, not to mention unladylike, and that nothing could be further in tone from the writings of Thomas than O'Connor's stories, in which atheist prophets blind themselves, sweet old grandmothers get shot, and clever college girls get their artificial legs stolen by itinerant Bible salesmen. But perhaps a modern follower of Thomas Aquinas, taking as her audience "the people who think God is dead",[11] would write not with the serenely ordered cadences of the *Summa Theologiae* but something more akin to the shocking, grotesque syncopations that one finds in O'Connor's novels and short stories.

Hillbilly Thomism: Mystery and Manners

Mary Flannery O'Connor was born and lived most of her life in the American South, including the last thirteen years when her health was ravaged by Lupus, which killed her at the age of thirty-nine. Her status as a "regional writer" was established at the outset: she stood in the line of William Faulkner and Eudora Welty and excelled in the subgenre of "Southern-grotesque" or "Southern-gothic". Indeed, so grotesque were her characters that many of her early readers took her for a misanthropic atheist and missed the profound influence that O'Connor's Roman Catholicism had on her writing, an influence that was made abundantly clear with the publication of her letters in 1979. In many of these letters she responds to misreadings of her stories that see them as fundamentally nihilistic. To one correspondent she wrote, "my stories have been watered and fed by Dogma",[12] and to another, who had claimed to see affinities between her writing and existentialist authors, she wrote, "My philosophical notions don't derive from Kierkegaard (I can't even spell it) but from St. Thomas Aquinas".[13]

But in what sense did Flannery O'Connor consider herself a Thomist? While she once described herself as "a Thomist three times removed", by which she meant "one who doesn't read Latin or St. Thomas but gets it by osmosis",[14] she clearly *did* read Aquinas, as well as having him mediated through secondary sources, particularly through Maritain's *Art and Scholasticism*, which she mentions on numerous occasions in her letters.[15] Yet hers is not the Cajetan-tinged philosophical Thomism of Maritain, nor the Thomism of the Twenty-Four Thomistic Theses, nor is it the strict-observance Thomism of Reginald Garrigou Lagrange. Above all, it is not the "rabbinic Thomism" that argues by way of citations from the *Summa*. Rather, it is the broad Thomistic humanism that was the shared inheritance of the Church from the *doctor communis*. In a letter to a college student troubled by religious doubts, O'Connor summed up her own beliefs:

I believe what the Church teaches—that God has given us reason to use and that it can lead us toward a knowledge of him, through analogy; that he has revealed himself in history and continues to do so through the Church, and that he is present (not just symbolically) in the Eucharist on our altars. To believe all this I don't take any leap into the absurd. I find it reasonable to believe, even though those beliefs are beyond reason.[16]

This summary of "what the Church teaches" certainly has a broadly Thomistic cast to it: natural knowledge of God, analogy, revealed knowledge of God, and even transubstantiation. And the "three times removed" character of it—Thomas mediated through the common tradition of the Church rather than Thomas as the object of intensive study by specialists—might seem sufficiently unsophisticated to warrant the "hillbilly" epithet.[17]

Yet I would propose that there is something still more distinctively Thomist in O'Connor's work. This is the conjunction of what she calls "mystery" and "manners". She writes in an essay, "The mystery . . . is the mystery of our position on earth, and the manners are those conventions which, in the hands of the artist, reveal that central mystery".[18] O'Connor names as "mystery" the irreducibly ungraspable reality that is at the heart of our existence: "our life is and will remain essentially mysterious".[19] Despite our attempts to capture the essential in concepts: "It is not answerable to any of our formulas. It doesn't rest finally in a statable kind of solution. It ought to throw you back on the living God."[20] At the same time, we never encounter mystery in itself, but always in conjunction with "manners", not only the stylistic manner of the artist, but also those highly particular traditions that accumulate like sediment over time, and which structure our lives and make them livable in the face of mystery. As she notes in one of her essays, "Somewhere is better than anywhere. And traditional manners, however unbalanced, are better than no manners at all".[21] But manners are not simply a hedge against the annihilating presence of mystery. Indeed, without the backdrop of manners—culture, tradition, custom, dogma—mystery cannot appear. As O'Connor writes to a friend: "For me a dogma is only a gateway to contemplation and is an instrument of freedom and not of restriction. It preserves mystery for the human mind."[22]

O'Connor believes that this conjunction of mystery and manners is something alien to modern people. We like our mystery neat, without dilution by manners. We prefer "spirituality" to "religion", with its overlay of dead customs. We are fascinated by the exotic customs of other cultures, while at the same time thinking that we are somehow beyond all that sort of thing. As O'Connor puts it, the modern writer is asked "to separate mystery from manners . . . in order to produce something a little more palatable to the modern temper".[23] Yet in separating them, we lose both, and thus we have the modern world, bereft of both mystery and manners, transcendence and tradition.[24] Those who still cleave to manners as the door into mystery inevitably appear to be a "hillbillies" in the eyes of the modern world, no different from O'Connor's backwoods prophets. They lack the sophistication (or sophistry) needed to strip themselves of manners in order to be cosmopolitan global citizens.

Aquinas does not make much use of the term "mystery" apart from formulae such as "the mystery of the Incarnation" or "the mystery of the Trinity".[25] Nor does he speak often of "manners" (*mores*), though he speaks frequently of "custom" (*consuetudo*). Yet in Thomas we find the same constellation of convictions that O'Connor indicates with her language of mystery and manners. Creation's rootedness in incomprehensible divine mystery is at the heart of Thomas' thinking. Our natural reason knows God best when it knows God as unknown: "the highest human knowledge of God is that which knows that it does not know God, inasmuch as it knows that what God is transcends whatsoever we conceive of him".[26] At the same time, Thomas devotes meticulous attention to human "manners". The second part of the *Summa Theologiae* is devoted to the virtues and vices that give structure to human cultural life, and in the third part of the *Summa* Thomas pays equally careful attention to the customary speech of the Church regarding the mystery of the incarnation. These are the things that form the backdrop against which mystery appears.

It is Thomas' conviction that it is only in the conjunction of transcendent mystery and human tradition and teaching that justice can be done to either. God's transcendence must be articulated in teaching and embodied in tradition in order for us to know the divine mystery as an abyss of light (to use Joseph Pieper's phrase) that gives us life, rather than an annihilating abyss of darkness. Yet those teachings and traditions, because they are instances of human language, must always be understood as articulations of a truth that transcends them and to which they are ultimately not adequate. As Thomas says, the human language with which we attempt to say something about God "leaves the thing signified as uncomprehended, and as exceeding the signification of the name".[27] In O'Connor's terms, dogma is not an end in itself, but a gateway to the contemplation of the divine mystery. Or, as Gregory the Great put it—in a passage quoted by both Aquinas and O'Connor—"Holy Scripture, in its manner of speaking, transcends all knowledge, because in one and the same utterance, while recounting an action, it discloses a mystery."[28]

To conceive of the conjunction of mystery and manners as being at the heart of Thomas' thought runs against the grain of what was, at least in years past, a prevalent image of Thomas. Thomas has been associated with a kind of apologetic rationalism—someone who thought that one could, by the exercise of reason, come to know quite a lot about God. In this view, what Thomas is primarily interested in are the things that reason can tell us about God and the world; the economy of salvation is given a peripheral place, which accounts for the way in which Christology is "tacked-on" to the end of the *Summa Theologiae*.[29] Again according to this view, his chief *intellectual* (as opposed to devotional or homiletical) interest in scripture and doctrine is in applying the tools of reason to them in order to forge a system that can draw conclusions with scientific certainty.[30] Not surprisingly, such of view of Thomas finds him far more interesting as a speculative metaphysician than as a theologian.[31]

This view of Thomas is increasingly rejected. On the one hand, numerous interpreters of Aquinas, while still approaching him primarily as a philosopher, stress the profoundly apophatic character of his thought, taking with absolute seriousness what he says about the fundamentally mysterious nature of God.[32] On the other hand, there has been a significant reassessment of both the depth and originality of Thomas' engagement with scripture and doctrine.[33] In other words, central to Thomas' work is reflection on the mystery of God and the scriptural manner of speaking of that mystery.[34] Thomas is not interested simply in the scientific ordering of discrete bits of revealed "data", but rather he seeks to discern the way in which the mystery of God is revealed in the *modo conversationis* or manner of life of Jesus of Nazareth, a manner of life that is not subject to *a priori* judgments of necessity precisely because it is the historical revelation of the divine mystery. There is a kind dovetailing between the historical contingency of Jesus' life and the mystery of God, because neither are subject to rational deduction.

While we do not find in Thomas the kind of appeal to "narrative" that became popular among theologians in the last part of the twentieth-century, we ought not to underestimate the importance to Thomas of the concrete events narrated in scripture, not simply as data upon which reason operates, but as in its totality a figure or image of the divine mystery.[35] As Thomas says in his Commentary on John's Gospel, "the teaching of the Father is the Son himself".[36] What is offered for belief is not "data", but the figure of Christ rendered in the Gospels—a figure that, by the beauty of its "fittingness" (*conveninetia*), draws one's will to assent to its truth even though that truth is beyond the grasp of reason. As Thomas himself says of theology: "the manner of proceeding of this discipline must be a narrative of signs, which serve to confirm faith".[37] Thus Thomas' theology serves as a kind of commentary on the narrative figure of Christ, pointing us to the mystery revealed in scripture's manner of speaking and Christ's manner of life.

Arguing in the Culture of Nihilism: Shouting at the Hard of Hearing

Of course, whatever the agreement they may have regarding mystery and manners, the works of O'Connor and Aquinas are inflected quite differently. And this is not simply because Aquinas is a theologian and O'Connor a fiction writer; the difference is deeper and has to do with audience or, more precisely, the context in which they are writing.

O'Connor was a self-consciously modern—indeed, even "modernist"—writer, with Henry James, Joseph Conrad and, later in life, Marcel Proust as literary heroes. More importantly, she was conscious that she was writing for an audience that did not share her perspective on mystery and manners. She wrote to a friend,

> One of the awful things about writing when you are a Christian is that for you the ultimate reality is the Incarnation, the present reality is the Incarnation, the whole reality is the Incarnation, and nobody believes in the Incarnation; that is, nobody in your audience. My audience are the people who think God is dead. At least these are the people I am conscious of writing for.[38]

One might ask, however, if a professed Thomist should not be able to surmount this difficulty by seeking a common basis in the truths of natural reason. After all, Thomas could enter into dialogue and disputation with Jews and Muslims who rejected the Incarnation. But as O'Connor sees the matter, she is in a fundamentally different situation from someone in the thirteenth-century. It is not simply that modern people do not share her convictions regarding Christ. Rather, the modern world lacks even the sense that there is some choice to be made between existence and nothingness, good and evil. As O'Connor puts it, "if you live today you breathe in nihilism".[39] We live in an age in which, "the moral sense has been bred out of certain sections of the population, like the wings have been bred off certain chickens to produce more white meat on them". O'Connor goes on to add, "This is a generation of wingless chickens, which I suppose is what Nietzsche meant when he said God was dead."[40] By contrast, even when he writes *contra gentiles*, Thomas is not writing for those who think God is dead.

Thus, O'Connor's writing must inevitably be inflected differently than that of an author writing in the thirteenth-century, and this inflection is one that gives her writing an extremely unstable or off-balance feel. Writing of Dante she says,

> I am often told that the model of balance for the novelist should be Dante, who divided his territory up pretty evenly between hell, purgatory and paradise. There can be no objection to this, but also there can be no reason to assume that the result of doing it in these times will give us the balanced picture that it gave in Dante's. Dante lived in the 13th century when the balance was achieved in the faith of his age. We live now in an age which doubts both fact and value, which is swept this way and that by momentary convictions. Instead of reflecting a balance from the world around him, the novelist now has to achieve one from the felt balance inside himself. There are ages when it is possible to woo the reader; there are others when something more drastic is necessary.[41]

While O'Connor shares the theological world view of Dante and Aquinas, her relationship to that world view is somewhat different. Religious faith is no longer woven into the fabric of a shared culture; rather, it has been interiorized. Whatever "felt balance" that the writer achieves interiorly will not externalize itself in "balanced" writing, precisely because there is no language shared between author and audience in which such a balance can be expressed.

As is well known, Thomas held that all arguments, including theological arguments, proceed on the basis of commonly accepted premises.[42] In some cases, where the premises of valid arguments are either self-evident or have been made evident by prior arguments, truth is clearly manifested to reason in such a way that reason cannot withhold assent: reason cannot deny the Pythagorean theorem without ceasing to be reason. However, there are cases where reason does not incline to either side of an argument, because the premises are not evident, and such is the case with those arguments that have to do with the nature of God. In those cases, the "wooing" of belief depends on our ability to recognize goodness where we cannot recognize truth. Thomas writes,

> In this situation our understanding is determined by the will, which chooses to assent to one side definitively and precisely because of something which is enough to move the will, though not enough to move the understanding, namely, since it seems good or fitting to assent to this side. And this is the state of one who believes.[43]

In the case of belief, what draws the will to move reason to assent is the perception of the good or fitting—*bonum vel conveniens*. This category of the "fitting" is woven through the *Tertia Pars* of the *Summa Theologiae*; confronted with the mystery of God incarnate, we discern a goodness or fittingness that attracts the will no less inexorably than truth attracts reason.

Yet even in this case there must be some shared sense of what constitutes goodness or fittingness in order for an argument *ex convenientia* to persuade. The perception of *convenientia* requires a sense of harmonious balance, an ability to see the way in which various contingent factors come-together (*convenire*) to form an object of compelling beauty. Thomas recognizes the analogy between aesthetic and theological persuasion in his Commentary on Lombard's *Sentences*, when he writes:

> Poetic knowledge is of things that cannot be grasped by reason, on account of a defect of truth, and therefore reason must be seduced by certain likenesses; theology, however, is about things that are above reason, and therefore the symbolic mode is common to both, because neither is proportioned to reason.[44]

Both poetry and theology exert a symbolic appeal that compensates for the disproportion or imbalance between reason and what is aesthetically represented.

According to O'Connor, this sense of balance, this ability to see goodness, much less to perceive truths of reason, is precisely what the modern world has lost, or rather, this is what has come to lodge within the interior space of personal artistic vision. But this is a forced confinement, which O'Connor refuses and meets with counter force: "Instead of reflecting a balance from the world around him, the novelist now has to *achieve* one by being a counterweight to the prevailing heresy."[45] Lacking a shared language of goodness or balance with which she can "woo" her readers, she sets out to shock. "When you can assume that your audience holds the same beliefs you do, you can relax a little and use more normal ways of talking to it; when you have to assume that it does not, then you have to make your vision apparent by shock—to the hard of hearing you shout, and for the almost blind you draw large and startling figures".[46]

The imbalance in O'Connor's writing is everywhere evident, and is usually identified by the description "grotesque". At times O'Connor seems annoyed with this description of her work, thinking it superficial and misapplied.[47] At other times, she acknowledges her use of "freaks" as a way of addressing the modern reader, in whom the sense of evil—and consequently the sense of good—has become "diluted" or is completely absent. Her stories are peopled by large and startling figures of both good and evil: child molesters, thieves and murderers, backwoods prophets, vacuous liberals, and pseudo-sophisticates. Her stories often end with a violent death or with a violent realization that one must endure the rest of life with crushing guilt or chronic illness. In the protagonist of her novel *Wise Blood*, Hazel Motes, we find a figure who is grotesque in the strict sense of the term: a fantastic combination of nihilistic atheism and evangelical fervor in a single figure.

O'Connor's characters are also "grotesque" in the etymological sense of the term: they emerge from the grottoes of her interiorized "felt balance". This felt balance is the concurrence of mystery and manners, transcendence and tradition, that she shares with Aquinas, but not with the contemporary culture of nihilism. Indeed, for the modern world the convergence of mystery and manners is itself a grotesque figure. In a world that lacks a language of truth or goodness or beauty, the mystery of God incarnate appears not as "balanced" or "fitting", but as ugly and horrific. In contrast to the fitting contingencies that Aquinas reads in Christ's manner of life, O'Connor's stories offer seemingly random violence that accompanies unexpected revelations. Perhaps she hopes that if goodness and beauty cannot themselves be perceived, then they might be glimpsed in their shadows—the evil and ugliness of which the modern world seems so enamored.

O'Connor herself was still able to believe, to be drawn by beauty and goodness to the truth. She was still able to say, in a letter to a friend, that "you can't have a peacock anywhere without having a map of the universe".[48] But she thinks that the ability to read this map is lost to the modern world. In her story "The Displaced Person", an unnamed priest comes to visit the Polish refugees working on Mrs. McIntyre's farm. When he sees a peacock spread his tail, he stands "transfixed, his jaw slack" and says in a loud voice, "Christ will come like that!".[49] But Mrs. McIntyre, hard-headed modern business woman that she is, for whom the peacock is just "another mouth to feed",[50] thinks him "an idiotic old man" and at the mention of Christ, her "face assumed a set puritanical expression and she reddened. Christ in the conversation embarrassed her the way sex had her mother."[51] A woman like Mrs. McIntyre cannot see a map of the universe in either the peacock's tail or in Christ; she is, as Walker Percy would put it, "Lost in the Cosmos", and even more lost for not recognizing her lostness.

It is only when she is confronted by the death of her Polish worker, in a random tractor accident that she could have prevented but chose not to, that she begins to sense that she may not know where she is or where she is going. The priest returns to the farm to give the Last Rites to the dying worker. Seeing the priest leaning with the man's family over his crushed body,

> She only stared at him for she was too shocked by her experience to be quite herself. Her mind was not taking hold of all that was happening. She felt she was in some foreign country where the people bent over the body were natives, and she watched like a stranger while the dead man was carried away in the ambulance.[52]

The story ends with Mrs. McIntyre abandoned by the rest of the workers on the farm, suffering a nervous breakdown and living her last days alone, with no visitors except the priest, who comes weekly to feed the peacocks and to "sit by the side of her bed and explain the doctrines of the Church".[53]

For O'Connor, this is a story of the way in which grace works in a world that can no longer be wooed by beauty. The thriving farm that Mrs. McIntyre seeks to build comes crashing down like the tower of Babel, and in the end, "nothing survived but [the priest] and the peacock and Mrs. McIntyre suffering."[54] Beauty is still present, in both the peacock and the teaching of the priest, but O'Connor does not seem to expect her audience to recognize that beauty or open themselves to its grace. Rather, she hopes that the grotesque fate of Mrs. McIntyre will act upon her readers as a disturbing grace, leaving them frightened, like the women at Jesus' empty tomb. But, in retrospect, O'Connor felt the story unsuccessful, precisely because her audience was unable to see the collapse of Mrs. McIntyre's world into suffering as the possibility of her redemption. "I missed making this clear but how are you going to make such things clear to people who don't believe in God, much less in Purgatory?"[55]

One always risks misunderstanding when shouting at the hard of hearing. O'Connor once wrote that, "Unless the novelist has gone utterly out of his mind, his aim is still communication and communication suggests talking inside a community."[56] But what community can O'Connor find with her audience? Certainly not the Christian community, but also not even the human community, since modern people have lost "even the sense of the human itself".[57] O'Connor seeks to communicate mystery in a world without manners, without the habitual ways of speaking and acting that make it possible for mystery to appear in a balanced and harmonious way. Yet she will not be deterred, for as a follower of Thomas she seeks to "take every thought captive in obedience to Christ" (2 Corinthians 10:5).[58] Though she once wrote that "The Church can't be identified with Western culture and I suppose the wreck of it doesn't cause her much of a sense of crisis",[59] in practice she recognizes that a retreat from engagement with that culture would amount to a retreat into a dualism of mystery and manners. While the Church is not identical with Western culture, neither does it exist in isolation from it. The mission of the Church is not simply to speak *contra gentes*, but to share in the apostolic movement *ad gentes*, a movement that was at the heart of Thomas' own vocation as a Dominican friar.

As O'Connor said, a hillbilly Thomist is likely to be mistaken for a hillbilly nihilist, precisely because she seeks a way of proclaiming the gospel through the guileful use of the nihilist's own idiom of distortion. But in robbing the modern world of its smug certainties, one might be seen as offering the abyss of nothingness rather than the abyss of faith. It is a risk O'Connor judges worth taking. She seeks to show that the human will cannot master the void, or even play safely within it, in order to open up the possibility that the void has already been mastered. She induces an awareness of lostness, so that we may recognize ourselves as found.

Gratia Turbit Naturam

If a hillbilly Thomist is likely to be mistaken for a nihilist, she is also likely to be mistaken, particularly by her fellow Catholics, for a Protestant. O'Connor mentions a review of her stories by "a priest who said that while my convictions may be Catholic, my sensibilities appeared to be Lutheran".[60] Presumably what this reviewer meant was that she was overly pessimistic about human nature, thereby denigrating the goodness of creation, a sensibility Catholics often identify with Protestantism. As one pair of authors put the matter, at the heart of Protestant theology is a conviction about, "the utter corruption of the human person as a result of the sin of Adam", with the result that "the individual, radically turned in on himself or herself and closed to any possibility of agapeic community, is locked into selfishness".[61] This is contrasted with Catholicism, which "has insisted in opposition to the darker views of the reformers that the human being, made in the image of God who is agape, remains in that image even after the fall and so is capable, even with great difficulty, of genuine other-directedness".[62] According to this view, we find in the case of Aquinas, with his belief that "grace perfects nature" (*gratia perfecit naturam*), a particularly ringing endorsement of human life and culture and a deep sense that grace, while distinct from nature, is at the same time in continuity with nature. In Thomas O'Meara's words, for Aquinas, "Grace is not a source of miraculous powers for curing cancer or handling poisonous snakes. Aquinas was little interested in the miraculous . . . but returned again and again to the invisible Spirit of Jesus working in people powerfully but respectfully."[63] Here, the claim that "grace perfects nature" seems to become the claim that grace *respects* nature.

Things seems otherwise in the world of O'Connor. There is nothing respectful about a grandmother shot by a serial killer or a child drowned in a river while seeking the kingdom of God. In O'Connor's fiction grace appears to be a profoundly disrespectful and disruptive force that might very well appear in the form of snake handling and cancer cures, or, even more likely, in the form of snakes that bite and tumors that kill.[64] Rather than perfecting nature and bringing it to fulfillment, the grace in O'Connor's stories seems to *disturb* nature: *gratia turbit naturam*. Whereas Thomas says that "grace does not take away nature but perfects it, therefore natural reason should assist faith",[65] O'Connor seems to be saying that natural reason hinders faith and, correlatively, faith overturns natural reason. Regarding the legal notion of "the reasonable man", O'Connor wrote to a friend, "Mine is certainly something else—God's reasonable man, the prototype of whom must be Abraham, willing to sacrifice his son and thereby show that he is in the image of God Who sacrifices His Son."[66] The example of Abraham evokes Kierkegaard far more than it does Thomas.

Does this mean that O'Connor's "hillbilly Thomism" is in fact an ersatz Thomism? Is it Protestant fideism in Thomist drag? There are two possible ways to address these questions. The first is to see if, in Thomas' account, grace is quite so "respectful" of nature as some have claimed; the second is to see if O'Connor really does pit grace against nature.[67] Is it possible to see grace taking the radically disruptive form that it does in O'Connor's fiction and still affirm the view that *gratia perfecit naturam*?

The difference between Thomas and Calvin or Luther is sometimes said to be that, whereas the Reformers taught that human nature is "totally depraved" by sin, Thomas holds that it is merely "wounded" and retains its essential integrity. And it is certainly true that Thomas holds the goodness of human nature to be diminished by sin, but not entirely destroyed,[68] and it is also true that he uses the language of the "wounding of nature" (*vulneratio naturae*) to describe this diminishment.[69] Yet he makes clear that this wounding is not on the order of a paper cut; rather it constitutes the *destitutio* of nature.[70] In the order of being, the goodness of human nature retains its fundamental integrity, inasmuch as the fallen human person remains a rational animal (otherwise sin would be impossible), but in the moral order the diminishment of the natural inclination to good can proceed, as Aquinas says, to infinity.[71] The integrity of human nature imposes no limits on human depravity.

But even if we grant, in theory, that the human inclination toward virtue can asymptotically approach zero, is this in fact our situation? Thomas certainly says that human beings, even in the state of corrupted nature, can do particular good acts, such as building houses or (what is a far more significant moral achievement) having friends,[72] and we ought not to underplay Thomas' insistence on these things as genuine goods. At the same time, we should not overlook Thomas' statement that these are *particular* good acts; our doing of them is contingent and circumstantial and they do not move us toward our ultimate end. And whereas prior to sin human beings could fulfill God's commands in such a way as to be pleasing to God, after sin and without grace, this is simply impossible.[73]

Thomas does say something that is akin to the claim that grace is "respectful" of nature in *Summa Theologiae* 1.62.5, where he writes, "grace perfects nature according to the mode of that nature, just as every perfection is received in what it perfects according to its mode".[74] Thomas says this in reference to the angels, whom God rewards with grace according to their natural perfections, something that is not true of humans.[75] But with regard to human beings, he also says that "divine providence provides for everything in accordance with its mode".[76] We might say that, while grace is never a reward for the good that is in human nature, in observing the "way of being" (*modus*) of a nature, the grace bestowed by divine providence does show a certain "respect" for that nature. Grace can not operate by external coercion (*coactio*) upon human nature precisely because to do so would be to destroy human nature, to which it belongs to act voluntarily. Put in the simplest terms, human beings do not have to become something other than human, whether angel or beast, in order to attain the vision of God.

But we should be clear about what this does and does not entail. We ought never to forget that the respectful *cooperation* of grace with the human will that makes human merit possible is founded on the prevenient *operation* of grace, in which "the will is the thing moved and God is the mover".[77] Ultimately, grace is something added to human nature from outside, not something that grows from within it. In saying that grace "perfects" or "realizes the potential of" human nature, we should keep before our mind the analogy with a form perfecting matter, or an agent perfecting that upon which it acts.[78] If Thomas' thinking has any sort of metaphysical lynchpin, it is that something that is in potentiality can only be actualized by something external to it. In the case of perfections realized within the order of nature, that upon which the agent acts must have some potential that can be realized, and thus in some sense "anticipates" its own realization. But in the case of grace perfecting human nature, no such anticipation is possible precisely because the gift of grace realizes something that is in excess of human nature's potential. So grace may "respect" human nature in the sense that the beatified human creature remains a human creature, but at the same time nature is disturbed by grace, like the *aqua turbata* of the pool at Bethsaida (John 5:7), or Mary who, upon hearing the angelic greeting, *turbata est in sermone eius* (Luke 1:29). Thomas, whatever the coolness or dryness of his tone, never forgets that grace is a word at which we are disturbed, a word that stirs us to reach out beyond the confines of our nature.

O'Connor, in the same way, never forgets that grace aims at bringing human nature to fulfillment, not destruction. One might say that grace reveals the truth of our nature that has been obscured by sin. Writing to her friend Betty Hester, after Hester left the Church, O'Connor says, "this means a narrowing of life for you and a lessening of the desire for life".[79] In losing that which is beyond our nature, we lose our nature. The difficulty in the culture of nihilism is at root not the loss of a sense of grace, but the loss of nature. Just as modern culture wants its mystery without manners, so too it wants its grace without nature. Or, more precisely, it understands nature as an emptiness that is entirely subject to human manipulation; human nature is the object of self-actualization. For O'Connor, this spells death for nature. Cut off from grace, it cannot reach its destiny; cut off from its creator, it cannot even exist.

At the same time that O'Connor believes that grace serves the flourishing of human nature by piquing our appetite for life, she also believes that, "All human nature vigorously resists grace because grace changes us and the change is painful".[80] *Gratia perfecit naturam* does not exclude *gratia turbit naturam*; for just as form perfects matter by stirring it to act, "troubling" and "goading" it into actuality, so too grace perfects nature by disturbing it.

Nature resists, just as matter resists taking on a new form in the artist's hands, but this resistance is not the last word. O'Connor saw her stories as embodying the deeply Catholic view that, unlike the case of angelic natures, grace acts upon human nature independent of whatever natural moral goodness might be found there. "Grace, to the Catholic way of thinking, can and does use as its medium the imperfect, purely human, and even hypocritical".[81] Grace perfects nature, and the sinfulness of the nature that grace perfects becomes, in O'Connor's hands, a testimony to the radical gratuity of that grace. In her stories, grace appears like the angel who disturbs Mary, in events that stand out in sharp relief: "This would have to be an action or a gesture which was both totally right and totally unexpected; it would have to be one that was both in character and beyond character; it would have to suggest both the world and eternity".[82] The arrival of grace is, for O'Connor as for Thomas, both totally right and totally unexpected, because it is both in accord with and beyond our human nature.

Hillbilly Thomistic Commentary: Praestet Fides Supplementum
Sensusm Defectui

Flannery O'Connor only quotes Thomas Aquinas once in her fiction. In her story "A Temple of the Holy Ghost", she puts the Thomas' Eucharistic hymn *Tantum Ergo Sacramentum* into the mouths of two convent-school girls, who sing it to mock the two teenage boys who have been invited over to entertain them on their weekend away from the convent. The boys, who have just treated the girls to a couple of hymns from the Church of God, are perplexed by Aquinas' hymn, and after a moment of silence one of them replies, "That must be Jew singing."[83] On the lips of the girls, the sublime theology of Aquinas becomes a tool to assert their own superiority, just as earlier they had, with shrieks of laughter, referred to each other as "Temple One" and "Temple Two", a reference to a lecture from an old nun at their school, who told them that if a boy were to " 'behave in an ungentlemanly manner with them in the back of an automobile' " they were to respond " 'Stop sir! I am a Temple of the Holy Ghost!' ".[84]

At the heart of the story are not the two adolescent girls, but the unnamed younger girl whose family they are visiting. When the two girls from the convent return after their evening at the fair with the boys, they tell the girl about the freak show they had seen: a hermaphrodite had exposed himself to the audience, but not before warning them, "God made me thisaway and if you laugh He may strike you the same way. This is the way He wanted me to be and I ain't disputing His way".[85] As the child lies in bed, slipping into sleep, she imagines the scene with the hermaphrodite—the freak show taking on the characteristics of a backwoods revival and blending with the image of the body as a Temple of the Holy Ghost:

> She could hear the freak saying, "God made me thisaway and I don't dispute hit," and the people saying, "Amen. Amen."
> God done this to me and I praise Him."
> "Amen. Amen."
> "He could strike you thisaway."
> "Amen. Amen."
> "But he has not."
> "Amen."
> "Raise yourself up. A temple of the Holy Ghost. You! You are God's temple, don't you know? Don't you know? God's Spirit has a dwelling in you, don't you know?"
> "Amen. Amen."
> "If anybody desecrates the temple of God, God will bring him to ruin and if you laugh, He may strike you thisaway. A temple of God is a holy thing. Amen. Amen."
> "I am a temple of the Holy Ghost."
> "Amen."[86]

The story concludes with the girl going with her mother to return Temple One and Temple Two to the school, where she goes into the convent chapel and kneels to pray during the service of Benediction of the Blessed Sacrament, as they sing the *Tantum Ergo*. Looking at the Host, ivory colored and pure, she thinks of the freak show and the hermaphrodite saying, "This is the way He wanted me to be." Later, as she is returning home, she looks at the evening horizon: "The sun was a huge red ball like an elevated Host drenched in blood and when it sank out of sight, it left a line in the sky like a red clay road hanging over the trees".[87]

O'Connor offers us here something normally absent from her stories: Catholic ritual and symbolism. And she places it in a complex juxtaposition with images of Protestant revivalism and the grotesque figure of the hermaphrodite. It is as if O'Connor is straining in the story to get at the very heart of the matter in depicting God's disturbing grace. She is reaching for the kind of distortion that will "make the reader feel, in his bones if nowhere else, that something is going on here that counts".[88] The image of the blood red sun descending like a Host upon the earth reflects the pure ivory Host in the service of Benediction, which in turn reflects the freak show in the girls imagination, where the hermaphrodite claims for himself the dignity of Christ's body: "I am a Temple of the Holy Ghost. Amen. Amen". These images bounce off each other, disorienting us, and yet conveying a sense of the immense importance of the identification of the freakish body of the hermaphrodite, whose very flesh violates all rules of order and division, with Christ's Eucharistic body. Faith supplies what the senses fail to perceive: the hermaphrodite's grotesque body is transformed by the grace of acceptance into an icon of purity. Thomas' hymn is freed from the confines of piety and smugness and becomes an exhortation to bow before the graced, freakish body, which has Christ as its head, and which extends to the farthest reaches of the horizon. In this single instance, O'Connor takes up the mantle of Thomistic commentator and casts a light upon Thomas' thought that makes its familiar words throw unexpected and luminous shadows.

Why be a hillbilly Thomist? Perhaps because pieties like "grace perfects nature", when found on the cool, dry lips of informed and responsible men, sound to modern ears like religious business as usual, and consequently of no interest. The culture of nihilism that O'Connor sought to address believes that it can have its grace without nature, its mystery without manners, its spirit without a freakish body to be transformed. O'Connor knows that, for the culture of nihilism, the alleged arrival of God in our world changes nothing, because that world is a void in which the human will plays endlessly. But for O'Connor, it changes everything, to a degree beyond what we can imagine, precisely because the world is not a void, but a creation that awaits the unexpected arrival of its maker. Thomas knew this. As highly as he prized human reason, he maintained that the event of the Incarnation, by which creation is brought to is proper end, is beyond the capacity for human deduction; it must therefore be announced in a way that can be heard and seen as a gesture that is both totally right and totally unexpected. In the land of the hard of hearing and the half blind, where we find ourselves today, it may be necessary to shout and draw large, startling figures if we seek, as Thomas sought, to take every thought captive in obedience to Christ.[89]

NOTES

1 Walter Farrell, O. P., *A Companion to the Summa*, vol. 1: *The Architect of the Universe* (London: Sheed and Ward, 1941), p. 44.
2 John Courtney Murray, S. J., *We Hold These Truths* (New York, NY: Sheed and Ward, 1960), p. 7. Speaking of the description of Aquinas' style as "dry", A. G. Sertillagnes compares it to Egyptian art or the metopes of the Parthenon and says, "a writer must be dry in that sense, if he is to say much in few words, and not put an obstacle between the mind and the truth" (*St. Thomas Aquinas and His Work*, Godfrey Anstruther, trans. (London: Burns Oates & Washbourne Ltd. [no publication date, but *Imprimatur* 1932]), 111.
3 For Murray's clearest analysis of "post-modernism", see *The Problem of God: Yesterday and Today* (New Haven, CT: Yale University Press, 1964), pp. 101–121. Murray's description is roughly equivalent to what O'Connor calls "nihilism".
4 *We Hold These Truths*, p. 293.
5 *Ibid.*, p. 128.
6 *Ibid.*, p. 317.
7 Thomas Franklin O'Meara, *Thomas Aquinas Theologian* (Notre Dame, IN: University of Notre Dame Press, 1997), p. 36.
8 Sertillanges, *St. Thomas Aquinas and His Work*, p. 109.
9 The secondary literature on O'Connor, like that on Aquinas, is voluminous. For a recent account of her life, which is particularly interesting for the way it interweaves it with accounts of the lives of three other American Catholic writers (Dorothy Day, Thomas Merton, and Walker Percy), see Paul Elie, *The Life You Save May Be Your Own: An American Pilgrimage* (New York: Farrar, Straus & Giroux, 2003).
10 Letter to Robie Macauley, 18 May, 1955, *Flannery O'Connor: Collected Works*, Sally Fitzgerald, ed. (New York, NY: The Library of America, 1988), p. 934. The remark is typical O'Connor—a humorously self-deprecating recognition that, in an upcoming television interview, she wants to come across as erudite and intelligent, but "will probably not be able to think of anything to say . . . but 'Huh?' and 'Ah dunno.'" At the same time, O'Connor is an author for whom the comic often serves as a delivery device for truth.
11 Letter to "A.", 2 August, 1955, *Collected Works*, p. 943. The woman identified in the published version of O'Connor's letters as "A." was Elizabeth Hester, to whom O'Connor addressed some of her most theologically searching letters. Hester, who briefly converted to Catholicism under O'Connor's influence, was also a longtime correspondent with Iris Murdoch. Her identity was finally revealed upon her death by suicide in 1998.
12 Letter to Thomas Mabry, 1 March, 1955, *Collected Works*, p. 929.
13 Letter to Helen Greene, 23 May, 1952, *Collected Works*, p. 897. O'Connor also saw connections between her identity as a Southerner and her identity as a Catholic. She writes in an essay, "There are certain conditions necessary for the emergence of Catholic literature which are found nowhere else in this country in such abundance as in the South" ("The Catholic Novelist in the South", *Collected Works*, p. 854).
14 Letter to John Hawkes, 20 April, 1961, *Collected Works*, p. 1149.
15 Her claim that she read the *Summa Theologiae* for twenty minutes each night before bed is quite possibly a joke (See her letter to "A.", 9 August, 1955, *Collected Works*, p. 945), but she did go to the trouble to obtain a copy of *De Veritate* in order to read what Aquinas had to say about prophecy (see her letter to "A.", 25 December, 1959 in *The Habit of Being*, p. 367). And while the mere presence of books in a personal library is no sure indicator of their influence, O'Connor did own several Aquinas anthologies, including Pegis' *Introduction to St. Thomas* and Gilby's *Thomas Aquinas: Philosophical Texts*. See Lorine M. Getz, *Flannery O'Connor: Her Life, Library and Book Reviews* (New York, NY: The Edwin Mellen Press, 1980).
16 Letter to Alfred Corn, 16 June, 1962, in *Collected Works*, p. 1166.
17 My own experience is that one only writes of Thomas with fear and trembling, because there is always some Thomist lurking around the corner, ready to leap out and demonstrate that you have focused too much on the *Summa Theologiae* and ignored the Aristotelian commentaries or, even worse, your Latin is so poor that you have failed to appreciate Thomas' use of the ablative absolute in a particular passage. Of course, one might respond that Thomas himself dared to interpret Aristotle without knowing Greek, making him perhaps a "hillbilly Aristotelian".

18 "The Teaching of Literature", *Mystery and Manners*, Sally and Robert Fitzgerald, eds. (New York, NY: Farrar, Straus & Giroux, 1969), p. 124.
19 "The Grotesque in Southern Fiction", *Collected Works*, p. 816.
20 Letter to Sister Mariella Gable, 4 May, 1963, *Collected Works*, pp. 1182–1183.
21 "The Catholic Novelist in the South", *Collected Works*, p. 856.
22 Letter to "A." August 2, 1955, *Collected Works*, p. 943.
23 "The Fiction Writer and His Country", *Collected Works*, p. 803.
24 See her letter to "A." August 2, 1955, *Collected Works*, pp. 943–944: "Henry James said that the young woman of the future would know nothing of mystery or manners. He had no business to limit it to one sex".
25 Thomas offers little sustained reflection on the term "mystery". Apart from the formulaic use, he seems to use the term, following the Greek usage, as a synonym for "sacrament".
26 *De Potentia* 7.5 *ad* 14: "illud est ultimum cognitionis humanae de Deo quod sciat se Deum nescire, in quantum cognoscit, illud quod Deus est, omne ipsum quod de eo intelligimus, excedere." As Karl Rahner comments on this passage: "it affirms that even in the beatific vision that which is known of God is known as the incomprehensible. The ultimate human knowledge of God is attained only when its character of mysteriousness is most forcibly displayed: supreme knowledge is knowledge of the supreme mystery as such." "The Concept of Mystery in Catholic Theology", *Theological Investigations* IV, Kevin Smyth, trans., (New York, NY: Crossroad, 1982), p. 59.
27 *Summa Theologiae* 1.13.5: "relinquit rem significatam ut incomprehensam, et excedentem nominis significationem". To put it in Thomas' typical language, our speech about God is true according to the *res significata* (i.e., we know that we can say true things about God) but not according to the *modus significandi* (we cannot know the *way* in which these things are true).
    It is worth underlining here that Thomas holds this radical inadequacy of language to be the case not only in what later thinkers would call "natural" or "philosophical" theology, but in "revealed" theology as well. A good example of this is the discomfort he feels (shared by Augustine before him and Barth and Rahner after him) with the dogmatic language of "persons" used in reference to the Father, Son and Spirit. Though firmly embedded in the tradition of the Church, the language of divine "persons" can be misleading if taken in the ordinary sense of "person". See *Summa Theologiae* 1.29.4.
28 *Moralia in Job*, 20.1: "sacra Scriptura omnes scientias ipso locutionis suae more transcendit, quia uno eodemque sermone, dum narrat gestum, prodit mysterium". Cf. O'Connor, "The Catholic Novelist in the Protestant South", in *Collected Works* p. 863, and Aquinas, *Summa Theologiae* 1.1.10.
29 The charge can be found in various places. See Karl Rahner, *The Trinity* [1967], Joseph Donceel, trans. (New York, NY: Crossroad Herder, 1997), pp. 51–2. With regard to the structure of the *Summa Theologiae*, and particularly the place of Christ, the debate in the past fifty years has been a busy one. For a recent discussion of these debates, as well as yet another constructive solution, see Jean-Marc Laporte, S. J., "Christ in Aquinas' *Summa Theologiae*: Peripheral or Pervasive", *The Thomist* Vol. 67 (2003), pp. 221–248.
30 For one example of this image of Thomas, see Adolph von Harnack: "Thus the theological science of the thirteenth century can be described as *the submitting to dialectical-systematic revision of ecclesiastical dogma and ecclesiastical practice, with the view of unfolding them in a system having unity and comprehending all that in the highest sense is worthy of being known, with the view of proving them, and so of reducing to the service of the Church all the forces of the understanding and the whole product of science*" (*History of Dogma*, vol. VI [third edition, 1900], Neil Buchanan, trans., (New York, NY: Dover Publications, 1961), p. 154, emphasis in the original). This characterization of Harnack's is not materially different from that of the neo-scholastic Ludwig Ott: "According to the teaching of St. Thomas, theology is a true science, because it uses as principles the securely founded basic truths of Divine Revelation and draws from these new knowledge (theological conclusions) by a strict scientific method and unites the whole in a closed system". *Fundamentals of Catholic Dogma*, James Canon Bastible, ed., Patrick Lynch, trans., (Cork: The Mercier Press, Ltd., 1958), p. 1.
31 On the other hand, there are also philosophers who greatly admire Thomas on questions of philosophical psychology, but reject his metaphysics. Anthony Kenny, for example, says of such venerable elements of "Thomist metaphysics" as the real distinction between

essence and existence and the account of God as *esse ipsum subsistens* that "even the most sympathetic treatment of these doctrines cannot wholly succeed in acquitting them of the charges of sophistry and illusion". *Aquinas* (Oxford: Oxford University Press, 1980), p. 60.

32 An early classic in this regard is Josef Pieper's *The Silence of St. Thomas: Three Essays* [1963], John Murray, S. J. and Daniel O'Connor, trans., (South Bend, IN: St. Augustine's Press, 1999). A more recent example would be Brian Davies' *The Thought of Thomas Aquinas* (Oxford: Oxford University Press, 1992), which is deeply influenced by Herbert McCabe's view that "when we speak of God, although we know how to use our words, there is an important sense in which we do not know what they mean". Herbert McCabe, "Appendix 3: 'Signifying Imperfectly'" in St. Thomas Aquinas, *Summa Theologiae* vol. 3 (New York, NY: McGraw-Hill Book Company, 1964) p. 104. Davies does not ignore Thomas' more explicitly Christian theological discussions, yet he pays far more attention to the *Prima Pars* than to the rest of the *Summa* and the picture we get of Thomas is that he was a philosopher first and a theologian second. Even with regard to the *Prima Pars*, Davies reorders Thomas' discussion, so that creation and providence comes *prior* to the doctrine of the Trinity, obscuring somewhat the explicitly Trinitarian basis Thomas given to his account of creation.

33 The significance of Thomas' official title at Paris—*magister sacra pagina*—began to be recovered by scholars in the middle of the twentieth-century. As Marie-Dominique Chenu wrote in 1950, "the *Summa* is embedded in an evangelical soil. By no means is this the result of some sort of devotion aiming to retain piousness within its rational systematization, but because therein is provided the law itself of its genesis". *Toward Understanding St. Thomas*, A.-M. Landry, O. P. and D. Hughes, O. P., trans., (Chicago, IL: Henry Regnery Company, 1964), p. 233. For two recent works in English that seek to undermine the view of Thomas as primarily a philosopher with a peripheral intellectual interest in scripture and doctrine, see Fergus Kerr, *After Aquinas: Versions of Thomism* (Oxford: Blackwell, 2002) and Nicholas M. Healy, *Thomas Aquinas: Theologian of the Christian Life* (Aldershot: Ashgate, 2003).

34 These two emphases on Aquinas as an apophatic theologian and on Thomas as a scriptural theologian converge in the work of the scholars associated with the Thomas Instituut te Utrecht. An introductory survey of "Utrecht-Thomism" can be found in Jozef Wissink, *Thomas van Aquino: De actuele betekenis van zijn theologie*, (Zoetermeer: Meinema, 1998).

35 Nicholas Healy makes the point that Thomas' emphasis on the literal sense of the Biblical text can be seen as a commitment to the primacy of the narrative sequence of events over all conceptual explication of those events. "Spiritual interpretations make connections between events and things that often break up the narrative structure of revelation. This is certainly permissible, even necessary, but the diachronic structure of God's actions in the world from Genesis to the Book of Revelation must take precedence over the synchronic explication of those actions." *Thomas Aquinas*, p. 43.

36 *Super evangelium S. Ioannis, lectura*, §1037.

37 *Scriptum super Sententiis*, prologue, q. 1 a. 5: "oportet . . . quod modus istius scientiae sit narrativus signorum, quae ad confirmationem fidei faciunt".

38 Letter to "A.", August 2, 1955, *Collected Works*, p. 943.

39 Letter to "A.", August 28, 1955, *Collected Works*, p. 949.

40 Letter to "A.", July 20, 1955, *Collected Works*, p. 942.

41 "The Grotesque in Southern Fiction", *Collected Works*, p. 820.

42 See *Summa Theologiae* 1.1.8.

43 *De Veritate* 14.1: "determinatur autem per voluntatem, quae eligit assentire uni parti determinate et praecise propter aliquid, quod est sufficiens ad movendum voluntatem, non autem ad movendum intellectum, utpote quia videtur bonum vel conveniens huic parti assentire".

44 *Scriptum super Sententiis*, prologue, q. 1 a. 5 *ad* 3: "poetica scientia est de his quae propter defectum veritatis non possunt a ratione capi; unde oportet quod quasi quibusdam similitudinibus ratio seducatur: theologia autem est de his quae sunt supra rationem; et ideo modus symbolicus utrique communis est, cum neutra rationi proportionetur".

45 "The Catholic Writer in the Protestant South", *Collected Works*, p. 862.

46 "The Fiction Writer and His Country", *Collected Works*, pp. 805–806.

47 O'Connor wrote, "I have found that anything that comes out of the South is going to be called grotesque by the Northern reader, unless it is grotesque, in which case it is going to be called realistic." "Some Aspects of the Grotesque in Southern Fiction", *Collected Works*, p. 815.

48 Letter to "A.", November 25, 1955, *Collected Works*, p. 971.

49　Flannery O'Connor, "The Displaced Person", *Collected Works*, p. 317.

50　*Ibid.*, p. 289.

51　*Ibid.*, p. 317.

52　*Ibid.*, p. 326.

53　*Ibid.*, p. 327.

54　Letter to "A.", November 25, 1955, *Collected Works*, p. 971.

55　*Ibid.*

56　"The Regional Writer" *Collected Works*, p. 844.

57　Letter to Dr. T. R. Spivey, October 19, 1958, *Collected Works*, p. 1077.

58　When Thomas first introduces the phrase *gratia perfecit naturam* in the *Summa Theologiae* in 1.1.8, he glosses it with Paul's phrase from 2 Corinthians 10:5: "take every thought captive in obedience to Christ".

59　Letter to Dr. T. R. Spivey, October 19, 1958, *Collected Works*, p. 1076.

60　Letter to "A." September 30, 1955, *Collected Works*, p. 960.

61　Michael J. Himes and Kenneth R. Himes, O. F. M., *Fullness of Faith: The Public Significance of Theology* (New York, NY: Paulist Press, 1993), p. 30.

62　*Ibid.*, p. 31. A similar characterization (from a different spot on the spectrum of Catholic theology) is made by John M. Hass, "One of the errors that arose in much Protestant thought, and persists to our own day even in secular culture, is that the natural and the supernatural orders are opposed to one another. Because of the doctrine of the total depravity of man, classical Protestantism tends to look at fallen man as radically over against God." "The Relationship of Nature and Grace in Saint Thomas", in *The Ever-Illuminating Wisdom of St. Thomas Aquinas: Papers Presented at a Conference Sponsored by the Wethersfield Institute* (San Francisco, CA: Ignatius Press, 1999), p. 63.

63　O'Meara, *Thomas Aquinas Theologian*, p. 115. O'Meara also writes, "The entire *S[umma] T[heologiae]* unfolds Aquinas' axiom, '*gratia perfecit naturam*,' 'grace brings nature to its full destiny.' Cosmos and church, being and life, art and ecstasy do not point to death but to life; the Catholic mind . . . delights in the ways in which the Incarnation continues." (p. 126).

64　For some insight on the workings of grace manifested in incurable cancer, see O'Connor's "A Memoir of Mary Ann", *Collected Writings*, pp. 822–831.

65　*Summa Theologiae* 1.1.8: "Cum enim gratia non tollat naturarm, sed perfecit, oportet quod naturalis ratio subserviat fidei".

66　Letter to "A.", November 10, 1955, *Collected Works*, p. 968. While O'Meara claims that Thomas' theology is "the polar opposite of any fundamentalism" (*Thomas Aquinas Theologian*, p. 116), fundamentalists are among O'Connor's favorite subjects, precisely because they offer us a Gospel that has no respect for our idea of what is reasonable, a Gospel that is, in fact, fanatical. Writing to sister Mariella Gable, O'Connor said,

>　About the fanatics. People make a judgement of fanaticism by what they are themselves. To a lot of Protestants I know, monks and nuns are fanatics, none greater. And to a lot of monks and nuns I know, my Protestant prophets are fanatics. For my part, I think the only difference between them is that if you are a Catholic and have this intensity of belief you join the convent and are heard from no more; whereas if you are a Protestant and have it, there is no convent for you to join, and you go about in the world getting into all sorts of trouble and drawing the wrath of people who don't believe anything much at all down on your head" (May 4, 1963, *Collected Works*, p. 1183).

　　O'Connor concludes her letter saying, "I am more and more impressed with the amount of Catholicism that fundamentalist Protestants have been able to retain. Theologically our differences with them are on the nature of the Church, not on the nature of God and our obligation to him." *Collected Works*, p. 1184.

67　A third approach would be to see if Catholic accounts of Protestant theological anthropology are accurate, or rather cartoonish caricatures.

68　See, e.g. *Summa Theologiae* 1-2.85.2. One might (forgiving the barbarous Latin) adapt Aquinas' adage about grace and nature to state his position on the effect of sin on nature: *peccatum non tollit naturam, sed defecit*.

69　*Summa Theologiae* 1-2.85.3.

70　*Ibid.*

71 *Summa Contra Gentiles* 3.12.7: "In infinitum igitur per malum moris bonum naturalis apti-tudinis diminui potest. Nunquam tamen totaliter tolletur, sed semper naturam remanen-tem comitatur [The natural tendency toward good can therefore be diminished infinitely through evil manners. Nevertheless it is never taken away totally, but always accompanies the nature that remains]".

72 Thomas mentions building houses, along with planting vineyards, in *Summa Theologiae* 1-2.109.2. The mention of friendship, usually overlooked by those commenting on this ques-tion, is in *Summa Theologiae* 1-2.109.5.

73 *Summa Theologiae* 1-2.109.8 *ad* 1: "homo potest vitare singulos actus peccati, non tamen omnes, nisi per gratiam [Human beings can avoid each but not every sinful act, except by grace]". In *Summa Theologiae* 1-2.63.2 *ad* 2, Thomas says that sin, even mortal sin, is com-patible with individual acquired virtues, since sin is an act and not a *habitus*. But in 1-2.65.1 he makes clear that acquired virtues must be guided by *prudentia* in order to be connected in what we might call a virtuous life. He further argues, in 1-2.65.2, that in order for pru-dence to operate correctly a person must be properly disposed toward his or her ultimate end, and that this disposition can only be brought about by grace, through the infused virtue of *caritas*. Thus it would seem that while all of the actions of a person in the state of corrupted nature are not themselves evil, such action are in no way salvific. See also *Summa Theologiae* 1-2.109.5 as well as Thomas' discussion in his *Super Romanos* §1140, regarding Romans 14:23, "whatever is not from faith is sin".

74 "gratia perficit naturam secundum modum naturae, sicut et omnis perfectio recipitur in perfectibili secundum modum eius".

75 See, e.g. *Summa Theologiae* 1.108.8 *ad* 1.

76 *Summa Contra Gentiles* 3.148.2: "Divina . . . providentia rebus omnibus providet sacundum modum earum".

77 *Summa Theologiae* 1-2.111.2: "voluntas se habet ut mota, Deus autem ut movens".

78 Thomas makes the analogy of form and matter in *Summa Contra Gentiles* 3.149 and that of an agent perfecting a potential (in this case, fire perfecting water's potential to be hot) in *Summa Contra Gentiles* 3.147.4.

79 Letter to "A", 28 October, 1961, *Collected Works*, p. 1152–1153.

80 Letter to Cecil Dawkins, 9 December, 1958, *Collected Works*, p. 1084.

81 Letter to John Hawkes, 14 April, 1960, *Collected Works*, p. 1125. In this same letter, O'Connor indicates that she holds the typical Catholic view of the Protestant theology of nature and grace, and distinguishes her own view from it: "In the Protestant view, I think Grace and nature don't have much to do with each other."

82 "On Her Own Work", in *Mystery and Manners*, p. 111. This is from remarks O'Connor made to introduce her reading of her story "A Good Man is Hard to Find" at Hollins College, Virginia in 1963.

83 "A Temple of the Holy Ghost" in *Collected Works*, p. 202.

84 *Ibid.*, p. 199.

85 *Ibid.*, p. 206.

86 *Ibid.*, p. 207.

87 *Ibid.*, p. 208.

88 "Novelist and Believer", in *Mystery and Manners*, p. 162.

89 My thanks to my colleague Trent Pomplun for his suggestions regarding this essay.

INDEX